Texas Woman of Letters, Karle Wilson Baker

Number Eight:

SAM RAYBURN SERIES ON RURAL LIFE

Sponsored by Texas A&M University–Commerce

James A. Grimshaw Jr., General Editor

TEXAS WOMAN *of* LETTERS, *Karle Wilson Baker*

SARAH RAGLAND JACKSON

Texas A&M University Press College Station

First edition

The paper used in this book meets the minimum requirements of the American National Standard for Permanence of Paper for Printed Library Materials, Z39.48-1984.
Binding materials have been chosen for durability.
♾

Library of Congress Cataloging-in-Publication Data

Jackson, Sarah (Sarah R.)
Texas woman of letters, Karle Wilson Baker / Sarah Ragland Jackson.—1st ed.
p. cm. — (Sam Rayburn series on rural life ; no. 8)
Includes bibliographical references and index.
ISBN 1-58544-456-1 (alk. paper)
1. Baker, Karle Wilson, 1878–1960. 2. Women and literature—Texas—History—20th century. 3. Authors, American—20th century—Biography. 4. Authors, American—Homes and haunts—Texas. 5. Texas—Intellectual life—20th century. 6. Texas—In literature. 7. Texas—Biography. I. Title. II. Series.
PS3503.A5435Z73 2005
818′.5209—dc22

2005005303

FRONTISPIECE *Portrait Photograph of Karle Wilson Baker. Karle Wilson Baker had portrait photographs made at the Sarony Photographic Studio in New York City in September 1940. (Daily Calendar Book, Private Collection, Baker Estate)*

For JLJ

CONTENTS

ILLUSTRATIONS

SERIES EDITOR'S FOREWORD

Karle Wilson Baker was one of the most recognized and honored poets in Texas in the twentieth century, and Sarah Ragland Jackson's biography of her literary life witnesses that claim. Ask most people today, however, and they will not have heard of her. Born to be a writer, Karle Wilson had a fire in her belly to write and found inspiration to fan those flames in deep East Texas after her parents moved from Little Rock to Nacogdoches in 1901. Her story, ably told, reveals the making of a writer, of a woman capable of balancing the responsibilities of a career and family during a time when the role of women tended to be subordinated, and of a person appreciative of the environment.

Karle Wilson was educated at the University of Chicago, Columbia University, and the University of California at Berkeley. In 1907 she and Thomas Ellis Baker were married; they had two children. Her desire to write began at an early age, and write she did. In her mid-thirties she became a frequent contributor of poetry to the *Yale Review*. Her writing expanded to children's stories and essays, and flourished until the early 1940s. In addition to being a wife, mother, and writer, she was a teacher at Stephen F. Austin State Teachers College from 1924–34. As if those pursuits were not enough, she also was actively engaged in lecturing around the country and participated in professional organizations such as the Texas Institute of Letters, of which she was a founder and the second president; the Philosophical Society of Texas in 1936, in which she was one of three women members; the Poetry Society of Texas; and Phi Beta Kappa. That is but a thumbnail sketch of a remarkable woman.

Elithe Hamilton Kirkland, Dorothy Scarborough, Katherine Anne Porter, and Naomi Shihab Nye are but four women writers for whom Texas has been an inspiration. Sylvia Ann Grider and Lou Halsell Rodenberger edited a marvelous collection of essays by and about Texas women writers: *Texas Women Writers: A Tradition of Their Own* (Texas A&M University Press, 1997). Spanning some 165 years from 1830 to 1995, the essays in this volume bring to life the works of many women writers who have gone unnoticed because they were overshadowed by the Texas mystique—the masculine interests in oil derricks, cowboys, ranches, horses, Texas independence—embodied in the works of popular writers such as J. Frank Dobie, Elmer Kelton, and Larry McMurtry. But now we can be grateful that Sarah Ragland Jackson has given us yet another name, Karle Wilson Baker, to add to that list of Texas writers. Undoubtedly, many more will be recovered in this century.

Established in 1997 under the umbrella of the Texas A&M University Press, the Sam Rayburn Series on Rural Life focuses on facets of rural life in East Texas in particular and in Texas and the surrounding region in general. Subjects that may be addressed include but are not limited to banking, public education, literary figures, cotton, oil/gas, sports, higher education, little theater, politics, social work, history, art, and agriculture. This eighth volume in the series, *Texas Woman of Letters, Karle Wilson Baker,* is the first to explore a literary figure. We encourage other authors to share with us their research in this and other topics.

James A. Grimshaw Jr.
General Editor

PREFACE

When my husband and I moved to Nacogdoches more than three decades ago, I heard right away about a local writer of children's books, Charlotte Baker Montgomery. Soon afterward I met Charlotte and became interested in her books. I learned that Charlotte's mother, Karle Wilson Baker, had been a local writer as well. Only later as I pursued my own research on the poetry of Robert Frost did I uncover information that Frost had spoken in Nacogdoches in 1933 at the invitation of Karle Wilson Baker. Following that lead, I published "Frost in Texas" and "Karle Wilson Baker Brings Robert Frost to Nacogdoches," two articles dealing with the Frost-Baker connection. From that time until this, I have remained fascinated with Karle Wilson Baker—both her life and works—as a subject for a biography.

Karle Wilson Baker received more recognition and honors than any other poet from Texas in the twentieth century. She was a charter member of the prestigious Texas Institute of Letters, the Poetry Society of Texas, and the Philosophical Society of Texas. Only the third person to be named a Fellow of the Institute of Letters, she followed J. Frank Dobie and Walter Prescott Webb in that honor. The exacting and highly respected Yale University Press published her first two books of poetry, *Blue Smoke* and *Burning Bush*. Indeed, she was the best known and most frequently anthologized poet from Texas in her lifetime. Baker received an honorary Doctor of Letters from Southern Methodist University in 1924 because of her widely recognized talent. In 1929, Dr. A. J. Armstrong, chairman of English at Baylor University, wrote to Baker asking her to introduce Edna St. Vincent Millay at a program there. He expressed the feelings of many in Texas when he wrote, "I conceived the idea that it would be nice to have the greatest of Texas' poets introduce the greatest woman poet in the world." The Southwest Press published a third book of collected poems, *Dreamers on Horseback* (1931), which was nominated for the Pulitzer Prize for Poetry.

However, Karle Wilson Baker was not only a poet but an essayist, novelist, and author of children's books. She prepared a children's reader about Texas history, *The Texas Flag Primer*, which was adopted by the Texas State Textbook Commission in 1925. The World Book Company published another reader, *Two Little Texans*. Yale University Press published her children's fantasy, *The Garden of the Plynck,* and a book of fables, *Old Coins.* Southwest Press published her popular book of essays on bird life and nature, *The Birds of Tanglewood,* in 1930. Later, she published two successful novels based on life in Texas: *Family Style* (1937), about the newly discovered East Texas oil field, and *Star of the Wilderness* (1942), set in Nacogdoches during the early days of the Texas Revolution. The latter was a Book of the Month Club selection.

In addition to her active writing life, Karle Wilson Baker taught at Stephen F. Austin State Teacher's College from 1924–34 during the college's formative years. She brought a dignity and national recognition that no other faculty member could. In almost every way Baker was ahead of the small village of Nacogdoches where she lived. Her intellectual interests advanced beyond most of her neighbors, and her "modern" lifestyle (living the life of the new, independent career woman) separated her from most other married women. Nevertheless, she was a devoted wife to Thomas Ellis Baker, her husband of forty-nine years, who respected his wife's career and encouraged her at every turn. The Bakers had two children, Thomas Wilson and Charlotte. Because of the strong support from all her family, Baker was able to balance an active career as a writer, college teacher, and public speaker. She often traveled across the country lecturing, attending university classes, researching, or conferring with publishers. Thomas E. Baker's family roots were deep in East Texas, and Karle Wilson Baker, who moved to the area from Arkansas as a young adult, became absorbed with the natural beauty and history of the area. She eloquently captures rural East Texas in her poetry, essays, nonfiction, and novels.

Charlotte Baker Montgomery grew up literally at the feet of this acclaimed writer. Karle Wilson Baker included her children in her early poems and even consulted with them when she wrote her first book for children, *The Garden of the Plynck.* Each day when Charlotte and Tomby returned from school, their mother would read a chapter or passages from the day's writing and ask for their opinions. Mrs. Baker dedicated the book "To Tomby and Charlotte, My Collaborators." In 1919 when Karle Wilson Baker enrolled at Columbia University, she took her children with her to New York City. When her children enrolled at the University of California at Berkeley, she accompanied them and enrolled herself. Several years later, Charlotte joined forces with her mother as the illustrator of *The Birds of Tanglewood.* They worked together again to produce Baker's children's book *The Reindeer's Shoe and Other Stories,* illustrated by Charlotte. They also collaborated on magazine articles. Charlotte Baker Montgomery has written and illustrated twenty children's books on her own.

My work on the biography of Karle Wilson Baker has given me much pleasure. What began as an intellectual interest has evolved into a genuine admiration for an extremely talented woman. Nevertheless, I am acutely aware that I have had to make choices and thus have not been able to include all of my findings from years of research. I would like to defer to Karle Wilson Baker's own words, "I know that even flattering portraits do not please the originals. I have long ago decided that it is impossible to write about anybody in a way that will satisfy him or his friends. . . . I am seldom satisfied either!"

Resource material for this project is abundant since Karle Wilson Baker was extremely self-analytical and wrote reams of information about herself as a writer of both poetry and prose. Also, she recognized early in her career that she was a writer of importance and faithfully saved correspondence she received and made copies of most of the letters she sent to others. This material is invaluable for the researcher of her life and works. Baker corresponded with virtually all the more prominent scholars and publishers in the state and with many nationally known authors, scholars, and publishers. The Steen Library on the campus of Stephen F. Austin State University is the repository for the rich collection of Karle Wilson Baker Papers. However, in addition to this public collection, the Baker family in Nacogdoches has a very large collection of private papers, journals, diaries, photographs, and unpublished manuscripts to which I have had unhindered access thanks to Charlotte Baker Montgomery, the literary executrix of the Baker estate. Both Montgomery and Thomas W. Baker graciously allowed me to interview them numerous times over a period of years. Charlotte Montgomery has been consistent in her support of this project and has generously shared both materials and memories. Also, I have had many other interviews either by letter or in person with former students of Stephen F. Austin State Teachers College. I want to thank the SFA Alumni Association, especially Betty Ford, for providing a list of alumni who studied under Baker. Participants from my survey as well as a large number of friends have shared anecdotes about Baker. I have tried to recognize all of them in the notes at the end of this book.

I must thank many professional people who have helped me to bring about this biography. A Faculty Research Grant committee from Stephen F. Austin State University, chaired by Dr. E. D. Malpass, provided funding for my research. The libraries outside Nacogdoches most useful to me from this funding were the Harry Ransom Humanities Research Center and the Center of American History at the University of Texas at Austin; the DeGolyer

Library and the Fondren Library at Southern Methodist University in Dallas; Northwestern Louisiana State Library and the Cammie Henry Research Center at Natchitoches, Louisiana; the Armstrong-Browning Library at Baylor University in Waco; Southwest Texas State Library (now Texas State University) in San Marcos; and the University of California Library at Berkeley. I owe a great debt of thanks to the many librarians who helped me at all of these institutions including those in the Steen Library. A grant from the Texas State Teachers Association allowed funding for research and travel that yielded papers on Karle Wilson Baker presented at professional conferences. I want to thank Dr. Archie McDonald, editor of the *East Texas Historical Journal,* and Dr. Earl J. Wilcox, editor of the *Robert Frost Review* for allowing me to quote from my articles on Karle Wilson Baker printed in those journals.

The Center for East Texas Studies, directed by Dr. Jere L. Jackson at Stephen F. Austin State University, has offered unwavering encouragement and assistance. In particular, I owe a debt of gratitude to Mary Devine and Melissa Darlington, proofreaders *extraordinaire* at the center. Jere Jackson, my husband, has been my most faithful supporter in this project. He has offered creative suggestions and has encouraged me to persevere when I had doubts. The Center for East Texas Studies has undertaken the reprinting of Karle Wilson Baker's selected prose and poetry accompanied by explanatory essays that I have provided.

Professor James Grimshaw of Texas A&M at Commerce, editor of the Sam Rayburn Series on Rural Life, saw the potential for this biography from the beginning, and I am indebted to him for offering me the opportunity of participating in the series. I would like to add a special word of thanks to editor Stephanie Attia for her professionalism and counsel. Mary Lenn Dixon, editor-in-chief at Texas A&M University Press, offered both the encouragement and scope that brought this book into publication.

Texas Woman of Letters, Karle Wilson Baker

"I cannot remember a time when I did not expect to be an author; but I remember announcing my decision to my family when I was eight."

CHAPTER 1
The Early Years

Karle Wilson Baker's lifelong love of East Texas began when she first arrived in the sleepy village of Nacogdoches in 1901. In a public speech after she had become a national literary figure, she commented:

> When I came home from college, at the University of Chicago, 'home' had moved in my absence: from Little Rock, Arkansas, to East Texas. I shall never forget how my father met me at the train, on a hot September night of brilliant moonlight, about half-past one o'clock, and brought me up through the sleeping town in the rattling old 'depot-hack.' And the thing I remember *most* vividly was the feeling of wonder—almost of awe—with which I looked up at the majestic old trees, as we drove beneath them—into their great blots of shadow and out again into the moonlight. I didn't know it at the time, of course, but I think that the process started then which finally resulted in *Star of the Wilderness.*[1]

Karle Wilson, named for her mother's brother, Karl, was born October 13, 1878, in a cottage on Louisiana Street in Little Rock, Arkansas. When she was four years old, the family moved to a new, finer two-story home on the same street.[2]

Kate Floy Montgomery Wilson, Karle's mother, was the daughter of John Rogus Montgomery, who had served as attorney general of Arkansas during Reconstruction after the Civil War. He had moved to Arkansas from Wisconsin, bringing his wife, Josephine, his two children, and his Northern attitudes with him. When the Southerners regained control of their affairs and threw the "carpetbaggers" out, Montgomery lost his position with the state; consequently, he bought property, "Linden Grange," twenty miles from Little Rock and started to farm. The farm was soon mortgaged, and in later years, the Montgomerys' son-in-law, W. T. Wilson, picked up the remaining payments. Karle Wilson Baker modeled the character Paul McAlpine in *Star of the Wilderness* on her grandfather's winning but somewhat irresponsible ways.[3]

Kate Floy became a primary school teacher in Little Rock. Her most persistent suitor was William Thomas Wilson, a widower ten years older than she, with two small children. He was handsome and a Baptist, two traits that certainly met with Kate Floy's approval since she was looking for a religious man, preferably a Baptist. Even though she was not physically strong, the young teacher was delighted to undertake the upbringing of the Wilson children, Bess and Mae.[4] Kate Floy and W. T. produced two children, Karle and her younger brother, Ben. In an autobiographical essay Karle described her mother as "the dominant, overshadowing, almost the sole influence upon my early childhood." She portrayed W. T. Wilson as "the typical business-absorbed parent" whom she knew less well than she knew her mother, even though she considered herself to be more like him. She stated that she knew little about her father's people except that the Wilsons had come as a pioneer family to Arkansas from Georgia and Tennessee. On the other hand, during her childhood she often visited her maternal grandparents at Linden Grange.[5] Most of the time the family went out to Linden Grange by train, and this initiated Karle's lifelong love of trains.

In early autobiographical notes she wrote of her foremost desire in childhood: "I cannot remember a time when I did not want to be an author; but I remember announcing my decision to my family when I was eight."[6] Karle Wilson recorded thoughts about her childhood in her diary, describing herself as a "moody" child who had "a morbidness in her temperament" that her mother "did all in her power to correct." She portrays herself as a brown-eyed, round-faced child, slow and timid, "very silent," and affectionate in a shy way to those who showed affection to her. She describes a "smouldering fire" and a "vast potential momentum" beneath her stolidity that was the cause of "a definite passionate ambition for literary achievement that began before I can remember." Her first poem, written at the age of eight, was "a production of some eight stanzas in iambic pentameter, upon 'Home.'" In the diary account, she laments the fact that even though she was from a fairly well-to-do home, she had grown up in the southwestern part of the United

States in a small city, "continents removed spiritually from any center of thought, any seat of intellectual activity."[7] Maintaining a daily journal was common among the women in the family. Both Karle's mother and her grandmother had a literary strain and enjoyed writing about daily events. Karle Wilson continued the tradition and wrote extensive journal entries. Very early in her career, she had an uncanny notion about the importance of putting her thoughts in writing. Numerous diaries, drafts of letters, letters received, and manuscript record books make up a voluminous account of the events that shaped her life.

Karle enjoyed a happy, normal childhood. She played with her sisters and brother, acting in home-produced plays, riding a pony, and bringing out a weekly handwritten magazine. She attended public schools and then the Little Rock Academy. She loved school (with the exception of arithmetic). English and history were her favorite subjects, but she enjoyed languages and learned Latin, French, and German. Years later she would add Spanish to her knowledge of languages. She took violin lessons for several years beginning at age nine and played in a student orchestra. As she grew older she became especially fond of tennis. She and her brother, Ben, continued to play the sport together when they were adults. But her greatest pleasures were reading, writing, and taking long walks.[8]

In 1895, Karle attended Ouachita Baptist College in Arkadelphia, Arkansas. She published a small article, "A Talk about the Weather," in the school journal, *Ouachita Ripples.*[9] Two years later, when she was nineteen years old, she enrolled at the University of Chicago for the June to August 1897 summer term. Founded in 1891, the university already possessed a large campus with impressive buildings. Courageously, Karle had decided to further her education in a big city far from home, but because of limited financial support from her family, she left the university in the Fall of 1897 to teach at the Southwest Virginia Institute, a school for young women in Bristol, Virginia. There, as a teacher of French and English, she earned money that allowed her to return to the University of Chicago for the summer term in 1898. In September 1898, she returned again to Bristol for a second year of teaching. She saved enough money to return to the university in the summer of 1899, and this time she remained until August of 1900.

While she lived in Virginia, Karle wrote to her mother that she liked the institute very much, commenting on the mountains, trees, and sky as beautiful beyond description. She wrote that she had confounded the headmistress of the school by her independent spirit: "Mrs. Morse was astonished that I had ventured to town alone—but anyone who is used to finding the way around Chicago could hardly get lost in this little mountain town!" The letters were often lengthy. Karle sent the first one, dated September 16, 1898, to her mother's Little Rock, Arkansas, address. By December 1898, she sent letters to her mother in San Antonio, Texas, where the Wilsons were living with W. T.'s brothers.[10]

When W. T. Wilson's successful grain and feed business in Little Rock fell victim to financial reversals, and the company went into bankruptcy, two of Wilson's brothers who had moved to San Antonio, Texas, encouraged him to join them in their successful business there. However, on a trip to San Antonio through East Texas, W. T. stopped for the night in Nacogdoches and stayed at the Banita Hotel near the train station. He was so impressed with what he found that he chose Nacogdoches as the place to relocate his family (Kate Floy, Karle, and Ben) and restart his business. Mae and Bess Wilson were young adults by this time and chose to remain in Little Rock.[11]

A superior student, Karle advanced rapidly at the University of Chicago and "placed out" of some courses and moved to the more advanced ones. She was fortunate to study with Robert Herrick and William Vaughn Moody and became a theme reader for both professors. Moody was her mentor, and after college, Karle Wilson Baker wrote a biography of his life. During her stay at the university, she established a lifelong friendship with Anna McCaleb. The two women shared interests in writing, and after graudation, Anna worked for a publishing house in Chicago.

In the spring and summer of 1900, Karle took frequent outings to Lincoln Park in Chicago where she wrote "The Poet," her first published poem.[12] During her college years, Karle had become a self-reliant young woman who enjoyed city life and loved the intellectual stimulation the University of Chicago offered. She found approval there as a writer as well. In 1901, the *University of Chicago Weekly* published a poem and a short story of hers.[13]

In a confidential letter written years later to her daughter, Charlotte Baker Montgomery, she confided that she had fallen in love for the first time while at the university. Writing to "Sharley," a name she sometimes gave to Charlotte, she described her feelings toward the young man as "almost pathologically infatuated" and his feelings as "pathologically jealous—really, not as a figure of speech." Karle's mother had insisted that Karle not see the young man until after college or else leave the college altogether. Karle wrote that she returned home to Nacogdoches and before a year had passed, the young man "broke the engagement—if it could be called that." After Karle returned home, she met Thomas Ellis Baker and fell in love with him. In the letter to Charlotte, she describes the first love as "the psychological opposite of 'Father.'"[14] In a personal essay on mother-daughter relationships, she refers to the incident that led to her return home. She wrote that her mother, who had always been a controlling force in her life, once again "took the same minute, detailed share [in the unhappy love-affair] by means of incessant letter-writing that she had always taken in my affairs. . . . My mother called me home receiving me back with infinite tenderness." But Karle realized that she had changed during her time at the university and that their relationship was forever altered. "We were no longer protecting mother and dutiful child, but two women. . . . My mother could not understand what had happened to her docile child." Even though Karle had left college of her own free will, she was resentful of her mother's influence over her: "I found myself committed to a life-and-death struggle for the right to call my soul my own."[15] She was determined to separate herself from her mother's too firm grasp, but Karle also recognized that her invalid mother was growing older and weaker and needed help at home, so she left Chicago to return to Nacogdoches. She proclaimed a dual purpose: to help her mother and "to dedicate myself definitely to the struggle to be a writer."[16]

From the time of her first arrival in Nacogdoches, the history of the area and its natural beauty fascinated her. Throughout her career, whether she was writing poetry, essays on birdlife or history, children's books, or novels, the absorption with Texas remained. She described Nacogdoches as she saw it in 1900: "It was wrapped in tradition as in a garment, permeated—not to say—drugged—by the perfume of its past. Yet the tradition was vague and nebulous; it was almost impossible for the inquiring newcomer to put his finger on a fact. . . . Nacogdoches, sitting beside her dusty streets, beneath her immemorial trees, was so proud of being "historic" that she had forgotten her history."[17]

After the Wilsons' first Nacogdoches home, "Pilgrim's Rest" on Mound Street, burned at Christmastime in 1902, they made plans to build on property they owned just across the street. Karle recorded in her journal the loss of her diaries in the fire: "This abruptly begins my fourth Journal; the other three having been beneficently burned with the burning of the house. It was a bereavement; but I was grateful on the whole that Fate has taken out of my hands a task which I suppose I should have nerved myself to sooner or later."[18] Two months later, she wrote again in her journal about the loss of college papers (which she considered more important than her diaries) in the Pilgrim's Rest fire:

> I wish I had not lost my college themes when the house burned. The other manuscripts I do not begrudge particularly, for I saved almost all my poems—many of which might have fed the flames very profitably—and the two long stories which I wrote with so much labor of copying and recopying and which I should never have had the energy nor the faith to reproduce. The other stories that were burned, I shall write over again and better; but my heart is often heavy over the loss of my themes. . . . How I bless the men who helped me, the men whose pencilled verdicts were upon those little lost manuscripts! . . . There were three at the University: Mr. Herrick, Mr. Moody, Mr. Bruyere.[19]

Karle Wilson's habit of faithfully recording her opinions in her journal covered a myriad of subjects. At the age of twenty-five she jotted down thoughts on religion:

> When I came back from the University I was about as un-orthodox as it is possible for anyone to be who has an irradicable instinctive belief in the nearness and the goodness of God. [She had joined the Baptist Church at the age of ten.] . . . I have never, since I can remember, been able to wear religion lightly—so far as my thoughts were concerned. The ease with which most people digest paradoxes has never ceased to amaze me.
>
> When I was about fourteen years old, I think, I formulated a creed for myself. . . . I considered it entirely original with myself, and that it ignored all established beliefs whatsoever, except the belief in God. . . . My attitude toward the religious teachings under which I had been brought up was one of scornful hostility. And there are traces of that attitude that persist in me yet, even after the pendulum has swung back a good way toward its original position. I have a horror yet of ever being drawn back into acceptance of the half-dead regime of the evangelical churches—the stock phrases, the ugly tunes, the dull and dreary hymns, the state of things typified to my mind by the Sunday School of my childhood. The Sunday School is a barbarous institution for a sensitive child. . . . The trouble is that there are two of me: one is a fanatic, an ascetic; and the other is a humanist, pure and simple.[20]

In later years her diaries indicate occasional attendance at Sacred Heart, the Catholic church. In 1945, she was confirmed in Christ Church, the Episcopal church in Nacogdoches.[21]

When Karle Wilson published her first poem in 1903 in *Harper's Maga-*

zine, she was ecstatic to receive a personal letter of acceptance from the editor. Later, when she received a check for twenty dollars, she purchased a bookcase. As she received other similar checks from writing, she used the money for travel "in a radius that twenty dollars would allow."[22] Thus, her patterns were set for years to come. In August of that year, she went farther afield and traveled with her half-sister Bess and Bess' husband, Maurice Wright, to Colorado Springs, Colorado. She recorded in her journal how she spent most of her time, "I sit beside my window, with the ink on the sill and write, write, write. If the people who live across the street think I am writing letters all the time they see me sitting here, they must consider me demented. I am writing stories; I have written four, and tomorrow I start on another; and there is still another I want to finish this week. The rest of the time I write poems,—and yes, and some letters."[23]

At the end of the summer of 1903, Karle, desiring to support herself, returned to Little Rock where she remained employed as a teacher until the end of the school year in 1905. She wrote in her diary of her frustrations with teaching and her desire to write: "The last month or so I seem to have got beyond the point where I can teach as an avocation. I'm tired of public life,—even if the public is only a constituency of school-children. I'm tired of responsibility, and I'm tired of being *seen;* . . . I both love and loathe this avocation of pedagogy. . . . Now what I want with the money is this: to buy me a year of leisure and quiet and comparative independence to write."[24] As a teacher, she had too little free time. She recorded in her journal an infrequent stroll in the National Cemetery in Little Rock where she had enjoyed the beauties of the natural world around her:

> I had such a splendid walk this afternoon: the adjective, if improper, is none too strong. I am ashamed that I get off for these rambles so seldom: my school-work and other labors keep me so busy. . . . On the few walks I have stolen this winter I have been struck afresh by the exquisite coloring of the winter landscape—the mystical greys, the phantom-blue of the haze and smoke, the strange, reticent rose of the after glow. . . . The birds pay man an odd compliment in their preference for haunting his graves. If I had time, I should learn them by name, and know something of their habits, in accordance with the naturalistic mania which is so prevalent just now. But my ignorance has its compensations: I think perhaps they gain in poetry.[25]

Her outing resulted in the composition of a sonnet, "In A National Cemetery," which *Scribner's* published in 1905.

Karle's studies of color in nature and birdlife began to appear more often in her poetry. She had taken up birding seriously when she first came to Nacogdoches to her parents' home in 1900. At that time, she purchased a birder's guide and began to record her observations. This early interest developed into an obsessive delight in birdlife and nature. She likely inherited her love of nature from Kate Floy Montgomery Wilson. After the fire at Pilgrim's Rest, the new home, Tanglewood, became her mother's labor of love even though her poor health forced her to limit her activities. Karle would immortalize Tanglewood years later in her book of essays on birdlife in Nacogdoches. During the time Karle taught in Little Rock, her mother wrote about the building of the new house and the landscaping she had planned.[26] In an unpublished essay, "The Magnolia Tree," Charlotte Baker Montgomery tells of her grandmother's gardening at Tanglewood:

> At Tanglewood, when she was able, Grandmother Wilson took her camp stool into the yard to oversee Charlie's work. [Charlie was the black hired man.] He planted fig trees along the tall board fence along Sam Houston Street [now Hughes Street], and crepe myrtles on both sides of the drive. He planted rose bushes in the side yard, bridal wreath near one front (Mound St.) gate, cape jessamines under the side porch. He set out hundreds of Emperor Narcissus bulbs bordering the long path past the front steps.[27]

The magnolia was among the many trees Karle's mother planted at Tanglewood. She wanted to add other trees to the old deciduous trees that were already there and wrote in her journal, "I was determined to have a home that should be embowered in some sort of green all winter. . . . On the north side of the house I have already the beginnings of my beloved 'Tanglewood.' Clumps of native evergreens—holly, cedar, sweet bay, magnolia grandiflora, wild peach . . ."[28]

Kate Wilson's landscaping was an inspiration to Karle. In a diary entry written in late summer 1905 while she was living with her parents, Karle Wilson mentions her "writing window" and the view from the window. She could observe the trees, the yard with its plants and shrubbery, and any wildlife in that area: "The bluejays are back again; they were not so numerous during July and the first weeks of August. Now the trees are full of them; just now I saw an unusually fine fellow hopping about under the tree within a few feet of my window."[29] In other early notes on birds, she writes: "Saw a real wren just now—the first time I ever identified one. I was attracted to my window by his urgent, squeakily musical little "Hick! Hick! Hick! Higgins!"

And there in my cannas, directly under the window, was his little brown back, his absurd little upturned tail, his striped profile with its bright eye turned up to look at me. I called Ben [her brother], and he confirmed my conjecture as to the name and family of the stranger."[30]

Karle Wilson received her wish "to buy a year of leisure and quiet and comparative independence to write" in June 1905, when she left the public schools in Little Rock and returned to Nacogdoches. The following summer, Karle spent from June 5 until July 10, 1906, at Port Bolivar on the Gulf Coast in a boardinghouse writing short stories and poems and reading.[31] Sometimes typing all day, she sent many manuscripts to prospective publishers. Her creative production during this time was amazingly prolific, but it is characteristic of her writing output throughout her career. In journal notes, she chides herself that she does not write enough, yet she fills page upon page of the journal with observations such as, "I wrote for seven hours almost constantly—the thermometer was at one hundred degrees" and records rewriting a story, reducing it from 5,000 to 3,500 words or reducing another from 7,000 to 5,800 words, simultaneously with reading biographies of literary figures such as Shelley and Wordsworth. She achieved such formidable production at Port Bolivar by following a systematic routine: she arose before five in the morning and walked to the marsh to watch the birds, then returned to her room and worked until four in the afternoon, stopping only for a light lunch in her room. In the evenings she walked and read. She wrote of her determination in her journal: "I am bent upon prose, just now."[32]

Even though Karle had returned to Texas to help her mother, she found her mother's depression and anxiety difficult to live with. "I can bear anyone else's despondency; but hers invades my citadel," she wrote.[33] Nevertheless, Karle and her mother collaborated to write a book. By the end of 1906, Karle Wilson had a manuscript of eighty thousand words ready to send to a publisher. The book was based on Kate Floy's childhood experiences. Karle encouraged her mother to write down the memories, and she handled the typewriting and revisions. (She revised the lengthy account three times.) Karle admitted that she and her mother could never decide whether they meant the book for a juvenile or an adult audience.[34] She posted "The Little Carpet Bagger" (originally titled "Union Forever") to Doubleday, Century, and Houghton Mifflin publishing houses, but they all rejected the manuscript. However, Karle published some short stories and poems of her own that year.[35] After her mother's death, Karle Wilson Baker submitted the manuscript to New York publishers again (1912–13) but was unsuccessful.[36]

On January 24, 1907, some citizens of Nacogdoches met to try and raise subscriptions to attract the Baptist college in Rusk, Texas, to Nacogdoches. The *Daily Sentinel* reported, "We are in this contest to win . . . to secure the East Texas Baptist College. . . . The result of the meeting was the adoption of a motion that Nacogdoches proceed at once to raise $20,000 as a bonus to the college. . . . Mr. E. A. Blount announced that he would start the subscription with one twentieth of the amount—$1,000."[37] About three weeks later, Karle Wilson wrote eloquently to the editor of the newspaper in support of the effort to transfer the college to Nacogdoches. She identified herself as a stranger who had come to a new place and stated that because of her fresh perspective she was perhaps more sensitive to the atmosphere of the place than the residents who were accustomed to it. She wrote:

> Now, Nacogdoches has a soul, a spirit, an atmosphere. She is no raw product of today or yesterday. There are ghosts on her streets. . . . Gentle Franciscan fathers and curious, credulous redmen; lordly Mexican alcaldes and courtly French adventurers; the hardy, high-hearted followers of Nolan and the young, ill-fated Magee; the stubborn, spirited, courageous American Empresarios; and finally that group of ardent strangers who swarmed through the gateway settlement to help Texas win her independence—men scholarly and grave like Rusk, picturesque like Crockett, massive like Houston, or simply young and winning and gallant like Travis, who at twenty-seven, died at his cannon in the court of the Alamo. Have you ever stood at the junction of LaNana and Banita on a spring afternoon, and turned the clock of your mind backward for two hundred years, and seemed to see the holy fathers in their coarse woolen gowns, barefooted, with the knotted rope about their waists, preserving their vow of silence as they built up the preliminary shelter of twigs and grasses while the curious Indians crowded about, watching their strange labor and their gentle ways? What were they doing? They were building the Mission of Our Lady of Nacogdoches for the future. . . . We are accustomed to thinking of them as rough frontiersmen perhaps. But the Franciscan friars were scholars, trained in the Spanish colleges at Zacetecas. Young Nolan, whose followers languished so long in the Old Stone Fort, finally to be marched out upon the square and driven off to slavery in Mexico, was an astronomer and geographer, who, it is said, made the first map of Texas. Rusk, our own particular possession, was one of the most persuasive orators of his time and country, trained in the colleges of one of the older Southern States. Even Houston, who was so close to primitive

> nature, so rugged and massive, that President Jackson's praise for him was that he was a "man not made by the tailor," knew all of Pope's Iliad by heart. . . . In his will, a document of singular impressiveness and dignity, he leaves explicit directions regarding the education of his children. . . . Why, if the projected college goes elsewhere, through the mere indifference and carelessness of Nacogdoches, there will be a mass-meeting of the ghosts. . . . Nobody need to be told what a college can do for the spirit and atmosphere of a town. The spirit of Nacogdoches today is a gift from the men of the past; the spirit of the future will be the gift of the men of today. . . .[38]

Her letter to the editor was the first time many of the citizens of the town had heard opinions expressed by this young woman who had only recently moved to their city. They must have been impressed by the well-informed, articulate letter that so obviously set Karle Wilson apart from the average inhabitant of the small town. Certainly it did not go unnoticed by a young banker, Thomas Ellis Baker.

Before Karle Wilson moved permanently to Nacogdoches, she had visited in her parents' home many times. Nacogdoches was a small village, and the social circles were small too: it seemed that everyone in the town was related or at least knew each other well. Charlotte Baker Montgomery has commented that during her mother's visits, Karle would have most certainly met Baker, a young businessman/banker who was active in almost every area of community life. He was born on Christmas Day in 1874 at Hickory Flat, a small community outside Nacogdoches near Central Heights. He started school there and worked on the family farm. (Charlotte still has the ten-dollar gold piece that her father earned as a boy when he sold his first cotton from the farm.) Thomas E. Baker's family moved into town in 1888, and he continued his education, attending public school in the Old University Building. He also took courses at Spencer's Business College. Tom Baker was a man of many talents and interests who worked at various jobs as a young man. He was in a printer's office for a time (where he later reported that he "learned to spell"). Because of his work at the print shop, he got free tickets to shows at the Opera House downtown when touring companies performed. He also acted in some of the local theatrical productions. Charlotte Baker Montgomery feels this accounted for his interest in cultural affairs. At one time Tom Baker was deputy county clerk and read law with Judge June Harris in Nacogdoches. He also worked at several dry goods stores in town. His industriousness led to his part ownership in 1901 with Sam Stripling and

R. W. Hazelwood in the Stripling Hazelwood Drugstore. At that same time, Baker was employed at the Commercial Guaranty Bank. Certainly a man of Baker's mettle was a very desirable bachelor in the town. The intimate social circle of the town's major families allowed ample opportunity for Karle Wilson and Tom Baker to cross paths. Karle would live in Nacogdoches only two years before they married.[39] Tom Baker won her hand in August of 1907, and they remained happily married for forty-nine years, until his death.

When Edward C. Marsh of the Macmillan Company wrote to Karle Wilson in late July 1907, asking her to participate in the publishing house's new series on American history by contributing the volume on Texas history, the young writer could not have been more pleased, but the project could not have been more ill-timed.[40] In only two weeks, Karle Wilson and Tom Baker were to be married. Nevertheless, Miss Wilson replied to Marsh within a few days accepting his proposal. She expressed curiosity about how he had come to know of her. She assumed he had seen some of her short stories or verse in popular magazines but was puzzled why he would select her, even if he had seen her work, since her publications were fictional rather than the nonfiction required for a work of history. Also, she had published under the pseudonym Charlotte Wilson; how did he know her real name to contact her?[41]

Marsh supplied some explanations in a return letter. He never mentioned having read any of Karle Wilson's fiction but said that he had acted on a recommendation from George P. Garrison, professor of history at the University of Texas in Austin.[42] Later, Karle Wilson Baker would learn that Macmillan had first approached Professor Garrison to write the volume on Texas, but he had declined. Only a few years earlier, in 1903, Garrison had published an important history of the state, *Texas: A Contest of Civilizations,* as part of the American Commonwealth Series for Houghton, Mifflin and Company.[43]

Some interesting observations can be made about the Macmillan offer. When Karle Wilson replied accepting the writing assignment, she mentioned that she could be in New York City about the first of September. In fact, after their wedding on August 8, the young couple had plans to honeymoon at Niagara Falls, New York.[44] The newlyweds must have mutually consented to spend some of their honeymoon time with a New York publisher arranging a contract for Karle. From the very beginning of their marriage, Tom Baker realized that his wife, unlike many women of her day, was interested in a career. Even during the early days of marriage, he understood and encouraged her expectations. Family members and friends have commented that Mr. Baker was devoted to his wife and "placed her on a pedestal."[45]

Another observation focuses on Prof. George P. Garrison. Garrison was later to become the father-in-law to Karle Wilson Baker's brother, Ben, when Ben and Elizabeth (Bess) Garrison married in 1910. In 1907, however, Professor Garrison did not have this family connection with Karle Wilson, but the Garrisons had relatives, the Perkins family, in Nacogdoches, and Bess Garrison regularly visited her cousins. George Garrison had lived in Nacogdoches years earlier.[46] Bess certainly would have been introduced to the newcomers, Karle and Ben Wilson. Very likely, Professor Garrison knew of Karle Wilson's persuasive letter to the editor in 1907 and recognized her interest in Texas history and her unusual talent for expression. Also, Karle had published three short stories that year in the months before her marriage.[47] Professor Garrison might have read them. As editor of the *Quarterly of the Texas State Historical Association* in addition to being a writer himself, he would have wanted such a skilled writer as Karle Wilson on the project. When Marsh described the type of book his company was looking for, he emphasized that it should be historically accurate but also highly readable. He wanted it to appeal to the general public and follow a narrative approach versus "a dry collection of historic facts." The title of the volume, according to Marsh, would be "The Story of Texas."[48] Marsh had written a similar description when he approached Professor Garrison about the project. Perhaps Garrison felt that the writing style a literary person could offer would better fit Macmillan's requirements than what he was willing to provide.

At any rate, quite unexpectedly, Karle Wilson was offered her biggest writing opportunity to date just two weeks before her marriage. After the honeymoon, she wrote to Professor Garrison for help with background information on Texas history. Garrison was most accommodating, sending her a reading list that began with his own volume, *Texas,* from the Commonwealth Series. He also recommended the text by Bolton and Barker, *With the Makers of Texas,* and Henderson Yoakum's two volumes on the history of Texas. In particular, he suggested the *Texas Quarterly of the Texas State Historical Association* as a source.[49] Issues of the *Texas Quarterly* from 1898 through 1905 contain translations of diaries and accounts of early expeditions in Texas that greatly enriched Karle Wilson Baker's background in Texas history. The articles included a four-part series on the route of Cabeza de Vaca and other important expeditions such as De León's expedition of 1689, the La Salle expedition, and the Magee-Gutierrez expedition of 1812, which included citizens from Nacogdoches.[50] A journal of Stephen F. Austin's first trip to Texas (1821), translations of early letters of Don Damian Manzanet, and letters from Sam Houston, Philip Nolan, and Adolpus Sterne were in some of the issues. Also included were articles on the Spanish abandonment and reoccupation of East Texas and accounts of the Tejas (or Asinai) and Cherokee Indians.

Always focused on characters and human relationships in her writing, Baker used a biographical approach for "The Story of Texas," introducing history through diaries and eyewitness accounts, some of which were based on the writings printed in the *Quarterly.* Her exceptional skill as a narrative writer made her work highly readable as well as informative.[51] While working on the project, she explained to Edward Marsh that the earliest part of Texas history, the Spanish and French explorations, was frequently ignored in textbooks and, to her knowledge, had never before been available for a popular audience.[52] Unfortunately, the responsibilities of married life (followed by the rearing of two small children) caused Karle to delay "The Story of Texas" project. She wrote to Marsh about her complications in 1908, and he replied that he could allow her more time.[53] When the Baker's first child, Thomas Wilson Baker (Tomby), was born December 1, 1908, at Dr. Felix Tucker's hospital in Nacogdoches on the corner of King Street near Tanglewood, Karle placed "The Story of Texas" "on hold" once again.[54]

Karle Wilson Baker often wrote fictional pieces that were partly autobiographical. These writings, among her family papers, offer insight into her early married life. In "Achieving Compatibility," an unpublished short story, she notes the community reaction when she and Tom (named "Peter" in the fictional work) married:

> When Peter and I were married there was no little shaking of heads. To the unsophisticated standards of our village I represented the pinnacle of intellectuality—none too desirable an eminence; where as they were quite proud of Peter, who had developed under their eyes from a little tow-headed chap delivering parcels to one of the influential businessmen of the community. They looked upon it rather in the light of an aberration that he should have chosen for a life-partner a "stranger," a migratory school-teacher who chanced to alight in passing, and whom nobody else would have thought of as a mere marriageable human being. That I was known to have literary aspirations, and that my name was actually to be seen occasionally in the magazines at the drug-store, only added to the enigma. My own friends, on the other hand, gave me an impression of politely suppressed uneasiness at the extraordinary step I had taken, and I think that both factions had visions—more or less definite—of our post-honeymoon days, which disclosed me read-

> ing Browning to a slumbering Peter, and looking up from my book at last only to burst into tears.
>
> Yet to Peter and I [*sic*], achieving compatibility has seemed, for the most part, a very simple matter. . . . Instinctively, we have built our temple of harmony upon the foundations of a mutual tolerance. . . . I have spoken of history; and here, indeed, we have instinctively come upon one of the intellectual regions common to our very diverse tastes. . . . but next to mother, home, and heaven, Peter loves hunting; if he has an earthly passion, it is for duck-shooting. . . . Armed with Peter's gun and my bird-glass, we have from the beginning spent every available minute in the open.[55]

In spite of their different natures, "mutual tolerance" became the cornerstone of their marriage, which was always filled with respect for one another.

The Bakers made their first home in Nacogdoches on the corner of North Street and Baxter-Duncan Street. The property behind the house sloped down to the Banita Creek and the railway station and then turned upward beyond the tracks into a heavily wooded area. This retreat into nature became a favorite place for Karle's birding and writing. A diary entry in February 1908 relates an incident she and her young husband experienced together:

> Yesterday afternoon—February 23—Tom and I spent walking in the woods. It was a mild, balmy day, without a hint of chill in the air, though, for the most part, with a drift of light clouds over the sun. Just before we crossed the creek we heard two owls 'talking' to each other over on the piney hillside—an odd sound in mid-afternoon. Just beyond the creek, in a rich, moist, grassy place, we found two or three clumps of fair little waxen, golden-centered flowers. . . . We startled a flock of slaty juncos out of a fallen pinetop, and found a hermit-thrush, who let us come within a few feet of him. Coming back across the pasture we came upon a single robin in the pasture-grass—a great, black-headed, ruddy breasted fellow.[56]

Karle Wilson Baker's diary entries demonstrate her dedication to observe everything in nature. Again in February, she recorded:

> For two weeks every day has brought new signs of Spring, although the weather, properly speaking, has been colder than usual. The pear trees are slowly making ready to blossom; one or two white flowers have

> already unfolded, but the other buds are doubtless awaiting the first warm day to burst into bloom. The japonicas bloomed two weeks ago; several days ago I noticed the first tiny radiating spikes of leaves on the weeping willow over at Dad's.[Tanglewood] The elms and some of the maples are all but in leaf, while others are still quite bare. A week ago tonight, about eleven o'clock, Tom and I first glimpsed Arcturus twinkling red and brilliant on the horizon, between the bare branches of the trees. Last night, at ten, he was well up in the sky. This morning as I went about my work I heard the bold, sweet whistle of the cardinal—not the short, experimental note with which he begins in the spring, but the long, full "Je-hu! Je-hu!" which marks the jubilant days of the early nesting season. In this climate he is the first of the birds to become conspicuous, to announce that the winter is over. His awakening begins in February, and he is in the flood-tide of his vernal ecstasy in March.[57]

Karle Wilson Baker increased her knowledge of birdlife by reading books by ornithologists. Later she took her daily diary entries (sometimes just jots of observations) and wove them into the poetic fabric of her sophisticated, first-person essays on birdlife in *The Birds of Tanglewood.*

In June 1909, Karle Wilson Baker heard again from E. C. Marsh of the Macmillan Company, who inquired about the progress of "The Story of Texas." On July 12, Baker sent the first four chapters (ninety pages) to Macmillan. Marsh replied that even though the editors were pleased with her work, the company had a policy to receive only complete manuscripts, and he needed the finished work as soon as possible before the editors could guarantee publication.[58] Karle was unable to meet the deadline for the submission of the complete manuscript, so the publication failed by default. In 1934, she sent a revised manuscript of "The Story of Texas" to the Macmillan Company, but the editors were not interested.[59]

The Baker family enlarged again when a second child, Charlotte, was born on August 31, 1910. In her diary, Karle named the occasion "Charlotte's Advent." Nine weeks later tragedy struck the family with the death of Kate Floy Montgomery Wilson. Karle noted in her diary that she stayed at her mother's house until midnight on November 6 and that she spent the night at her mother's home on November 7; Kate Floy Montgomery Wilson died at 4:45 P.M. on November 8.[60] Karle Wilson Baker wrote about her last hours with her mother: "I can see them [her mother's eyes] as they looked at me during her last hours, when she was too weak to talk. There was the old, imperious tenderness, still—and still the fire, burning through the dark anguish, demanding as its right the key to the mystery of pain. Few people have had more of physical suffering crowded into a moderate life-time than my mother; her one great achievement was *gallantry.* Few have ever had better right to boast, 'I was ever a fighter.'"[61]

For the next fifteen years, Karle Wilson Baker actively pursued her writing interests as she nurtured her young family. She faithfully recorded in a ledger the date when she submitted each poem or short story to a publisher, followed by the date on which the piece was either published or rejected. An examination of the record book, which is in the possession of the Baker Estate, gives evidence to her determination to write and be published. She received many rejections, but she remained undaunted and continued to submit material. With time, she experienced success in getting her short stories published, but her greater successes during these years came from her poems. Much of Karle's inspiration came from life with her family and her observations of nature. Both Karle and Tom Baker enjoyed the outdoors, and they wanted their children to learn the same appreciation. Between 1911 and 1925, Karle Wilson Baker, following her favorite method of recording her thoughts, used a large ledger book to record the Baker family's experiences at a cabin they owned outside Nacogdoches at Fern Lake.[62] The Bakers referred to this retreat in the woods as "The Camp." Naming her journal "The Log of Camp Billiken," she made the first entry on Saturday evening July 29, 1911. Charlotte was not yet one; Tomby was almost three. Karle Wilson Baker was determined that her own children would experience freedom and have liberties that she had not known as a child. Her own mother had been intent on "controlling" and "training" her children in a manner that had placed severe limitations on their activities.[63] The Bakers spent much of October that first year at the camp. Tom Baker enjoyed duck hunting at the lake; Karle enjoyed the serenity and beauties of nature. Tom gave Karle a rifle, but she never learned to shoot. Family members and friends joined them at the camp, sometimes for several days at a time. Frequent guests were Ben T. and Bess Wilson; Tom's mother and sister, Carrie, and Carrie's husband, Capt. I. L. Sturdevant; and Karle's father, W. T. Wilson. The children's cousins, Carolyn Sturdevant and Floy Lewis, also came.[64] Their cook, a black woman named Lucy, was on hand to help. The Bakers established a rhythm as to when they would go to the camp: the autumn months (September–November) were popular for duck shooting, and spring was a popular time for fishing (March and then again in May), but summer was too warm. Karle made many photographs of the children at Fern Lake fishing from the pier, sitting on logs, or just playing in the woods. Daily entries made at the camp describe the weather, the birds, the natural surroundings, and who was there.[65]

Instead of going to the camp in the summer months, the Bakers often vacationed with the I. L. Sturdevants, Karle's in-laws. Karle's son, Tom W. Baker, described a vacation with the Sturdevants (Aunt Carrie and Uncle Link) to San Antonio that took five days in a Model T; they camped out in tents along the way. His cousin, Carolyn Sturdevant Miller, recalled the trip too.[66] Tom W. Baker also recalled an unpleasant incident on the road when the two families vacationed in Eureka Springs, Arkansas (about 1917). The families traveled in two cars. Tom Baker commented that his uncle had a big Franklin automobile with an air-cooled engine. The black man who worked for both families traveled with them and helped with the driving. They had plans to spend the night in a downtown hotel in Henrietta, Arkansas, along the way. When they were told that the black man could not stay in the hotel, the ladies and children stayed in town, but Capt. Sturdevant and TEB (the manner in which Karle often referred to her husband) drove outside town and all three men slept in the car.[67]

Each autumn the best duck-hunting day was noted as "The Day of the Big Flight," and sometimes the campers killed two dozen or more ducks at a shooting, but most days they shot many fewer. Karle's friend from college, Anna McCaleb, visited Nacogdoches in April 1913, and they spent most of the time at the camp. During Anna's visit, they had a "Limerick Day" when Karle wrote humorous verses about those at the camp. About Tom Baker, she wrote:

> A banker named Baker once said,
> "Don't bother to fix me hot bread;
> Just save me cold slabs,
> With grease-gravy in dabs,
> And let me rush madly to bed."

A limerick about herself:

> A muscular person named Karle
> Said, "It puts brain and nerves in a snarl
> To look after the kids,
> Or to wash up the lids;
> But water I'll tote by the bar'l."[68]

When Karle Wilson Baker wrote in her diary in 1913 that she was "just a writing person" she also noted that Herrick at the University of Chicago had written on her themes, 'You write charmingly about nothing.'" She added to her diary entry, "My particular age of the world wants the man who writes briefly about something. . . . That is why I am, at age thirty-five, an unknown author."[69]

That she was an "unknown author" was not due to lack of trying, nor was she really "unknown." In 1913 alone, she submitted to publishers at least thirty-five poems and about twenty-two essays or short stories. Most of the poems were accepted for publication as were about half of the short stories and essays. She submitted works to a wide variety of magazines including *Harper's, Century, Forum, Poetry, Smart Set, Lippincott's, Scribner's, Atlantic, International, Life, Delineator, Ladies Home Journal, Saturday Evening Post, Munsey's, Red Book, McCall's, Holland's,* and *People's Home Journal.*[70] *The Craftsman* published her article "Helpful Facts in Building a Summer Camp: By A Woman Camper Who Knows All About It." The article described the family's life at Fern Lake and included pictures of Tomby and Charlotte at the camp.[71]

In the early years at Fern Lake, the Bakers sometimes went to the camp in a buggy, which took two hours from their home in Nacogdoches. Ben T. Wilson sometimes came on horseback. Tom Baker drove an automobile into town to the bank each day except on weekends. Often Karle and Tom went boating on the lake before breakfast or took a walk together before he drove to town. When Tomby and Charlotte became school age, they rode to town with their father and out to the camp again after his workday at the bank.[72] Karle Wilson Baker remained at the camp where she could walk in the woods and take her writing box. In 1916, Karle noted that from October 20 to November 14 when they were at the camp the children did not miss a day of school and only spent one night in town (Halloween). Also that year she wrote an article titled "Camping with the Kiddies: By One Who Has Tried It," and enclosed photos of the cabin at Fern Lake, the woods and lake, and her children. In the article, she stated that the experiences at the camp "steadied" her as a new mother and brought back her vigor and sanity: "To my mind it is as indispensable as a baby-carriage or a bath-thermometer." She described her freedom: "Nowadays I can spend the whole day on the lake if I like, or in the woods with a book; for they [Tomby and Charlotte] go in to school in the morning with 'Father' and come back with him in the evening."[73] Baker gave the camp another fictional name, "Camp Peterkin." She wrote that even though the camp was only seven miles from home, "After I have had a few hours there, in which to let the silence of the pines 'slide into my soul,' I could not be happier if it were seventy or seven hundred." She felt that the time spent at the camp was equally important for the children:

> Altogether, unless you are completely and incorrigibly urban in your tastes—unless you are the sort of person who thinks the frogs sound "lonesome"—you have only to contrast this method of taking a vacation with the usual one of taking it at a hotel to see how much more naturally the children fit into it. . . . And how they have enjoyed it! As I watch them day by day acquiring the curious lore of the woods; as I watch their eyes shine over the wonder of a new butterfly or the note of a new bird; as I see them growing up in intimate friendship with earth and air and sky, I think of the intensity of my own childish memories, and I know that our camp in the woods is laying up for them a treasure-store upon which they shall continue to draw as long as they live in the world.[74]

According to Charlotte Baker Montgomery, the family members took turns writing in the "Camp Log."[75] Thomas E. Baker made entries in the camp journal for 1919 and 1920. On November 13, 1919, the childish handwriting of Charlotte (age nine) appears. When the Bakers were at the camp in 1920, Tom Baker wrote about President Harding's election on November 2 and notes that the bank took a holiday for the first time on Armistice Day, November 11; the holiday allowed him to have a full day shooting duck at the lake. He also wrote in 1920 that *The Garden of the Plynck*, Karle's first children's book, came by special delivery while they were at the camp.

Karle Wilson Baker resumes writing the log in 1921. In October 1922, she mentions that they are taking "both cars" to the camp and that she is busy typing while she is there. In 1925, the days at Fern lake ended. Tom Baker wrote in the log, "We sold the camp. . . . We regret giving it up, but it seemed impractical for us to use it, so we decided to let it go. We hope new occupants will have as much fun as we did with it."[76] During the years at Fern Lake, Karle Wilson Baker realized the first part of her dream to become an established writer: she gained national recognition as a poet. This achievement is the subject of the next chapter.

"Writing my poems is seldom more laborious than skimming the cream from my thoughts. It just needs time and quiet to rise."

CHAPTER 2
The Poet Emerges

Even though Karle Wilson Baker had confided in her diary in September 1913 that she was "a writing person," she had to confront the reality that with her children, Tomby and Charlotte, ages five and three, family life demanded most of her attention.[1] She frequently composed short lyrics, but she never could find enough uninterrupted time for a long prose work. She also supported the interests of her husband and her father, who were active in the Nacogdoches community. Thomas E. Baker was an officer at the Commercial Guaranty Bank, and W. T. Wilson still ran his grain and feed business and was a member of the Citizens Committee for Stephen F. Austin State Teachers College, which was dedicated to bringing a college to the town. But even in the face of such diversions, Karle Wilson Baker managed to forge what would become a long and active association with the important scholarly journal, the *Yale Review.*

Between 1914 and 1920, the shy, retiring, but talented young woman from Nacogdoches, Texas, became the most frequent contributor to the *Yale Review.* Because of the recognition she received from the *Review,* Karle Wilson Baker became one of the most famous poets in the South. How did a female poet from a small town in Texas reach such heights of fame? The answer is found in the combination of the unconventional publishing initiatives of the *Yale Review* and the remarkable talent of one of the *Review's* earliest and most prolific contributors. The alliance demonstrates how an editor's discernment, encouragement, and advice can move a gifted but unknown writer into the national spotlight. Wilbur L. Cross conceived the creation of the *Yale Review* in 1911 as a national quarterly devoted not only to literature, the fine arts, science, and philosophy, but also to current issues of import to all citizens interested in the economic, social, and political life of the country. The new editor exhibited courage and creativity when he took risks and published little-known writers alongside famous authors in the same issues. Also, he challenged the publishing establishment in yet another way by supporting and publishing works by female writers and writers who lived in places other than the East Coast. These initiatives persisted in spite of wartime restrictions on paper and publishing that forced editors to be even more selective. Karle Wilson Baker benefited from all these factors.

Poetry came naturally to Baker, and the ease with which she wrote is reflected in her verse. Her first efforts at writing were poems or diary entries. A diary entry in 1917 expresses her feelings: "Writing my poems is seldom more laborious than skimming the cream from my thoughts. It just needs time and quiet to rise."[2] Later, after much success as a poet, she wondered if it had come too easily. Oddly, her notion that writing should be more difficult motivated her to turn to writing novels, which often was more challenging for her.[3] Her poetic forms include the lyric, sonnet, ballad, and ode, where she incorporates a strong sense of imagery and figures of speech, especially metaphor. A wide range of interests occupied her writings, and her personal life strongly influenced her early poems that focused on family, religion, and nature. These were followed by contemporary concerns and the role of women. Her later poems reveal her lifelong interest in Texas history. Much of her poetry portrays the natural beauty of East Texas, but she is more than a local colorist or regionalist. Regardless of the subject matter, she goes beyond the specific to a larger lesson. Careful reading of her poetry reveals universal themes, which she herself recognized in her work and noted in a diary entry made when she was seventy-seven years old: "Throughout my life I have had one theme: the universal set in the common place, the essence piercing the husk—at first instinctively and graspingly, next confusedly, now freely and in the light."[4]

Karle Wilson Baker's national reputation as a writer was established by her poetry. The *Yale Review* enjoyed a nationwide distinction that created respect for Karle Wilson Baker in the literary world in America. A regional press or popular magazine could not have achieved the same results for her. Even though Baker had published in other journals, her real breakthrough came when the *Yale Review* published "A Group of Sonnets" in October 1914. The issue included two previously unpublished poems by Robert Browning as well as these four sonnets by Karle Wilson Baker, "The Young Poet to Italy," "Evening," "Desire of Fame," and "To My Enemy."[5] Baker was still writing under the name of Charlotte Wilson. Upon receiving the sonnets, the assistant editor, Edward Bliss Reed, wrote enthusiastically to Baker: "This is the first time I have had the pleasure of seeing anything of your work, and I should be glad to read anything you may wish to submit." Reed also added, "Will you kindly send me a few items about yourself, for we always publish brief information about our contributors."[6] Baker responded:

> As to myself, I am a Southerner born and bred and—with exception of about two years spent at the University of Chicago, where I studied English Composition under Robert Herrick & Wm. Vaughn Moody—I have lived all my life in the South. I was born in Little Rock, Arkansas, in 1878. Before my marriage, nearly seven years ago, I taught two years in Virginia, and two more in Little Rock. Outside of the magazines (which I inhabit none too frequently) I am Mrs. Thomas E. Baker, and I have a "husband of my own" and a small son and daughter. I am a "self-made author" (what there is of me) and have never achieved the dignity and solidity of a book. Perhaps a dozen published stories and some fifty poems in various magazines constitute my title to a right to exist.[7]

Although Baker had published some fifty poems in a variety of magazines, she was still not well-known nationally. By nature she was retiring and modest, yet senior editor Wilbur L. Cross fueled her ambition and creativity by enthusiastically supporting most of the poems she sent to the *Review*. Karle Wilson Baker published some twenty-six poems with the *Review* in a six-year period, becoming the *Review's* most frequently published poet in those years. Along with his assistant editor, Helen McAfee, Cross offered Baker both criticism and encouragement. Comments such as "We like every one of your poems" and "Let me see more of your poems" reflect how he felt toward the newly discovered poet.[8] Karle Wilson Baker had never before received this kind of support from an editor. Cross's skillful, conscientious editing helped to improve her poems, but on the other hand, she did not always feel obligated to accept outside advice. When Cross wrote to her regarding the sonnet "Desire of Fame," suggesting that she change the accent in the fourth line, Baker replied courteously that she did not resent his suggestions but welcomed them. However, she noted that "In regard to the irregularity in the fourth line, . . . I did it on purpose." She added, "What I mean to say is, that the altered accent, by relieving the steady tramp of the verse, really heightens the effectiveness of the whole. It is not at all unlikely, however, that my ear is at fault; and I feel sure I should concur most heartily in any amendment you might wish to make." Cross responded immediately: "You are probably quite right about the irregularity in the fourth line of your sonnet on 'Desire of Fame,' and it will be set up as it stands."[9]

"At the Picture-Show," which appeared in the *Review's* October 1915 issue, is an example of a poem that benefited from Cross's editing skills when he suggested changes: "I like very much your poem 'At the Picture-Show,' and will publish it in the course of the year. In this kind of verse, of course, you intend to come at times rather close to prose. I think that you reach the point in 'Out of the fragments; that is plain to see.' Again, 'with damask cheek' is rather stale. If you wish to look over the poem again, we should like to send it to you. Otherwise, it will go to the printer as it is. On the whole, the poem seems to me one of the best that I have seen in the new style."[10]

Later correspondence indicates that Baker welcomed Cross's recommendations. He replied to her, "I thank you for returning "At the Picture-Show," with the changes, all of which seem to me to be for the better. I do not see any "weak spots" in it as it stands, though the repetition of *all* in the two lines—"Through all her wholesome days; but when, at night, They all go voyaging across the screen"—troubles me a little. What do you say to making a change here?"[11] About two weeks later, editor and author reached an agreement: "I think your emendation of 'They all go voyaging' to 'They go a-voyaging' a very good way out of the difficulty, and will have the poem set up as it now stands. It seems to me perfectly clear."[12] By accepting Cross's advice, Baker improved her poem. She rarely received advice from other people, however; after all, she was writing in a rural area of East Texas, far removed from sophisticated editors, writers, or others who could read her work critically or with whom she might even discuss her work. In a diary entry years later, Baker noted that in her youth she had felt a great desire, which she described as a "famine-like craving," for association with other writers, "if they were right for me." Wilbur Cross met this qualification, and she welcomed his editorial suggestions. One the other hand, she wrote that "much contact with would-be writers, the members of authors' clubs, even the 'little great,' fills me with a deep impatience approaching disgust, and does me more harm than good."[13] She was always very much aware that she was working alone and that seeking outside help from just anyone would not prove beneficial.

In contrast to her poetry, Karle Wilson Baker's first attempts at publishing essays in the *Yale Review* were unsuccessful. She submitted an article on William Vaughn Moody in May 1914, but the editors rejected it.[14] The next month, Baker sent an essay titled "The New Religion and The Woman's Problem" to the *Yale Review* for consideration. Cross replied that he found her article very interesting but that he could not use it because he "had already arranged for several other contributions on this general subject."[15]

Baker's early poems and short stories were rarely published in Texas. Not only was the literary climate male oriented, but also the more important and influential journals were located in the North and East. However, in 1915, she submitted "Poet Songs" to the *Texas Review*. The editor, Stark Young, published it, calling it the best of the poems in the *Review*.[16] "Poet Songs" is a lyric poem in three parts. The last section became one of Karle Wilson Baker's most famous little poems:

Dropp'd feathers from the wings of God
My little songs and snatches are,
So light He does not hear them fall
As he goes by, from star to star.

Dropp'd feathers from the wings of God
I find, and braid them in my hair;
Men heed them not—they only make
My soul unto herself more fair.[17]

That same year, again submitting to a journal other than the *Yale Review*, Baker published "The Housemother" in the new periodical out of Chicago, *Poetry: A Magazine of Verse*, edited by Harriet Monroe.

On November 22, 1915, Cross wrote another letter to Baker encouraging her to send more poems to him. "We like every one of the poems which you have let us see, and are keeping "A Little Boy's Bath," "A Clear Night," and "The Family.". . . I wish that you would let me see some more of your poems in the course of a month or two. Perhaps additions might be made to the group."[18] The eloquent little poem "A Clear Night" demonstrates Baker's command of metaphor and imagery:

I have worn this day as a fretting, ill-made garment,
Impatient to be rid of it.

And lo, as I drew it off over my shoulders
This jewel caught in my hair.

During these exciting years of early publication, Karle Wilson Baker found her verse published in journals and magazines throughout the country.

However, the lyric poems that came so easily for Karle Wilson Baker did not take up her total writing life. She continued making her extensive diary entries. Her interest in birdlife, which she recorded in her diary, continued to grow, and her observations soon became the subject for essays as well as verse. In a diary entry while she was still living on Baxter-Duncan Street, Baker mentions a technique she had for feeding birds that she would use later at her homes Tanglewood and West Windows: "I got my lunch-counters up last Friday but this morning was the first time I have caught anybody using them. When I first got up, a little wren was picking around on the shelf, trying the popcorn grains and picking the suet from under the screen; and another was eating the suet I had tied in the window-bush. Monday I fixed up a little 'Christmas-tree' on the shelf, and this morning I tied some suet in it, and an ear of corn for the Cardinals."[19]

The year 1916 was an especially good one for Karle Wilson Baker at the *Yale Review;* seven of her poems appeared in the October issue. Cross wrote enthusiastically, "I am delighted with the poems which you sent in, and am keeping the following: 'Wild Geese,' 'Stillness,' 'The Rain-Pool,' and 'Apple and Rose.' They seem best adapted to my use. I am returning 'Bright Angel Trail,' 'Fairy Mountains,' 'Altair,' and 'The Earth's Child.'"[20] Cross titled the poems that appeared in the October 1916 *Yale Review* "A Group of Lyrics." Subject matter for the lyrics "A Clear Night," "Stillness," "Wild Geese," "Street Doves," "The Family," "A Little Boy's Bath," and "Apple and Rose" focuses on nature and domestic life—natural themes for a woman living in a rural area with a young family. "Apple and Rose" is a gentle dedication to her two children:

My little daughter is a tea-rose,
Satin to the touch,
Wine to the lips,
And a faint, delirious perfume.
But my little son
Is a June apple,
Firm and cool,
And scornful of too much sweetness,
But full of tang and flavor
And better than bread to the hungry.

O wild winds, and clumsy, pilfering bees,
With the whole world to be wanton in,
Will you not spare my little tea-rose?
And O ruthless blind creatures,
Who lay eggs of evil at the core of life,

Pass by my one red apple,
That is so firm and sound!

Three other poets contributed to the October 1916 issue: Edward Bliss Reed, an editor at the *Yale Review;* John Masefield, who would become poet laureate in England in 1930; and Lee Wilson Dodd, an essayist, playwright, and poet. Each of the men published one poem.

In Baker's personal life, 1916 was not a good year. On September 20, Baker's beloved father, W. T. Wilson, was struck by a train in Lufkin and killed. Wilson was a tall, strong, and active man who never drank; his ill-fated death always remained a mystery to his family. The tragedy came as a shock to Karle, who had grown closer to her father after her mother's death.[21] The Bakers decided to move from their home on Baxter-Duncan Street to the Wilson homestead, Tanglewood. Karle had always loved her parents' home, and now she would rear her children there. Her brother Ben T. Wilson, his wife Bess, and their one- year-old daughter, Florence (Toncie), lived across the street. Toncie was a favorite niece of Baker. Ben, who with Tom Baker owned the Ford agency and sold Model Ts, built a tennis court beside his house where he and Karle sometimes played tennis together; he and his sister were good friends and kindred spirits.[22] When she was an adult, Charlotte Baker wrote about her aunt and uncle: "Aunt Bess was my favorite aunt. My uncle, Ben T. Wilson, was commonly called Ben [T.] . . . Living just across the street from one another, the Bakers and the Wilsons were closely associated. I was allowed to call them 'Bess and Ben,'. . . We alternated Sunday dinners at the two houses. At the Bakers, the main dish was fried chicken; at the Wilsons, it was chicken pie. . . . When radio came along, Ben T. was the first in town to have one."[23]

Florence Wilson Reavley felt similar affections toward her aunt, Karle: "When I was growing up I simply thought of KWB as my aunt—a close, loving member of my family in whose presence I felt thoroughly comfortable and accepted. It was a joy to visit her home which had an aura of refinement and culture—but a 'down to earth' informal quality as well. Hers was a gentle, sensitive spirit with a deep underlying strength and ready, but low-key humor. She was warm but undemonstrative."[24]

Jenny Harris held her school for children in the reconstructed Old Stone Fort located just across the street from Tanglewood. After moving to this house, Tomby and Charlotte could walk from their new home to school, which allowed Baker more time to write.[25] Charlotte Baker Montgomery recalls her family's move to Tanglewood in 1916, when she was only six years old:

Charlotte's drawing of Tanglewood (the home) in The Birds of Tanglewood. *Kate Floy and W. T. Wilson, Karle Wilson Baker's parents, built their home, Tanglewood, on Mound Street in Nacogdoches in 1903. The Thomas E. Baker family moved into the house after W. T. Wilson's death in 1916. The name became immortalized in Karle Wilson Baker's book of essays,* The Birds of Tanglewood. *(Private Collection, Baker Estate)*

> After Grandfather's death, my parents moved to Tanglewood, it became even more tangled and woody. My mother was as ardent a gardner [*sic*] as her mother had been. She—and Charlie—filled the space within the loop of the driveway at the back of the house with flowers: four-o-clocks and cosmos and gallardias I remember especially. They planted hollyhocks and castor beans against a tall board fence, and grew asparagus and ferns for greenery to go with cut flowers. There were hyacinths and jonquils and violets. But I associate trees with my mother more than flowers. She spoke eloquently of them in her verse—as friends, teachers, guides and companions.[26]

In the summer of 1917, the Nacogdoches Citizens Committee achieved its goal when the state of Texas selected the town as a future site for a college. Karle Wilson Baker's dream for a college expressed in 1907, would become a reality, but Stephen F. Austin State Teachers College did not open until six years after the first announcement. W. T. Wilson had not lived to hear the good news. Karle Wilson Baker continued to create a steady stream of poetry, and Wilbur Cross continued to press her for more poems. He wrote in December 1917, "A group of your poems is appearing in the present number of *The Yale Review,* and I am herewith sending you a modest honorarium. Have you in your desk some more very fine poems which you would like to let me see?" "Leaf Burning" and "Vanity" were among the poems the *Review* chose to publish. "Leaf Burning" became the introductory poem to her first book of verse. She renamed the poem "Blue Smoke":

> The flame of my life burns low
> Under the cluttered days,
> Like a fire of leaves.
> But always a little blue, sweet-smelling smoke
> Goes up to God.[27]

By 1918, Karle Wilson Baker was well established as one of the leading female poets in the South. In February, Wilbur Cross admonished her for sending some poems elsewhere. He wrote, "I was glad to receive your poems the other day. I particularly like 'Stars' and 'Fairy Fires,' which I am keeping. . . . You say that you have formed the habit of thinking of *The Yale Review* first. I hope that you will not lose the habit. I fear, however, that you really did lose the habit when you did not let me see "William Vaughn Moody."[28] The *Review* also accepted "November" and two poems about the

First World War, "Eagle Youth" and "Graves of France" in 1918.[29] "November" is made up of four short lyrics; the first one is titled "Leaves":

> My great trees are stripping themselves,
> Throwing away their gauds,
> Preparing for the winter of their souls.
> But my little cedars
> Are picking up the twisted golden baubles
> And sticking them in their hair.

At this time, Baker began preparing a book of her poems for publication, and naturally she turned to Wilbur Cross for advice. *Yale Review* had already published many of the poems in her collection. Cross encouraged her to submit the prospective book to the Yale University Press; doubtless, Cross's introductions helped to pave the way for Baker at the university's press. In the next five years, Yale University Press published her first two books of poems, *Blue Smoke* (1919) and *Burning Bush* (1922), a children's book, *The Garden of the Plynck* (1920), and a book of fables, *Old Coins* (1923). A letter from Wilhelmina Day, the editor at Yale University Press, acknowledges Baker's talent, describes the hardships of the University Press during wartime, and explains the exacting nature of the Press as a part of Yale University:

> Your letter of April 9th to Mr. Cross has been referred to the Yale University Press. I find that I am tempted to do something which we had decided not to do and that is, consider another volume of poetry. We had fairly definitely decided not to bring out any poetry until 1919 as our lists have been rather overbalanced on this side. I will, however, esteem it a favor if you let us examine your manuscript [Blue Smoke] and I would also be glad if you would let us see "Old Coins." The Press would not be able to promise a speedy publication . . . since publishing conditions are very uncertain owing to the war. The Government may at any time cut off our full supply of paper and the manufacturers of book cloths are becoming nothing less than brigands in the attacks that they make upon our financial resources.
>
> I shall await your answer with much interest, and hope that even without the promise of speedy publication, you will be willing to allow us to examine your work. . . . I must tell you that everything submitted to us has to go to the Council's committee on Publications of Yale University; and that we are not allowed to bring out anything without their permission.[30]

By July 15, 1918, Baker had a letter from Yale University Press confirming that it would publish *Blue Smoke* in the fall of 1918. In September, Day wrote to Baker that the U.S. government had asked Yale Press to cut back by 25 percent because of the war; as a result, the Press postponed the publication of "Blue Smoke" until spring 1919.[31] Karle Wilson Baker's first published book of verse, *Blue Smoke,* finally came out on August 29, 1919.[32]

The summer of 1919 was pivotal for Karle Wilson Baker's career in several ways aside from the publication of *Blue Smoke.* That summer Baker registered for classes in psychology at Columbia University in New York City to study personality development. She believed such studies would enhance her skills in analyzing character traits for her stories. In addition to the psychology classes, she began to learn about a new movement, Spiritualism, popular in Europe and America since the First World War. These two influences led to another new interest: extrasensory perception. Her study of ESP lasted for the remainder of her life. The events of the summer began with a trip by train to New York City. Karle Wilson Baker took her children, Charlotte and Tomby, with her. While she was in class at Columbia, the children attended the Horace Mann School.[33] During their summer in New York, she and the children traveled by train to New Haven, Connecticut, to the offices of Yale University Press to check on the progress of the publication of "Blue Smoke."[34] She also took her manuscript of fables, "Old Coins," and some ideas for a children's book for the editors to consider for publication. Traveling by train had always fascinated Baker. When she was a young woman she had traveled on the train to Chicago to attend the university. She also went by train to Virginia to teach. She wrote several poems about trains including "From the Pullman" which appeared in *Blue Smoke.* This little lyric poem also reflects Baker's interest in women, especially the downtrodden:

> All day I have sat gazing out of the window,
> Blessing my eyes with the silver of the little bare trees.
> But now, in the dark,
> I am haunted by the faces of women in lonely shanties—
> Here an old one, there a young one, but always a woman
> In the half-opened door,
> Watching the world go by.[35]

When Baker and the children arrived at the Yale University Press offices, the senior editor, Wilbur Cross, was not there, but they met with G. G. Wyant, the advertising editor. Baker left the manuscript of "Old Coins" with Wyant. After she returned to New York City, he wrote to her, "I have been reading over your manuscript, 'Old Coins,' with very much pleasure—and indeed I may say that I was charmed with some of the little fables. I am sending it over to our committee for their consideration."[36] Also, while Baker was in Wyant's office, she brought up the subject of publishing a children's book with Yale Press. They would pursue this possibility in the months to come.

After the publication of *Blue Smoke,* Wyant wrote to Baker that the critic and columnist for the *Boston Evening Transcript,* William S. Braithwaite, had written the Press requesting a photograph of Baker. Braithwaite had said that he could do a lot for the book and for Karle Wilson Baker.[37] Baker's new book impressed Yale University Press as much as her poetry had impressed the editors of *Yale Review* earlier. The Press editors realized they had found a new, sophisticated talent. One of them, W. S. Lewis, wrote to her about *Blue Smoke:* "I think you have an altogether rare and major poetic conciseness of phrase combined with such directness of emotional appeal that no one can escape you! . . . People, you know, once they have read them ['At the Picture Show,' 'From the Pullman,' 'A Clear Night,' 'Reprieve,' 'Apple and Rose,' and 'A Little Boy's Bath'] won't let them willingly out of memory. Decidely, I think, they will 'stick' and I do wish you would 'drop some more down.'"[38]

Another admirer, Katherine Lee Bates, head of the Department of English at Wellesley College, wrote to Baker after the publication of the book: "I cannot put aside your exquisite *Blue Smoke,* even for a brief absence from home, without sending you my word of delight and gratitude. To have written only *Eagle Youth* would have won my heart, but your pretty volume is stained and shabby because of all the journeys it has made with me. . . . I know many lovers of your songs; boys not yet in college, busy people in the age of middle-life, white-haired women. You must not forget that we are all listening and waiting. What a group that was in a recent issue of the *Yale Review!*"[39]

Karle Wilson Baker's book was well received at home too. *Blue Smoke* received a glowing review from Edmond Trombly in the *Texas Review:*

> "Blue Smoke" is not only a deliberate book; it is unpretentious, honest, and entirely wanting in that sensationalism for which publishers clamor so loudly. . . . Again and again in this little book you sense the cry of one hungering for more elbow-room—spiritual, of course,—and for contact with one's fellows. . . . Still the small town has its compensations; and the soul will never starve which can find in village streets in trees, birds, clouds, spires, in rising smoke, and in children what is revealed to us here.

> . . . She is interested in her town, her townspeople, in her family, in the great war, and in a host of other things. . . . It is a brave, as well as an excellent book.[40]

Her friend, *Yale Review* editor Edward Bliss Reed, reviewed *Blue Smoke* with great perception:

> *Blue Smoke,* a volume whose very form is a delight, will place its author in the foremost ranks of our lyric poets. In every page there is distinction, a power of suggestion, an emotion deep in its restraint, clear in its freedom from the blight of sentimentality. . . . This poet gives only her best. Her style is simple, vivid, . . . there is perfect ease in all the beauty of these songs. . . . To find much in little, to hold the world in a grain of sand, to see where two worlds meet is, in part, the endowment of a poet, and Karle Wilson Baker possesses it.[41]

Yale University Press's publication of *Blue Smoke,* combined with the earlier publications in the *Yale Review,* placed Karle Wilson Baker in a larger arena than any other poet in Texas at the time. Academics around the state took note of the book. In particular, *Blue Smoke* caught the attention of Rebecca W. Smith, an assistant professor of English at Texas Christian University. A teacher of American literature, Smith wrote to Baker that she liked the book very much. She sought Baker's advice and asked for her opinion of the important tendencies in American poetry.[42] Baker's letter of response gives insight into her thoughts about poetry:

> Let me thank you very much for your kind words for "Blue Smoke." They are very heartening. . .which brings me indirectly to one of your questions: what I think of the tendencies in current poetry. I think the *aliveness* of it—even including the extravagances, the quarreling, the clamor, . . . is 'all to the good.' It stirs people up. It sets them to asking, in self-defense, what is Poetry, any how. . . . Nobody knows what is great and what is worthless in contemporary work; what is indispensable is that it all be given a hearing, and Time will do the winnowing. My own favorites among our outstanding poets are Lindsay, Sandburg, Frost and Sara Teasdale.[43]

Baker wrote to G. G. Wyant at Yale Press about the vigorous reception *Blue Smoke* had received in Texas: "I have been greatly and agreeably surprised at its reception in Texas. . . . I have been especially pleased by the enthusiasm of the English departments of colleges and schools from which I happen to hear."[44] Further national recognition came in 1921 when a tribute to Karle Wilson Baker appeared in the *Library of Southern Literature,* submitted by the Texas writer Dorothy Scarborough: "Karle Wilson Baker is an author of whom the South may well be proud . . . she is an authentic poet . . . worthy to stand beside Sara Teasdale and Edna St. Vincent Millay in the 'essential fire' of her poetic thought and the tooled beauty of its form."[45]

After the publication of *Blue Smoke,* Baker wrote to Wyant reminding him that she had a manuscript for a children's book that she wanted him to see. "I hope to have it ["The Garden of the Plynck"] in your hands by the middle of February, at the latest—earlier, if I can. You may remember that I told you of its being lost by the express company. . . . However, I shall give it first place on my working program."[46] She did not realize it at the time, but Yale Press would place "Plynck" ahead of "Old Coins" in their publishing schedule.[47] A few months later, Baker wrote to Wyant of some concerns about her children's book: "Anyone who attempts a tale of this kind, particularly with a little girl for a heroine, is dogged by the implacable shadow of 'Alice.'" *Alice in Wonderland* was the measuring stick for all children's books at the time. Nevertheless, Baker defends her manuscript and relates her daughter's involvement in the book: "The atmosphere of their worlds is different: Alice's is the world of a frolicsome logician and mathematician, and Sara's (I speak with due humility) of a poet. . . . Moreover, I think it will be found that Alice is a man's little girl, and Sara a woman's. I hope I have avoided sentimentalizing her; but the real little Sara [Charlotte] at my elbow was constantly warning me with big grieving, startled eyes, away from anything which she calls 'too sad.'"[48] In the same letter, Baker refers to comments made by a friend (probably Anna McCaleb Sheets) about the book and gives her own rationale about children's books. She also mentions that she has another children's book underway:

> One of my friends who has seen the manuscript has suggested that the "big words" might prove a stumbling-block to children. She admitted that she would be dreadfully loth to see them sacrificed, but her experience with children's books . . . had impressed her with the conviction which possesses most people that a children's book must contain only words of one syllable and ideas to correspond. . . . I think a child, whose taste is not corrupted, likes books to grow up to. He enjoys the mind-stretching process of which he is vaguely aware, even while it tantalizes him. . . . No "grown-up" work has ever had more loving care from me, or been nearer my heart. I wrote it more than two years ago in about

three weeks. . . . I am at work now on a group of separate stories for children—with Tomby's and Charlotte's help. We have finished "Pilio," and "The Storm-King's Plume."[49]

On April 29, 1920, editor W. S. Lewis at Yale Press wrote to Baker of his interest in "The Garden of the Plynck" and that in his opinion, "it stands up very well against *Alice in Wonderland.* We are counting upon it to be one of our very best Christmas books and are prepared to make a great flutter over it." In addition, Lewis included some constructive criticism of the first chapter.[50] Baker replied that she was pleased to discuss the manuscript with a competent and friendly critic and that she was already making some alterations with his suggestions in mind. In the letter she instructed him how she wanted the dedication to read: "To Tomby and Charlotte, my Collaborators, and To all mothers who read stories to children."[51] During the writing of the book, Baker had consulted with Tomby and Charlotte each day when they returned home from school by reading a new chapter or episode to them and soliciting their opinions about the plot and the characters as the story developed.[52]

With today's copy machines, one can forget how difficult it was to make extra copies of manuscripts in the 1920s. G. G. Wyant wrote that Yale Press was planning the illustrations of "The Garden of the Plynck" and that the editors anticipated the publication of the book in time for the Christmas market. He also mentioned that they needed another copy of the manuscript, one for the printer and another for the illustrator.[53] Somehow Baker was able to supply another copy. Wyant wrote a week later that the publications committee had accepted "The Garden of the Plynck" for publication (Fall 1920), but he added that they would postpone publishing "Old Coins" until the next season. He wrote: "Now I have a little bad news for you, but I can assure you that we are giving the situation our most careful attention and will do the best we can in it. And that is that probably we shall have to postpone 'Old Coins' from this fall to the next season. This is only a tentative arrangement, and it is still possible that both of your books can be published this year. But if we find it inadvisable to do so, I will ask your kind pardon in advance for the delay."[54] In reply, Baker signed the contract for "Old Coins" to come out in the spring of 1921, adding some comments about the illustrations for "The Garden of the Plynck." "Your letter of April 29 was received in the household of the Plynck with great interest. Charlotte and I are delighted that there are to be 'colored illustrations'—Charlotte had been holding her breath in the hope that there would be." She also addressed the problem of revisions to the book, stating that her family seemed to resent any changes but that she felt she could persuade them to allow some revision.[55]

Baker continued to follow "The Garden of the Plynck"'s path to publication with interest. She also made comments and suggestions for advertising the book and showed an interest in the posters and circulars that the Press was preparing.[56] She urged one of the sales managers to emphasize that she was an author from Texas: "I've had a strong feeling for some time that a lot of my books—or any other Texas author's—could be sold in Texas if it were made known that the author was a resident of the Biggest State in the Union. Local pride and a sort of vague but powerful aspiringness are more abundant among us—as yet—than aesthetic discrimination. . . . I feel sure there are hundreds of libraries in Texas that would add my books if they realized it to be a patriotic duty!!!"[57] On October 26, 1920, W. S. Lewis wrote that the book was out: "Today marks little Sara's appearance and it is a red letter day for all of us. There is always something distinctly festive about a publication date. The job which has required so many hands and so much time is at last finished and there is a great desire to fling one's cap. . . . But Sara is no ordinary child—even for the Yale Press—and, in strict confidence of course, I must confess to a desire to fling my cap far higher than usual over her debut."[58]

Baker wrote back enthusiastically, "We are all more than charmed with her, too; thank you for your cordial and generous letter written on publication day. I hope she and Sara will never disappoint your expectations."[59] In addition, Baker, who was ever alert to other publishing opportunities, reminded Lewis that in his letter he had asked about another book of verse [the future *Burning Bush*]: "It will be a year or two yet before I have another ready to submit to you. I want it to be so much better than "Blue Smoke.". . . I admit that that is a "vaulting ambition," but I cherish it none the less. However, I have begun on a new Plynck book, to be called "Pilgrims to the Plynck," in which Jimmy makes an entrance into the Garden."[60] (Perhaps she intended in the sequel to give a young boy the major role.) She also noted, "But ahead of both these projects, in my hopes and affections, is 'Old Coins.'. . . I think it is my favorite child, not even forgetting Sara."[61] Baker was constantly writing and planning ahead for future publications. Unfortunately, by 1929, buyer interest in *The Garden of the Plynck* had ground to a halt. The sales manager, Norman Donaldson, wrote the sad news that the Press still had one thousand bound copies in stock: "Your book, 'The Garden of the Plynck' seems to have run its course and we do not see much possibility of any further sales through the regular trade channels. The failure of this book to take hold the way we all thought it would is one of those unanswerable questions which always rise up to puzzle a publisher."[62] He asked Baker to give up her royalty rights and allow the Press to sell the book to a firm that would take over remaining copies and distribute the books, adding that the Press was as disappointed as she that the book had not done better.[63] Baker agreed to the plan.

In 1920, while Karle Wilson Baker was making final adjustments on *The Garden of the Plynck* and awaiting its publication, she was also actively pursuing her interest in birdlife. Writing simultaneously on a variety of subjects and writing poetry and prose at the same time was a common work habit for her. To continue writing her observations of birdlife in her own garden was not at all unusual while she was considering revisions for *The Plynck*. The notes Baker had collected on birdlife in the early 1900s prepared her for writing the essays that she would send to the *Yale Review* in the 1920s. Understandably, since she had published so many poems with the *Review*, she sent her essay, "The Birds of Tanglewood," to that journal in the fall of 1920. The assistant editor, Helen McAfee, replied in November that the editors were interested in publishing the essay but that they felt it was a little too long. Also, McAfee pointed out, "Our readers are, of course, nearly all Northerners, and therefore are quite unfamiliar with your setting. Would it be possible to introduce a little more 'local color' into the first paragraph or two in order to make your Texas garden as vivid as may be to the reader who has never seen it?"[64] Baker responded by shortening her text by a thousand words and rewriting the opening paragraphs bearing in mind McAfee's suggestions. In addition, she expressed gratitude for the editor's help but insisted on her own literary integrity:

> If I have failed with this introduction, I hope you will frankly tell me so, and send it back that I may try it once more. . . . There is no excuse for doing this sort of thing at all unless one loves it enough to take any amount of pains. . . . I notice you entertained some doubts about the title. Perhaps it does sound a trifle self-important. But I can't accept your suggestion because, as I have said, Tanglewood isn't, or hasn't, a garden in any proper sense. Would you like "Bird-Neighbors in Texas" better? . . . I only want you to be very sure that I am most glad to consider suggestions. One is often distressfully conscious of being too close to one's material; anything that helps one to see around it is a gift to be grateful for.[65]

She attached her revised introduction for the essay to the letter:

> Tanglewood is just a big "yard," where you may happen to stumble, almost anywhere, over a vaulting-pole, a baseball bat, or a story-book lying open, face downward, on the grass. But the birds do not mind the children, nor value immaculateness any more than they do. Their concern is with the great oaks and sweetgums, wreathed with wisteria, grape, and wild smilac; with the rich crimson seeds of the young magnolias, the little cedars which provide such snug storm-shelters, and the loaded hackberries and hollies, but most of all, perhaps, with the unpruned shrubbery, cunningly planted years ago by hands that now lie quiet, in casual-looking clumps in the angles of the house and along the inconsequent little paths. Tanglewood takes its name from the riot of sumac and muscatine and Virginia creeper that it was when my father bought it. Before that, there had been a pond in the midst of it, where the boys came to shoot the wild ducks that came down for water and rest on their long flight to the Gulf in November. The new owner did not at once build a house on his property.[66]

On November 29, Helen McAfee replied: "It is refreshing to know that 'Tanglewood' is not a garden but just a 'southern yard,' and we are glad to make its acquaintance a little more intimately in the new introduction which you have written to your delightful sketch. It is wholly to our minds as you now have it, both for manner and for length, and about the time the blue birds return to us (after, perhaps, paying you a visit) we shall get about having it set up. Soon afterwards you should receive proofs."[67]

Yale Review senior editor Wilbur Cross wrote to Baker ten months later that "The Birds of Tanglewood" would appear in all their "fine feathers" in the October *Yale Review,* the journal's tenth anniversary issue. Cross wrote that he was particularly glad to have Karle Wilson Baker in it. He enclosed a check by way of honorarium for her essay.[68] The essay was so well received by *Yale Review* readers that the *Review* was quick to accept Baker's second bird essay, "Window Lore." Once again the *Yale Review* contributed to her literary prominence by recognizing her as a talented essayist.

Another of the bird essays, "An Aerial Harvest," was published locally as an article for the town's newspaper, the *Daily Sentinel.* An unusually severe rain and ice storm had caused hundreds of migrant birds to die or be downed in Nacogdoches. On that occasion, Baker was able to see more specimens up close than she had ever seen before. Neighbors brought birds for her to identify; she and her family tried to save some of the birds that were only crippled, but most were lost.[69] Her account exhibits sensitive observations viewed through trained eyes. Over the years, Baker became an expert on birdlife, identifying hundreds of species in the East Texas area. People came to her with questions as if she were an ornithologist.

In September 1921, Baker received a note from her friend Katherine Lee Bates, to whom she had written about the naming of a second volume of verse. Bates replied, "It is glorious news that you have a new volume on the way. Either title is a lovely one, but my own preference is for *Burning Bush,* both because of its suggestion or reminder of *Blue Smoke* and of its inherent expression of the quality of your work. It has seemed to me from the first that common sights and simple experiences flame at your touch."[70] The following October, Baker wrote to W. S. Lewis of her hopes that Yale Press would publish a second book of her collected poems. The reply came in February from a new editor at the Press, Wilson Follett, who had replaced Lewis. Follett wrote that the committee had approved the publication of "Burning Bush," and he suggested that the book should come out in the fall of 1922, but he added that they would have to postpone the publication of "Old Coins." On February 28, Baker answered Follett, stating that "Old Coins" originally had been set for publication for the fall of 1920 but postponed for the publication of *The Garden of the Plynck* and that she was unsure about a second delay.[71] The opinions of the editorial staff prevailed, and "Old Coins" went once again to a "back-burner." Baker wrote back with suggestions of poems that could be omitted if "Burning Bush" were too long; she mentioned "Song to the Beat of Wings," "Tree Talk," "The Window," "Hymn," "Dogmatic," and "Sunset Song" and added that other poems could be excluded if necessary, but she wanted the last word.[72] She wrote to Mr. Follett again in March 1922 about revisions for "Burning Bush" and "Old Coins":

> I should have answered it [his letter] sooner, only we have been running a sort of hospital at our house lately, and I have been by turns patient and head-nurse. The scourge seems to have passed, and I hasten to send you the revisions. . . . Applying your suggestion, I want "Hymn" omitted. . . . I like your suggestion about Old Coins. I'll get it off to you in a day or two. If you don't like them, I think I shall just trundle them back to my garden and bury 'em again where I dug 'em up in the first place—awaiting some last trump of authentic inspiration about them.[73]

"Old Coins" would wait another year before publication; Yale University Press published *Burning Bush* on August 23, 1922. "Courage," a small lyric with great substance from *Burning Bush,* immediately gained wide popularity:

Courage is armor
A blind man wears;
The calloused scar
Of outlived despairs:
Courage is Fear
That has said its prayers.[74]

Not long after its publication, Karle Wilson Baker spoke in a public lecture about *Burning Bush* and the kinds of poems she liked to write. Her extensive comments offer insight into the poet as well as the poetry:

> Not very long ago, I read a review by a young and very blasé poet, of another poet's new book. After praising it very generously, he arrived at this climax: "One of the best things about his volume is that it does not contain a single poem about a tree, and has nothing else wooden in it."
>
> Now, my books contain more poems about trees, I think, than about any other one subject. Doubtless the young reviewer would be very sorry for me; but I, too, am very sorry for him. I am very sorry for any poet who thinks that trees are made of wood. . . . A lumberman's trees are made of wood; but a poet's? Never! To tell you what things that seem wooden are really made of is a poet's essential business. . . .
>
> What our haughty young poet probably meant was that he was personally very bored, and very tired of reading people's unsuccessful efforts to make the real, green life of a tree shine through the bark. Since he was himself a poet, I cannot think that he meant to imply that common things, like trees, are not fit subjects for poetry. Poetry, being a Protean and god-like thing, has doubtless many functions; but to me it seems clear that the function which should be recognized as especially precious to a democracy, is its function of rescuing common things from commonness. . . . The only way it can be done is by seeing through the common, to the stream of spiritual fact that flows behind it, like Dante's river of light, ceaseless and ever-renewed; by catching and reflecting a glint or glimmer of that intenser, more luminous vitality which works through the web of appearance which we know as the everyday world. So I make no apologies to the haughty young critic for writing mostly about common things, and, especially about trees. I do apologize to the trees; because, in spite of all my much speaking about them, and tiptoe as I might, I have never really touched the lowest twig of their beauty and their mystery. . . .

> [She listed several groups of poems she intended to read.] The next little group of poems I shall read is in free verse. I don't know how you feel about free verse: some people like it and some people hate it. . . . Not long ago, just before a reading I gave in Dallas, one of the club-women asked me what I thought about Amy Lowell's poetry. I told her I admired some of it very much. "Well," she said, "what is there in it?" That was rather a poser to answer offhand, but I did the best I could. "Well," I said, "there's a great deal of color in it, for one thing; it's full of splendid *pictures:* it stirs up your memory and imagination, makes you *see* beautiful images. And there is *music* in it, if you listen closely for it—the verbal music of beautiful words, cunningly chosen. And there is rhythm in it, even when there isn't any regular metre. And often there is the enthusiasm, the intensity, the *feeling,* that distinguishes it from prose." I saw that my eloquence wasn't making much impression, and before I had hardly got the last word out of my mouth, she put in impatiently, "Oh, yes, I know all that. But where's the *poetry* in it?"
>
> So I am warning you about the things I am going to read next, so that you won't be looking for the *poetry*—if that's the way you feel about free verse. [She then read what she called "a set of homely characterizations in free verse": "A Flock of Birds."][75]

"Good Company," an example of her "tree poetry" and her admiration of nature, became one of her best-known poems:

> Today I have grown taller from walking with the trees.
> The seven sister-poplars who go softly in a line;
> And I think my heart is whiter for its parley with a star
> That trembled out at nightfall and hung above the pine.
>
> The call-note of a redbird from the cedars in the dusk
> Woke his happy mate within me to an answer free and fine;
> And a sudden angel beckoned from a column of blue smoke—
> Lord, who am I that they should stoop—these holy folk of thine?[76]

The poems about birds in *Burning Bush* reflect the study Baker had made of birdlife in East Texas. "The Cardinal and His Lady" from "A Flock of Birds" reveals imagery through metaphor in only two lines: "The redbird is the core of fire at the heart of my still living; / And his little lady is the soft ashes covering the half-seen embers." Tree and bird imagery are the most common symbols in Karle Wilson Baker's poetry. She often walked in the forests of the East Texas piney woods admiring the trees and birds. Her notebooks on birding illustrate how she identified with birds. Her poem, "The Tree," from *Blue Smoke* characterizes this bond.

> My life is a tree,
> Yoke-fellow of the earth;
> Pledged,
> By roots too deep for remembrance,
> To stand hard against the storm,
> To fill my Place.
> (But high in the branches of my green tree there is a wild bird singing:
> Wind-free are the wings of my bird: she hath built no mortal nest.)[77]

Baker articulates her basic philosophy of life and art in this poem. Like most artists, she often found herself torn between responsibility and creative ambitions. Dr. Leonidas Payne, chairman of English at the University of Texas, once introduced Baker as "Domesticity—with Wings." "The Tree" expresses that duality.

In January 1921, Wilhelmina Day of the Yale University Press notified Baker that the Press would not publish "Old Coins" after all. Baker wrote back immediately reminding Day that she had a contract for "Old Coins" and suggesting publication be delayed for twelve months while she revised. In March, Baker sent word to Wilson Follet that she was sending the revised manuscript of "Old Coins" to him. She admitted in the letter that Yale's returning the manuscript to her had been a blow to her self-esteem and had confused her judgment on the merits of the book.[78]

Even though she was a successful poet, essayist, and writer of children's stories, Karle Wilson Baker still had the desire to write longer prose. In another effort to improve her prose-writing skills, she responded to an advertisement in the *Atlantic Monthly* (summer 1921) for a course in short story composition taught by Walter Pitkin, a professional psychologist. Pitkin, by correspondence from New York, would become her teacher/adviser on prose style. Baker felt she needed the psychological insight that the course offered, but she was also attracted to Pitkin because he claimed that he could help writers produce commercially sellable prose material.[79] For years Baker had experienced conflicting concerns over having time to write, making a living at writing, being a good wife and mother, and being an independent woman. She wrote to Pitkin, "One of the problems of married life that interests me is the economic basis of it."[80] Later she wrote in her diary that she had thought at the time of her marriage that she would write while her husband was away at work and while her babies were asleep, and that thereby she would become financially independent. At the time of the diary entry, written after sixteen years of married life, she calculated that her average annual income had been only $118.15.[81] She had confessed her great ambition to Pitkin: "What I desired was literary success: the high, permanent, liberal success that comes to very few in a generation. It had been my mother's ambition before me, and her mother's before that: and, so far as I can tell, I was born with it. It was so complete and so genuine that it possessed me; it was not necessary for me to make myself stick to it, it held me, determined the direction of my whole life."[82]

Pitkin became the perfect sounding board and outlet for her prose writing. In October 1921, Baker wrote to him about her new interests: "I think it is plain that my interest is in psychological stories. . . . I have been especially interested in 'Psychic' stories, and stories of the so-called 'supernatural.'"[83] The courses that Baker had taken at Columbia University in the summer of 1919 had not only strengthened her skills in characterization, they had also stimulated her interest in studying human nature and the human psyche. After she returned home, she continued her research in psychological development and became fascinated with the study of extrasensory perception, purchasing many books on the subject for her personal library. Today the Stephen F. Austin State University Library has a collection of books on psychic phenomena donated by Baker. The earliest publications date from 1917, but the inscriptions show that she purchased many of the books in 1920 when her interest in ESP began in earnest. The titles themselves—*How to Speak with the Dead; The Psychology of the Future; Our Hidden Forces, Hints and Observations for those Investigating the Phenomena of Spiritualism;* and *Voices from the Void (Six Years' Experience in Automatic Communications)*—echo the content inside the books. Such books would lead Baker to experiment with the methods and techniques of ESP in her prose writing (see chapter 5). Throughout her correspondence with Pitkin from August 1921 until May 1922, Baker revealed private thoughts about her writing and its problems, but even more interestingly, she discussed personal feelings about herself and her relationships with others with this professional psychologist. Obligingly, Pitkin offered psychological analysis of the writer as well as an analysis of the writer's work. As a result, Pitkin became an unusually strong influence on Baker. Many letters the two exchanged are of a personal nature, dealing with Baker's self-analysis and philosophy of life. Pitkin's letters often encouraged her to write about subjects that were close to her. He wrote in October 1921, "In your next letter I wish you would tell me point-blank about some problem in adult life which you would gladly write reams about."[84]

At the beginning of the course, Baker had admitted to Pitkin that even though she had published some short stories, she had not found the success that she had experienced in poetry but felt a strong need to write in prose.[85] Pitkin responded by reinforcing Baker's desire to shift to prose: "It is refreshing to come upon a poet who frankly admits that her verse cannot express everything she has to express. After reading some of your poems and your other work, I must agree with you absolutely: you simply must find yourself in prose."[86] Pitkin's willingness for her to cast poetry aside—because it did not fulfill all she might express—may have been influenced by his overeagerness to recruit her as a student. Karle Wilson Baker had already gained national recognition and had "found herself" through her poetry.

In some instances, Pitkin showed a paternalistic attitude toward Baker. Like most writers, she dreaded receiving rejection slips from publishers, and her success with publishing poetry had spared her from the dreaded slip most of the time. She had experienced rejection from prospective prose publications, however, and she wrote to Pitkin about her fears. He suggested that she submit all stories prepared for market to his office so that his business manager could forward them to prospective publishers. He wrote protectively, "You will never get a rejection slip, nor any report until it is a favorable one."[87] Earlier, she had confided to him that her rejection slips for short stories usually mentioned that the works needed "busy, plotty stories" and "more action." But she explained that she wanted more depth in her stories: "I find the mysteries of character and temperament unexpressibly fascinating. And over against my despair of ever being able to try seriously to write 'busy, plotty stories,' I place my firm belief that, in his own way, everybody else is interested in 'the significance of life,' too."[88] Pitkin responded: "When an editor says he wants 'more action,' he does not mean less thought and fewer ideas; he means that the ordinary reader has to grasp your ideas through the medium of *events*. . . . It is chiefly a piece of careful psychological analysis. . . . Send me anything further about yourself that occurs to you, together with your comments on this letter. A few weeks of this progressive analysis, and you will be ready to write a story for me."[89]

Walter Pitkin and the editors at Yale University were among the few people Karle Wilson Baker ever looked to for advice in her adult writing career. Pitkin felt that a writer must establish some clear personal beliefs before credibility and identity could be expressed in fictional characters. After Baker had shared some of her strongest feelings with him, he replied bluntly:

> You dislike practical life *because it interrupts your thoughts*. . . . It means that you have an instinctive feeling toward being interrupted in meditation. . . . You say that you have a vague notion of becoming a public speaker when your children are older; but you hate the gush and frothiness of the Woman's Club; and you feel that such success as you might gain thus would be "too easy and hence demoralizing.". . . You presuppose that what is easy is demoralizing. . . . Obviously you resent tinkering with your philosophy.[90]

She responded forcefully with her philosophy of the creative life:

> . . . I have explored, like every other thinking person, all the ways [of seeing life] I could become aware of, and have finally found the one that for me is workable. . . . I did not say or suppose that all easy things are demoralizing or that all hard things are good; I implied that "*too*-easy" things, when they make up the greater part of one's performance, certainly have a tendency to be demoralizing. . . . When people, because they have not yet learned to discriminate, praise alike extravagantly your successes, your half-successes and your near-failures, you are like a wrestler without an opponent, and your spiritual muscle suffers.
>
> . . . You tell me that I must tinker with my philosophy, and that the first thing you must learn, no matter with how much pain, is that "actions speak louder than thoughts." But I have already learned it. . . . If you mean that the thing I must learn first of all is that the only way to make the inner life effective is to *embody* it in some way, to *live it* into visibility, so to speak, then I am already converted. . . . The plain truth is that I must write, I must be an artist, or else become aware in my secret soul, that for me life is not worthwhile. . . . The ultimate intolerable burden of the common lot is not its hardness, but its meaninglessness.[91]

Following his suggestion to write about herself and people she knew, Baker sent manuscripts to Pitkin ranging from autobiographical writings such as "In Search of Myself" to short stories on various subjects taken from her life experiences.

During the time she was developing her prose style with Pitkin's help, Baker also played an active role in the formation of the Poetry Society of Texas. In October 1921, Therese Lindsey of Tyler wrote to Baker about creating such a society in Texas patterned after the successful Poetry Society of South Carolina.[92] Even though Baker stated up front that she wanted to be a mere "private" in the organization, she joined with Lindsey and Hilton

Greer of Dallas to organize the group. The state chartered The Poetry Society of Texas in November 1921 with 182 founding members.[93]

The following spring, Baker wrote to Wilson Follett once again expressing self-doubt about the manuscript of "Old Coins," which was still under contract at Yale Press: "I want to be exceedingly sure that it is good enough for 'me an' the Y. P.' to publish—that it wouldn't endanger or impair our joint prestige! . . . If your matured and considered judgment is against, then I want to withdraw the manuscript, have the contract annulled by mutual consent, and erase the whole transaction from the tablets of our memory."[94] Follett replied that the Press had set a publication date of May 5, 1922, for "Old Coins,"[95] but he would later amend that date to February 15, 1923.[96] In a speech about *Old Coins,* after publication, Baker explained, "The name, 'Old Coins,' is meant to suggest that the *themes* they deal with are as old as the wisdom (and the folly) of man: the ageless and universal truths that have been rediscovered and restated by generation after generation since the beginning of time. I was thinking of the rediscovery and restatement when I called them "small, *rubbed* coins."[97] Baker's friend, Hilton Greer, reviewed *Old Coins* for the *Dallas News:*

> It is a little book of etchings which a reader can finish at a sitting, or one to which return can be made for a reading of a single sketch, as the mood impels. Mrs. Baker is a Texas writer who has published four volumes, two of poetry and two of prose, all of them conferring distinction not only upon the author, but upon the State in which she resides.
>
> This latest collection, as might be expected and desired, is prose so touched with poetry that it falls little short of being sheer poetry itself. . . . "Old Coins" will make a pleasant clinking in the reader's memory and the literary numismatist will delight in the exhibit.[98]

When the reviewer for the *New York Times Book Review* mistakenly referred to Karle Wilson Baker as a man, Upshur Vincent of the *Star-Telegram* in Fort Worth wrote a letter of complaint to the *Times* even though the review had been favorable.[99] The reviewer for the *Times* had written about *Old Coins:*

> Twenty-seven "small and rubbed coins" are here offered to the reader, and by "coins" the author means those experiences, universal to all mankind, the common knowledge of which has helped to spread far and near among both ancient and modern peoples that wise understanding of human conduct which is often most gracefully and aptly expressed by allegory, parable or fable. Mr. Baker uses all three forms with a good deal

> of success. Several of his little stories possess a rare degree of merit. His English has often an almost bell-like clearness and will be read for its form and diction alone. But almost all the "coins" are to be enjoyed for content as well as form. Mr. Baker employs delectable symbols.[100]

The mistakes in the review were not retracted. Vincent's own complimentary review of the book appeared in the *Fort Worth Star-Telegram*. However, his review digressed to include comments on Baker's short story set in East Texas, "The Porch Swing," published in *Century Magazine* (1921). He described the story as one "whose people are types of those who have made East Texas the God's country of today." This long review also referred to Baker's active speaking agenda: "Mrs. Baker left Ft. Worth Friday night for Amarillo where she talked before the Panhandle Penwomen Saturday afternoon and read from her poems under the auspices of that organization Saturday night. She came to this city from Houston where she read Tuesday night before the Y. W. C. A. On May 11 she will read before Baylor College for Women at Belton."[101]

An important change appeared in Baker's writing when she turned to a subject that would interest her in both poetry and prose for the remainder of her writing career: Texas, its history, and its people. A poem pivotal to her career, "Song of the Forerunners," won first prize at a poetry contest sponsored by Southern Methodist University in 1922. The poem, an excerpt of which follows, was about the men and women who pioneered Texas:

> The men who made Texas
> Rode west with dazzled eyes
> On the hot trail of the Future,
> To take her by surprise:
>
> They were dreamers on horseback,
> Dreamers with strong hands,
> Trailing the golden Lion
> Who couches in far lands:
>
> Old men and young men, little men and tall,
> Bad men and good men—but strong men, all.
>
> . . . .
>
> But the men who made Texas
> Left their work half-done—
> For nothing stands full-finished
> Beneath the spinning sun;

And the women who dreamed Texas
Had much work to do
When they lay down for their last sleep
In a land still new; . . .[102]

Harriet Monroe remarked about the award in an issue of *Poetry: A Magazine of Verse*, "John Hall Wheelock, gave first place to Karle Wilson Baker's 'Song of the Fore-runners,' and probably the state of Texas will endorse his verdict by remembering it longest."[103]

Although much of Baker's writing that followed focused on Texas and its fascinating history, she continued her interest in nature. In April 1923, Baker wrote to Follett at Yale Press her ideas for a book based on some of her bird essays. She pointed out that the *Yale Review* had already published two of the essays, "The Birds of Tanglewood" and "Window Lore." As she described the book to Follett, she wrote that she planned more essays about birds, trees, moths, butterflies, and "other winged affairs" of the East Texas woods. She described the setting for her research: "Much of it gathers around our family migration to a camp in the woods [Fern Lake], where for years we have spent a month every fall when the wild ducks are going over."[104] Her interest in butterflies, chrysalises, and cocoons led her to create a collection of mounted butterflies at her home. Her son recalled that she had a cyanide jar with a cloth lid and made her own butterfly nets that she used to catch, kill, and then mount butterflies and moths for study.[105] On the same day that she wrote Follett, Baker sent a query letter to Wilbur Cross at the *Yale Review* exploring the possibility of their publishing her paper on William Vaughn Moody. She reminded Cross that the *Review* had turned down her essay on Moody in 1914 but that the *Forum* had published one of her Moody essays in the fall of 1922. She said she planned to compile a series of such papers as a study of the man and his work.[106] *Yale Review* declined to publish her essay on Moody. Helen McAfee, the assistant editor, replied, "We feel rather doubtful about the possibility of using your paper on William Vaughn Moody. It is only once in a long time that we allow ourselves to publish a study of a single writer; an in this case, as you know, we have already had a criticism of Moody's work by Professor Lewis, who recently died."[107]

In late August 1923, John E. Rosser, editor of The World Book Company, approached Baker with the proposition to write a primer for use in the first grade of the Texas public schools. He wrote, "Texas is so large, and the number of pupils in the first grade so great, that publication of a book indigenous to that State and limited to it in sale might be profitable to author and publisher."[108] Baker wrote back the next day that she had just returned from a six thousand mile trip by automobile to the Far West where she "fell in love with a number of things—among them the Pacific Coast," but she assured Rosser that she would like to undertake the work on the primer.[109] In October, Rosser sent twenty leading published primers, primary school vocabulary lists, and instructions on the amount of material and number of pictures she should have per page. He added that he would bring in an outside illustrator and that the primer should not exceed three hundred words.[110] When the materials arrived, Baker was making a speaking tour around Texas. In November 1923, she spoke at Baylor University, Southern Methodist University, and to a convention of the State Federation of Women's Clubs. After she had completed the speaking engagements, she responded to Rosser regarding her progress on the primer and noted that she was consulting her niece, Floy Lewis, who was head of the kindergarten department at California State Teacher's College at Fresno, for advice.[111] Baker completed the primer in a few months, but she had to wait until 1926 before the state of Texas adopted *Texas Flag Primer* for classroom use.

The *Yale Review* and Yale University Press had launched the poet on the national scene, but her continued success was due to her talent and hard work. Baker had always been interested in being a "modern" or "new" woman with a career and the ability to earn an independent income. Always self-analytical, she admitted in a public speech that she owed all her national recognition to her poetry: "It began to come to me as a curious surprise that whatever recognition I had managed to achieve was as a poet. I had gone on writing poetry because life had to be expressed."[112] While her children were small, Karle Wilson Baker chose to write lyric poetry, explaining that she simply did not have enough concentrated time to write long prose works such as novels. In a letter to Pitkin, she referred in good humor to the interferences that come with family life and how they affect writing: "The cook has been sick—which is equivalent to saying that Fate has hit the Muse over the head with a poker."[113] In the family-intensive decade of 1914–24, Baker made significant professional advancements, publishing two books of verse, a children's storybook, and a book of fables. By the time the decade came to a close, she was adding to her literary output by producing more short stories, essays, and even a primer. In addition, Karle Wilson Baker had established a network of friends such as Hilton Greer, Leonidas Payne, W. H. Vann, and A. J. Armstrong, whose invitations to speak at their campuses would help further her career. When a new college was founded in her hometown of Nacogdoches in 1923, she agreed to teach the next year.

"The so-called woman's movement is to me the most thrilling thing in an age so full of intellectual and spiritual adventures that one grows positively greedy in contemplation of it."

CHAPTER 3
To Fill My Place
The SFA Years

When the Board of Regents came to dedicate Stephen F. Austin State Teachers College on April 30, 1924, the Rotary Club sponsored a luncheon in the board's honor. A. W. Birdwell, the president of the college, chose Karle Wilson Baker to be a major speaker on the program; she read her recently completed ballad "Within the Alamo" and "The Pine Tree Hymn," the poem she had written the year before honoring the new college.[1] Baker was further recognized for her poetry on June 10, when Southern Methodist University awarded her an honorary doctor of letters.[2] That summer she began a ten-year teaching position at Stephen F. Austin State Teachers College, taking a leave of absence in 1926–27 to attend the University of California at Berkeley. These ten years, 1924–34, in addition to being years of great service to the East Texas community, were possibly the most productive in Baker's career.

Stephen F. Austin State Teachers College first opened its doors in Nacogdoches, Texas, in the fall of 1923. When Baker joined the faculty the following summer, she was one of seven members in the English Department. The college enrollment was quite small, approximately 350 students. Baker and her husband were personal friends with Birdwell and his wife. Birdwell had recognized the value the poet would add to the faculty when he asked her to accept a teaching appointment. No other faculty member had the national recognition she enjoyed; indeed, no other college or university in Texas could boast of having a poet of such acclaim. She was regularly sought after as a visiting speaker at many of the other universities in the state and at some out of state. Already Baker had published her first four books at one of the nation's most important scholarly presses, and during her years of teaching at Stephen F. Austin, she would publish more: *The Birds of Tanglewood* (1930), a book of essays on birdlife in Nacogdoches; *Dreamers on Horseback* (1931), her last book of collected poems; and *Family Style,* a novel about the newly discovered East Texas oil field (completed in 1932 but not published until 1937). In addition, Baker was nominated for the Pulitzer Prize for Poetry while she taught at Stephen F. Austin; thus, the small town of Nacogdoches became further celebrated in the state because of her.

Early in 1924, the college had acquired a grand piano for the music department, but there was no auditorium on campus to house it. Ida Pritchett, the head of the department, placed the piano temporarily in the Sara Richardson house on North Church Street. A gathering of college dignitaries and supporters heard "The Pine Tree Hymn," Baker's poem set to music by Pritchett, played there for the first time. Those present included A. W. Birdwell and his wife, John Crawford, Emory Monk, F. F. Davis and his wife, Thomas E. Baker and his wife, the Deans of the College, and Guy Blount, Lois Foster, Eleanor Atkinson, Grace Bailey, Ardath Ellington, Bernice Mallory, Loulein Harris, Dera Willingham, and Ida Pritchett. The double quartet that sang that day performed "The Pine Tree Hymn" publicly at the new college auditorium in late spring 1924.[3]

In March, Baker wrote to Harriet Monroe, the editor of *Poetry: A Magazine of Verse,* about her summer teaching appointment at the college. She also mentioned to Monroe that she had asked the college librarian to subscribe to *Poetry.*[4] In the same month, Dorothy Scarborough wrote an article, titled "Karle Wilson Baker: Poet of Quiet Things," for the *Dallas News* "Contemporary American Poets" series. Scarborough's article introduced many Texans to Baker's work:

> Karle Wilson Baker has a gifted and versatile pen, as is shown by the fact that she has been successful in various forms of prose, as well as verse, in the short story, the informal sketch, the intimate essay. And her book of fairy tales, "The Garden of the Plynck," is a delightful volume, with charm for adults as much as for children, which is rare. . . .
>
> But it is as a poet that she commands more attention, for she has done more of her work in verse. Her prose is the prose of a poet, but her poetry is never prosaic. . . . She does not disregard the little daily things which a less discerning mind might think trivial. . . . Life to her is never

> commonplace, but each recorded hour has its own significance of fancy or spiritual emotion. . . .
>
> She finds beauty everywhere, in the sky-lines of the cities, in old buildings, in pictures, but most of all in nature. . . . One is a fondness for trees. She is fortunate in that she lives where she can have them for daily companions. . . . Birds are another favorite subject, and both in her prose and verse she shows affection for familiarity with them. . . .
>
> No one can read Mrs. Baker's poetry without being impressed by her strong religious feeling, her faith in God, her steady optimism. . . . Her songs are musical, her art practiced to avoid clumsy lines and awkward phrasings. . . . She is the singer of quiet things, and she is greatly loved.[5]

Such recognition in the state made Baker an important attraction for the new teacher's college in Nacogdoches, which college administrators did not fail to grasp. Her picture was the only faculty photograph in the summer catalog, which was also the first catalog the college had produced.[6] Also, the inaugural issue of the campus newspaper, the *Pine Log*, featured a large picture of Baker accompanied by the heading, "Will Teach in the Summer School."[7]

Baker wrote the descriptions of the courses on Contemporary Poetry that appeared in the school *Bulletin:* "The first aim of this course is to give students the essential basis for judging, appreciating, and enjoying poetry. The material of the course will be both critical and creative. English 215 will deal with the poets of America since 1890, important among whom are Moody, Lindsay, Frost, and Robinson. English 216 will deal with British poetry since 1890, giving special attention to Noyes, Masefield, and Yeats. Throughout these courses the student will be led to think of poetry as a living art, a contemporary activity in which he may share by means of creative appreciation."[8]

Assuming the appointment of college instructor at age forty-six, Karle Wilson Baker had to make certain changes in her life. Her time was now regulated by the rigors of class preparation and presentation, faculty meetings, and other responsibilities that come with teaching. Even though Baker had intended to teach only one summer at the college, she stayed ten years. She grew to appreciate the students she taught and felt they could teach her even as she taught them. She wrote to a friend, "In teaching literature to these young people I was making a vital and illuminating sort of contact with a whole new world. . . . These boys and girls were the sons and daughters of the little farms and the red hills and in the sandy flats under the pines; and in studying poetry with them I came to know that little world as it presented itself to the wistfulness and eagerness of youth."[9]

Birdwell made an exception to the Texas state rule that barred married women from teaching at a state university when he hired Baker. She had the distinction of being the only married woman in any department at the college. Birdwell remained one of her great admirers; after he read her novel, *Family Style*, he commented: "*Family Style* will be more popular a quarter of a century from now than now. It would not surprise me to see English teachers putting it on the required reading list as an example of realistic and yet beautiful English."[10] At a meeting of the Panola County Education Association, Della Thompson, a former student of Baker's, related an incident that occurred between Birdwell and a male student:

> When Mrs. Baker first began teaching English at SFA, a man trying to register noticed that the English he must take was taught by her. Of course, he didn't know her, but he did think that he knew he didn't want a woman teacher, so he went to Dr. Birdwell to try to have something done about it, but Dr. Birdwell advised him to go ahead and take the course, telling him that he was sure he would enjoy it. When the term was over, this man went to Dr. Birdwell and told him how much he enjoyed the course; he also told Dr. Birdwell that he thought that it should be compulsory for every one to take a course in English from Mrs. Baker![11]

In replies to a survey sent to more than two hundred SFA alumni who attended the college during the years Baker was a teacher, an overwhelming majority refer to the excellent quality of her classes.[12] Many students who responded to the survey were only sixteen years old at the time they were in her English class, yet they have clear memories of the experience. In answer to the request to describe Baker, students typically responded that she was "gracious," "stately," "dignified," and a "wonderful teacher." Some students included a well-loved Karle Wilson Baker poem in the reply; some recalled Baker's bringing the poet Robert Frost to the campus to speak; others remembered hearing her read poetry in her garden.[13] Students who responded to the survey but who were not English majors usually remembered Baker because she wrote the poem that became the school song, "The Pine Tree Hymn," or because of the Karle Wilson Baker Dramatic Club named in her honor.[14] Albert Thompson, a former student, wrote of Baker's teaching method, "She always had time for the students, whether in class or after class. She was very thorough and went into great detail when studying a poem. Instead of discussing a wide variety of writers, Mrs. Baker would select very few writers and discuss their works in great detail. . . . The head of the department substituted for her. He expressed amazement that she would spend an entire week [on] one poem. However, she never changed her method of teaching."[15] Her former student Inez Washburn Gilmore recalled the day of a test: "I remember one occasion, an important blue book exam. Mrs. Baker was ill. She sent the printed test and left us to our honor—no supervision. One outspoken student asked the group if we should share answers, or be honest. We voted one hundred percent that we had too much respect for Mrs. Baker, and we would not violate her trust. Not a single student cheated." Gilmore also remembered with fondness Baker's melodious speaking voice as she read poetry aloud to the class. She said the class preferred Baker's poems above all others and that they often pled with her to read to them.[16] This statement is verified in the Karle Wilson Baker Papers. Among class notes and assignments, a petition signed by thirty-six class members, including Inez Washburn, states the request: "Mrs. Baker, The class would be glad to have you read some of your own poetry to us."[17] Another student, Victor Fain, who was a reporter for the *Pine Log* and would, in later years, become the editor of the Nacogdoches *Daily Sentinel,* affirmed that students were aware of Mrs. Baker's fame: "All of us seemed to be fully aware and appreciative of Mrs. Baker's talent and contributions. I know I felt it an honor to be in her class, and as young and naïve as I was, I realized what an enhancement she was to our college."[18]

In the winter term 1929, Mrs. Baker's English 216 class presented a program on the "new poetry" (contemporary and experimental) to the student body assembly. One student, Francis Rudisill, gave the introduction to the program, "Poetry in Our Times," remarking that earlier she had known "practically nothing about the modern movement or present day poets. . . . My entire view of poetry has changed. . . . I made the surprising discovery that poets are people. . . . Poetry is life in words."[19] Some of Mrs. Baker's poetry had appeared in a nationally recognized text, *The New Poetry: A Study Outline,* by Mary P. Parsons.[20] Other students participating in the assembly read poems by contemporary American poets. A student, Denard Haden presented two poems as dance interpretations.[21] Another student from the survey recalled the assembly: "When Dr. Birdwell introduced her [Mrs. Baker] as speaker in Special Assembly, the entire student body waved, clapped hands, and called for 'more.'"[22] Curry Herrington retains in her memory an unfaded portrait of Baker through one of her poems and answered the alumni survey in this manner:

Let me grow lovely, growing old
So many fine things do:
Trees, and ivory, and gold,
And silks need not be new.

The writer continued:

> Her own poem described her. Mrs. Baker walked with dignity and poise. Even before she entered the classroom, I thought of lavender perfume. Her lovely gray hair was puffed up on the sides and brought to a bun on the top of her head. She had a natural charm and a very droll sense of humor. I visited in her home. There she sat in a high-backed chair with the same dignity she carried everywhere. The little things she cared about most were around her—a few books, a new magazine, a writing pad, and I think, either a kitten or a dog. In teaching, she brought out the beauty in all literature, never raising her voice above its normal pitch. Her students had to listen intently to follow her thoughts.[23]

Karle Wilson Baker's earliest impressions of college teaching are recorded in a letter to her friend, Professor J. B. Hubbell at Southern Methodist University:

> I have been having a fascinating time—especially with the work in contemporary poetry. I hope to be able to repeat the course this fall, for I have really spent the time this summer learning *how* to teach it.
>
> They [students] have the scantiest of backgrounds to build against, for the most part, but they have been delightfully responsive, and the work has been a joy. I have an ambition to gather together a nucleus of poetry-lovers, and to build up a good working-library of recent poetry, including the publication of the various poetry societies and student-clubs, before I leave Nacogdoches and Texas. I feel that to get such a seed really planted in a new school is something worth working for.[24]

The Karle Wilson Baker Papers include assignments and lesson plans for Contemporary Poetry 215 that illustrate what she expected of students. She assigned the following work for the class to complete while she was away for a speaking engagement:

- Make a study of the poetry of Robert Frost, in the same way that we have studied Moody and Robinson. However, since there will be no class meetings, you should have time to read more widely. I shall

Karle Wilson Baker in March 1926, at the time she was teaching at Stephen F. Austin State Teachers College. (Private Collection, Baker Estate)

expect you to get acquainted with all the more famous poems, and to make a few personal discoveries on your own. Begin with "The Death of the Hired Man," "Home Burial," "A Hundred Collars," and "The Code." There will be a test at the second meeting after my return.

- Hand in a bibliography of critical material on Frost. I hope you will be interested in making this as complete as possible. Indicate how much of it you have read, and mark with an asterisk the three sources which you found most helpful. I shall return these for your notebooks.
- This is your opportunity to work on your term themes. The other poets to be studied are Vachel Lindsay, Carl Sandburg, and Amy Lowell.
- Study the chapter in *New Voices* entitled "Nature in Contemporary Poetry." You will probably have a question on this in your next test.
- Hand in a paragraph (not over one page) on "Nature" as it appears in Moody, Robinson or Frost. If you prefer, you may contrast or compare all three, or any two. This may be as brief as you like, provided it contains at least one point that you have observed or thought out for yourself.[25]

Shortly after Baker started her first summer of teaching, she received a letter from Jay B. Hubbell, who had assumed the editorship of the *Texas Review.* Under his direction, the *Texas Review* moved from Austin and the University of Texas to Dallas and Southern Methodist University. Hubbell wanted Baker to serve as an advisory editor and asked her to send him ideas about what the "new" *Review* should be like. He wished to pattern his review after the *Yale Review,* which he considered to be the best in the country. He knew that Baker was a logical choice to turn to for advice since she knew more about the *Yale Review* than anyone else in Texas. Hubbell also mentioned that he wanted to change the quarterly's name from the *Texas Review* to the *Southwestern Review.*[26] Baker responded favorably to Hubbell's letter:

> I am delighted that you are to take over the *Review,* and I shall be glad to serve on your advisory board, so far as my time will permit. I shall enjoy the work, and I shall be proud of the distinction. . . . I feel very strongly that, to make it the sort of magazine you plan, it should deal in a thoroughly professional (or shall I say business-like?) manner with contributors. . . . I think its professional relation to writers, as much as the Yale prestige, has given the *Yale Review* its pre-eminence in its field.
>
> We (my husband and I) differ as to the change of name for your projected quarterly. He like the suggested "Southwestern Review"; but I

> should be reluctant to see the old name go. Texas is beginning to have a glamour for the East. . . . Wouldn't it be better to win for Texas the glory of standing for the whole—Southwest—of gathering it all under the banner of her name?[27]

Baker taught at Stephen F. Austin for the next fifteen months (April 1925–June 1926), balancing her teaching load, speaking engagements, and writing projects as her fame continued to grow nationally. Her poems were frequently included in anthologies of poetry. Louis Untermeyer's *American Poetry Since 1900* (1924) and an anthology published in England, *The Best Poems of 1923*, included one of her most enduring poems, "Let Me Grow Lovely." Leonidas Payne, the chairman of the Department of English at the University of Texas, included "Good Company" and "Winter Flowers" in his new book of poetry (1925). In Payne's letter requesting permission to use the poems, he also suggested that she join the faculty at the University of Texas, but she declined.[28] In a later anthology, Payne used "I Shall Be Loved for Quiet Things" and "Within the Alamo."[29] Also in 1925, Baker was awarded the "Southern Prize" by the Poetry Society of South Carolina for the poem "The Lost Grove." The recognition included a monetary prize of one hundred dollars.[30] Two years later, Hilton Greer included her poetry in his anthology, *Voices of the Southwest.* The next year, her poems appeared in another anthology, *The Lyric South,* edited by Addison Hibbard. V. S. Montgomery included Baker's poems in *Texas Poets and Poetry* (1934).[31] Karle Wilson Baker became the most anthologized poet in Texas in her lifetime. In addition, she continued to publish poetry in national magazines and prepare her last book of collected verse, *Dreamers on Horseback.* During this busy time, Baker also managed to write another book for children.

In March 1926, John Rosser and the World Book Company published *Texas Flag Primer* that Rosser had commissioned Baker to write in 1923. About the book, which was adopted by the state for use in the public grammar schools, Baker commented, "I have always been interested in children's literature, and having already made a close study of Texas History ["The Story of Texas"], I was glad to undertake the production of a Primer of this kind. . . . There is a lack of good realistic literature for children, and what there is of it is likely to be too wooden and stolid. My effort was to write something real yet imaginative."[32] Rosser wrote that he would soon send 110,000 copies of the *Texas Flag Primer* to the state. The World Book Company also printed 7,500 circulars advertising the new book. The circular was actually a three-page biographical sketch of Baker that included a portrait drawing taken from her photograph. In addition, it described the contents of the primer and included a page of reviews of the book by educators and parents praising Baker's contribution to the state.[33]

That spring, Karle Wilson Baker was busy with speaking engagements in addition to her teaching. She spoke to a Dallas women's club, the Craig Class. The Craig Class would become one of her most frequent speaking commitments over the years.[34] About that same time, Hilton Greer and the Poetry Society of Texas arranged to present a radio program of poetry readings from the WFAA station at the Baker Hotel in Dallas. This was the first radio program of poetry readings ever offered in the state. The program featured four poets, all members of the Poetry Society. Pearl Wallace Chappell of Dallas read Karle Wilson Baker's "Song of the Forerunners" and "Good Company." The Baker family, along with others including the Birdwells, heard the program at Ben T. Wilson's home. *The Daily Sentinel* reported:

> The program was heard on the radio instrument Tuesday night at the home of Mr. and Mrs. Ben T. Wilson, the sounds coming with clearness that made the entertainment almost like being in the next room to it. . . . The Dallas News, in commenting upon the meeting [the poetry reading], gave a list of those present and the poems which were read in their broad-casting program. Only one of the list was commented upon and this was Karle Wilson Baker of Nacogdoches, of whom it was said, "She is recognized as one of the foremost of living poets."[35]

Greer also asked Baker to present a program to the Poetry Society later that month. Focusing on Texas as the subject at the meeting, she read from her sonnet group "Some Towns of Texas" and "A Ballad of the Alamo." The program closed with the reading of "The Lost Forest."[36]

Throughout her life, Karle Wilson Baker saw herself as a student and was ever desirous of increasing her knowledge. Even though she never graduated from college, the University of Chicago, Columbia University, and the University of California at Berkeley contributed to her education. Opportunity came in 1926 for Baker to further her education at the University of California at Berkeley. Charlotte and Tomby had completed their freshman year at Stephen F. Austin, and the Bakers wanted their children to begin their sophomore year at Berkeley. Baker, Tomby, and Charlotte drove to California in their new Essex automobile. According to her daughter, Karle Wilson Baker's interest in accompanying her children to the University of California was twofold. Not only did she want to continue her own education, but she also had reservations about sending Charlotte (only sixteen years old) to such a large university so far away. At that time, UC–Berkeley had an enrollment of approximately ten thousand students. The Bakers had not seen the campus previously, and when they arrived, they were very favorably impressed.[37] An amusing situation occurred in the Contemporary American Poetry class. The professor read a poem and then proceeded to explain to the class what the poet had meant. He did not realize that Karle Wilson Baker, his student, was the author because he thought the poet was male. After the professor had spoken at some length about the poem, Baker hesitatingly raised her hand, identified herself as the poet, and offered the intended meaning of the poem.[38]

Baker published four poems in the *University of California Chronicle* (July 1927) while she attended UC–Berkeley. Also, the California Writer's Club asked her to speak at one of their meetings. In her lecture, she commented that she had found what was truly good in literature through her experience in teaching. Specifically, she referred to the challenges of teaching literature to a classroom filled with college athletes and the success she had with them.[39] Even though Baker was away from Nacogdoches, she remained mindful of the small college back home. On November 6, 1926, she wrote an account of campus life at Berkeley to the *Pine Log*, comparing the two schools and the role she had assumed as teacher-turned-student:

> . . . I am often reminded of our old library difficulties at S.F.A. Here we have access of reading-rooms, hundreds of chairs, and thousands upon thousands of books, but there seems to be almost the same disproportion between the number of students and the number of books, that there is with us.
>
> . . . I think it's excellent discipline for the teacher to turn student occasionally—it certainly gives one a fresh insight into the student's point of view. On the other hand, if one has stayed awake at night trying to distribute A's and B's and C's justly (we won't mention the other) it makes one more patient with the "Prof." So the teacher-students profit in both directions.[40]

When the Bakers returned to Texas in December for the Christmas holidays, they were delayed by bad roads and car trouble. Baker sent a telegram from Gallup, New Mexico, to her husband on December 15, 1926: "Were held up here all day by road conditions and necessity of relining brakes which were cut out by yesterdays mud. Sorry to lose time but all have had a comfortable days rest leaving at six in the morning end of fifth inning no hits no runs no errors."[41] After they arrived in Texas, Baker spoke to the Craig Class in Dallas shortly before Christmas, reading her own poetry and selections from her short stories.[42] When they returned to the University of California the next month, Baker enrolled in courses in creative writing. She joined Charlotte in a class on the history of art and Tomby in a philosophy class. After her fifteen-month stay at Berkeley, Baker left her children at school in California and returned to Nacogdoches in August 1927 to resume her teaching responsibilities.[43] Upon her return, the Department of English gave her the title of assistant professor. The Bakers also began the project of building a new house, "West Windows," on North Street and took up temporary residence at 577 King Street.[44]

The year 1928 was a busy one in the Baker household. Thomas E. Baker became the new president of Commercial Guaranty State Bank, which entailed many extended duties and responsibilities. Once again, Karle Wilson Baker balanced household involvements with writing, speaking engagements, and, of course, teaching; she continued to be one of the most sought-after instructors on campus. That year a student writer for the *Pine Log* commented on Baker in the classroom: "She brings with her into the room a calm and a repose, yet at the same time an expectant atmosphere conductive to the enjoyment of poetry. And because she is the creator of enduring poetry herself, she is able to so present a poetry course that the most prosaic student will get everything possible out of it."[45]

In March 1928, at the request of Leonidas Payne, Baker lectured on the poet William Vaughn Moody in Austin at the University of Texas.[46] Because of the anticipated large audience of students and townspeople, the lecture was held in Garrison Hall. Payne also asked Baker to read her own poetry the next day to English classes at the university. He introduced her saying, "Not only is Mrs. Baker recognized as among the best lyric poets in America today, but she is also recognized as a master of prose. In my judgment, she is the most gifted lyricist in Texas today."[47] As was her habit, Baker sent copies of her books to her host in thanks for the visit. He received copies of *Old Coins* and *Burning Bush,* both of which were already out of print. *Blue Smoke* was out of print as well, and Baker could not find a copy to send to him.[48] While she was in Austin for the Moody engagement, Baker stayed in the home of Annie L. Perkins Garrison, the mother of her sister-in-law, Bess Wilson. Bess was at her mother's home at the time, and Baker wanted to spend any extra time during the Austin visit with her.[49]

As the president of the Poetry Society of Texas, Hilton Greer wrote to Baker in April 1928, asking her to judge a contest sponsored by the Poetry Society. He also accused her of losing interest in the society. Baker replied with a list of reasons why she had been less active, including building a house, school responsibilities, taking part in a biennial celebration program in San Antonio, and planning a return to California to be with her children for the summer. She did, however, agree to judge the poetry contest for Greer in May before she left.[50]

After another summer in California with her children, she returned to Nacogdoches to resume teaching and to move into West Windows, the Baker's new home on North Street. Tomby and Charlotte remained in California, he at Berkeley and she at Mills College. The first faculty meeting for the fall semester 1928 was on September 21; a week later, on September 28, the Bakers moved to West Windows.[51] She describes the new house in her diary: "Essentially the house of my dreams. . . . Windows that commanded a sweep of landscape and sky, and a quiet room just for my books and writing . . . I have dreamed of a house with high windows that faced the sunset."[52] She had already published essays in the *Yale Review* on birdlife based on observations at her home Tanglewood. Now she added a last essay, "Domesticity—with Wings," written at West Windows. At West Windows she observed birdlife on extensive property behind the house that she sometimes described as "The Thicket." According to her niece, who lived next door, the family often called it "The Grove" as they had referred to property below the house on Baxter-Duncan Street.[53] She would put the bird essays together in a delightful book titled *The Birds of Tanglewood.*

By November, Baker was off again on a speaking engagement. This time she traveled by train to Wellesley College in Wellesley, Massachusetts. Katherine Lee Bates, professor emeritus at Wellesley and the author of the famous patriotic anthem "America the Beautiful," had invited her to speak at the college's annual Speaker's Day. Baker's national reputation as a poet brought about the invitation.[54] Boarding the train in Nacogdoches, she made a stop in St. Louis to visit her half-sister, Bess Wright, and her family. When she reached Boston on November 5 at 9:45 P.M., a faculty member from Wellesley met her. During Baker's visit she took a tour of Boston and Harvard University, and Bates took her on a special trip to Longfellow's Wayside Inn.[55] Baker recorded in her notes on the speaking engagement that she was not totally satisfied with the program she presented at the college. For material, she had relied heavily on her book of fables, *Old Coins,* and she felt the students were not particularly responsive. She was heartened a few days later, however, when she spoke to the Boston Authors' Club. Katherine Lee Bates had been scheduled to speak at the exclusive club, but due to illness, she was unable to attend and asked Baker to speak in her place. Baker

Winter photograph of West Windows by Charlotte Baker. The Bakers built West Windows on North Street in Nacogdoches in 1928, near Stephen F. Austin State Teachers College. West Windows is the house on the right side. The house on the left belonged to the Baker's in-laws, the I. L. Sturdevants. (Steen Library, Stephen F. Austin State University, Karle Wilson Baker Papers Box 52/33)

recorded the events of the evening in her diary: "The dinner was as other dinners of the sort, but very nice. The toastmaster was as all toastmasters should be—indefatigably but genuinely witty; and one of the speeches was excellent. I read well, and consequently felt more satisfaction and less disgust, than usual. The audience was wholly kind."[56]

A couple of days later, Baker traveled to Mountain Lakes, New York, and spent two nights with Julia Moody Schmalz, sister of the late poet William Vaughn Moody. For several years, Baker had been writing a biography of her former teacher, who she considered to be the most outstanding poet in American letters. She taught Moody's works in her classes at Stephen F. Austin.[57] Reams of correspondence exist between Baker and Schmalz from 1924 to 1934.[58] During their visit, the women discussed the progress and direction of a book that Schmalz was compiling of articles about her brother. Baker hoped to be a contributor, but she found Schmalz's manuscript to be unwieldy and far too long. Schmalz was not open to suggestions, and Baker was unable to help her with revisions. Some of Baker's own contributions intended for the book had already been published as magazine articles: "A Poet of the Lean Years" *(The Forum,* 1922) and "William Vaughn Moody: A Recollection" (*Christian Science Monitor,* December 1923). Later Baker tried to publish another article on Moody, "The Firebringer in the Classroom," but was unsuccessful.[59]

Baker began the long trip home from New York on November 11, 1928, making a stop in Atlanta, Georgia, to speak on November 12 at Agnes Scott College, where she read selections from Moody's works as well as some of her own poetry. The next day she attended some conferences at the college and visited Stone Mountain. She finally reached Nacogdoches again on November 14.[60] Traveling such distances by train alone in the 1920s to meet demanding speaking engagements would have deterred many women of the time, but Karle Wilson Baker thoroughly enjoyed the opportunities afforded by travel, sight-seeing, and meeting with interesting people. Thomas E. Baker often testified to this fact when he quoted from the poem, "Box-Car Letters," where his wife writes, "I would not stay when I want to go!"[61]

When Baker was ready to publish a book of her essays on birdlife, she turned again to the Yale Press, but even though the *Yale Review* had published two of the essays, the Press editors were not interested in publishing an entire book of essays about East Texas. She began looking elsewhere for a publisher. In early January 1929, while attending a meeting of the Poetry Society in Dallas, she discussed prospective publishing opportunities with Hilton Greer. On January 10, Baker wrote to Greer asking for information about the publisher P. L. Turner of the Southwest Press. Greer encouraged her to publish with Turner and also spoke to the publisher on her behalf.[62] Southwest Press published *The Birds of Tanglewood* the next year and a book of poetry, *Dreamers on Horseback*, in 1931. On March 20, 1929, Baker once again gave a program for the Craig Class in Dallas. The next day she traveled on the interurban to Denton to present a program on William Vaughn Moody at Texas Woman's College, where she was honored at a luncheon given by the Karle Wilson Baker Literary Club.[63]

Charlotte's graduation from college allowed Baker and her husband the opportunity to travel together to California. After they attended the Stephen F. Austin graduation at the end of May, Karle and Tom Baker left on June 3 by train for California and Charlotte's graduation from Mills College. The school festivities preceding the commencement exercises spanned several days. While there, Baker met Charlotte's art instructor and good friend Florence Minard. Years earlier, Minard had illustrated *The Garden of the Plynck* for Yale University Press. Tom Baker had arranged to be away from the bank for nearly three weeks, but after that time, he had to return to Nacogdoches. Charlotte began graduate studies in art at Berkeley and Baker remained in California with her, but this time she did not enroll in classes. In early August, she returned to Nacogdoches and finished her articles for the Moody book, but Julia Moody Schmalz was too disorganized, and the book never reached completion.[64]

The failure of the Moody book to come to fruition did not keep Baker from continuing her own writing projects. Commenting on her writing habits on October 13, 1929, her fifty-first birthday, Baker wrote: "I am using the loose-leaf method so that, when looking back over the material, I can easily weed out whatever I find too wearisome or distasteful. . . . I wish to leave behind me the double distilled—triple-distilled."[65] In response to a student who asked advice about writing, she once said,

> Of course, as with most writers, I have almost as many more manuscripts that have never been published, and I haven't kept count of the number that have been written and destroyed. I know all about that bane of a writer's life, the "printed slip,". . . I think what anybody needs to be a writer, granting a little talent, is the ability to keep trying in the face of all discouragements. With that, a little talent will take him farther than a big one without it.[66]

In November, Anna McCaleb Sheets, Karle Wilson Baker's dear school chum from the University of Chicago, visited in Nacogdoches again. Sheets worked for a publishing house in Chicago and was to some degree a writer herself. While she was in Nacogdoches, she lectured to Baker's classes on the poet Carl Sandburg. The Bakers entertained Sheets by taking her out to Fern Lake and to Natchitoches, Louisiana. During Sheets's visit, Baker received a long letter from Schmalz asking her to come for another visit. Sheets knew of the problems Baker had been having with the difficult Schmalz and advised her friend to be wary of her.[67] When Schmalz encouraged Baker to submit a study of William Vaughn Moody's works to Houghton Mifflin Company, Baker followed the advice and was encouraged by the reception her book received, but the publishing house eventually declined to publish it.[68]

Baker sent a query letter in December to H. S. Latham, an editor at the Macmillan Company, exploring whether or not they would be interested in publishing a book of her collected poems from *Blue Smoke* and *Burning Bush* along with some new poems. She wrote, "[I] would like to have my books sponsored by a firm which, in addition to the distinction which it stamps upon its publications, also concerns itself with marketing them. From the first, the people who are interested in my books have complained of the difficulty of getting them." She listed her four books published with the Yale University Press, the primer published with the World Book Company, and her contract with Southwest Press to publish "The Birds of Tanglewood."[69] On January 21, 1930, the Macmillan Company responded that the poems "do not prove to fit in with our needs" and declined to publish them.[70]

As usual, Baker's speaking engagements occupied as much time as her writing projects. A. J. Armstrong, chairman of the Department of English at Baylor University, wrote to Baker asking her to introduce Edna St. Vincent Millay at a program scheduled for February. In his request he wrote, "I conceived the idea that it would be nice to have the greatest of Texas' poets introduce the greatest woman poet in the world."[71] Baker accepted the invitation, but family illness that February kept her from introducing Millay. In May, the Texas Alpha chapter of Phi Beta Kappa at the University of Texas elected Baker an honorary member of the society.[72]

Baker wanted to take her chances with her own biography of Moody at the University of Chicago Press, and she also wanted to meet Moody's widow, Harriet, who lived in Chicago. So in September 1930, she combined a visit to Anna McCaleb Sheets in Oregon, Illinois, with a visit to see Harriet Moody. While she was at Anna's, she received "The Birds of Tanglewood" proofs to review, and she posted a short story, "Devious Paths," to a publisher. On September 12, she and Anna went to Chicago and called on Harriet Monroe at the *Poetry* office. Baker recorded the visit in her diary:

> She looked older than when I last saw her, frailer, and withal, more distinguished looking. . . . She asked about my work, and was interested in hearing that I had left the Moody manuscript at the University of Chicago Press. . . . When we rose to go, she said, "There is an alphabetically arranged collection of poetry in English since 1912—all we have kept of it. Your book is there." She produced *Blue Smoke,* and was surprised that she did not know of *Burning Bush.* I told her of the forthcoming *Birds of Tanglewood,* of the *Southwest Review,* and the Southwest Press. . . . Finally we bowed ourselves out, pleased and happy, to burst into simultaneous speech on the curbstone opposite.[73]

The next day, Baker called alone on Harriet Moody. She found the poverty-stricken widow preparing a cookbook for possible publication. Her home, an old three-story mansion located in a run-down part of Chicago, was both sad and eccentric. (Baker mentions an upholstered sofa-swing suspended from the ceiling of the Moodys' living room.)[74] Following the visit, Baker commented in her diary, "I did find it tragic—oh, so tragic and pitiful! It was a sort of cave of memory, where this once resplendent old soul was keeping all that was left of Moody . . . to have come to this dark shrine!"[75]

Recognition was waiting for Karle Wilson Baker upon her return to Texas. Southwest Press published *The Birds of Tanglewood* (her first book of prose to achieve a large circulation) in the fall of 1930. Because the artist assigned by Southwest Press to illustrate the text had been unable to do the work, Baker had seized the opportunity to recommend her daughter, Charlotte, who had recently graduated with a master's degree in art from the University of California at Berkeley.[76] P. L. Turner agreed to the new arrangement, and mother and daughter joined efforts. Charlotte provided thirteen pen and ink illustrations for the text.[77] After its Texas publication, *The Birds of Tanglewood* was an immediate success across the state and received favorable reviews from every prominent newspaper in Texas and from newspapers as far away as the *New York Sun.* Congratulatory letters arrived from critics and friends such as Louis Untermeyer, Derrick Lehman from the *University of California Chronicle,* J. Frank Dobie's wife, Bertha, and Charles G. Smith at Baylor University. In addition, requests poured in for public appearances.[78] Publicity from the book brought new attention to the town of Nacogdoches and to the young college. In November 1930, Baker and her daughter drove to Dallas to attend the Dallas Woman's Club annual exhibition of fall books, honoring the authors published by Southwest Press. P. L. Turner, the president of the Southwest Press, wrote to Baker that she and Charlotte were

Karle Wilson Baker taking bird notes. Drawing by Charlotte Baker used as an illustration in The Birds of Tanglewood. *(Private Collection, Baker Estate)*

invited to the Dallas Women's Club tea. Lena Rogers, a member of the organization, invited the Bakers to stay at her home. The Bakers allowed an extra day in the city so that Charlotte could look for an advertising job in hopes of putting her drawing skills to "practical use."[79]

Baker had revised the first paragraph in *The Birds of Tanglewood* from the introduction written for the earlier *Yale Review* essays. Her Texas readers did not require the explanations the Northern reader needed, and she took the opportunity to set the locale firmly in Texas history:

> My introduction to Tanglewood was concerned with thrushes. It was a tangle of grape-vines and underbrush and great forest trees, which my father had just bought in the little town to which he had lately moved. . . . When I first came from college to live in the little house across the street, the birds had no knowledge of its change of ownership. They went on singing and rioting and nesting there just as their ancestors had done through immemorial summers, untroubled by perplexities as to whether it belonged to France, to Spain, to one Sam Houston, to the Republic of Fredonia, or still to the friendly Tejas. All had claimed it at one time or another, but my own conviction is that the wood-thrushes were and are the rightful owners of the place.[80]

Earlier in 1930, Baker had told Leonidas Payne that she intended to give up writing verse. After he had read some of *The Birds of Tanglewood*, Payne wrote to Baker: "I have read about half of the delightful essays on birds in Birds of Tanglewood. I can see why you are deserting poetry for prose, but in reality not deserting the Muse at all, for there is much poetry in your essays."[81] Bertha Dobie, reviewing *The Birds of Tanglewood* for the *Dallas News*, agreed: "It is a poet's book, always in feeling and often in language. Small yellow birds are 'flying daffodils,' 'the creek—like a poetic gloss to a line of prose—meanders along beside the railroad.'" Dobie also related Baker's memorable description of the mockingbird: "He is a worldling, and no worldling can be a great poet. As an artist, he is one of the dazzling second-raters."[82]

An already overwhelming calendar of speaking engagements for poetry now swelled into many requests for lectures on *The Birds of Tanglewood*. During the SFA years, Karle Wilson Baker spoke frequently to groups both large and small. The Baker Papers are filled with correspondence from organizations asking her to read her works or to lecture on a literary topic.[83] Since she viewed writing as a career that should yield monetary rewards as well as aesthetic ones, she had charged a speaker's fee since the 1920s. However, the fee rarely deterred organizations from requesting a speaking engagement. Also, Baker's early uneasiness about public speaking relaxed over the years. A student journalist had observed her anxiety: "She [Baker] is extremely reticent about doing things of this nature [public readings]. She does them almost under cover of night and is careful that it doesn't by any chance leak out in time for her intimate friends or family to be present at the performance."[84] On several occasions Baker depended upon her son, Tomby, to drive her to speaking engagements.[85] Even though she was modest and retiring, Baker was an energetic woman with a strong determination. The rigorous agenda of teaching classes at the college, traveling distances by car or train to give speeches, and maintaining a publishing schedule were possible only because of her own industriousness and the support and encouragement she consistently received from her family. As her number one fan, Thomas E. Baker was proud of his wife's writing and the recognition she received.[86]

When *The Birds of Tanglewood* came out, Baker dedicated it "To the Memory of My Father and Mother—the Builders of the Vanished 'Tanglewood.'" A review of the book in *Texas Outlook* in 1931 noted that Baker described characteristics of the different species in such a personal manner that they became vivid in human terms:

> In her non-technical approach to birdlore, and in her frank delight in every personal discovery of well-known scientific facts, Mrs. Baker writes nature essays much in the manner of John Burroughs, whose nineteenth century studies of the out-of-doors have become classics. Like Burroughs, she delights to attribute human traits to the birds, and like him, she uses them as a starting point to philosophize about life in general. However, she goes farther than he does in finding a symbolism everywhere she looks, in seeing a kind of allegory in birdlore. This mysticism, which is the core of Mrs. Baker's poetry, stamps her nature essays as distinctively her own.[87]

Karle Wilson Baker felt that most bird books could be confusingly technical. To her, a bird's one striking peculiarity was more helpful as an aid to identification than the most painfully accurate and exhaustive inventory of markings. An experienced birder conscious of the awkwardness of man in nature, she was always aware of herself as a potential intruder into another world. Appreciative that sometimes she was tentatively allowed to join the lives of her bird friends, she begins and ends *The Birds of Tanglewood* with sympathetic accounts of the life of the thrush family:

I suddenly saw, not six feet over my head, as plain as the sun, a most delicate golden-brown nest; and, rising above the rim of it, the soft, spotted breast, bright brown head, and still, watchful eye, of a brooding wood-thrush. Of all the birds that had particularly belonged to us, the wood-thrush had always been first and dearest. . . . For several days the father would not even sing his evening song if I were near. I would hear him singing, and steal to my seat under the tree to listen; but the song would cease, and the singer slip away. Before many days, however, he consented to my presence; for a little while before sun-down, and a little after, rain or shine, he would take his station near his family, and pour out, softly, his bell-like song. Even so, at these times I could never quite find him. I knew that, if I did not sit quietly, he would not let me be one of the family; so I kept very still, and merely knew that he was among the leaves above me, quite close over my head. . . . Yet is life kind to the stumbling worshipper of wings. For there is no end to her surprises. Flashing at us through the high branches, shooting into our lives the beam of life so much swifter and intenser than our own, yet somehow native and familiar—there is always some uncaptured marvel.[88]

Rebecca Smith, a professor at Texas Christian University in Fort Worth and a friend of Karle Wilson Baker's, reviewed the new book: "Our most distinguished Texas poet has turned essayist. Karle Wilson Baker's latest volume, rather overlong awaited by her public, is *The Birds of Tanglewood,* four descriptive essays set among the tall trees of her East Texas home." Smith outlined the book:

The first, "Birds of Tanglewood," constitutes a social register of the birds who come during her first Texan summer to the "tangle of grapevines and underbrush and great forest trees" about her father's newly purchased home. She finds that the thrush looks middleclass although he is a poet at heart; her favorite bluebird has a "high seriousness" of soul; the mockingbird is not the Shakespeare of birds as Lanier declared, but a dazzling second-rater. "Window Lore" was written after an illness had imposed upon the author a close-up view of the visitor to the window sill by which she lay for months and observed their habits of feeding, the color of their eyes, the shape of their eyebrows, and the ways of special crippled fellows. "An Aerial Harvest" is the record of a storm in April, 1922 that strewed the little East Texas town with a brilliant wreckage of dead and wounded birds. The final essay, "Domesticity—with Wings," describes Mrs. Baker's new home, West Windows, successor to Tanglewood as a haven for birds.[89]

Baker was a practical woman who was always looking for ways to use her talent to earn an income. Among the pages of the handwritten manuscript of *The Birds of Tanglewood,* Baker left a note to herself: "Be planning a 'Bird and Tree Program' for next summer, for summer camps, summer schools, etc. Try to get an engagement with a lyceum bureau. Have 'Birds of Tanglewood' done and accepted."[90] She had the skills and experience from the early days at Fern Lake with her own children to handle a summer camp for birders, but the camp never came about. However, in her notes she sketched out general headings to develop for the project: "How to Begin Bird Study," "Why Study Birds," and "Puzzles and Pitfalls."[91] She also included advice for the novice birder: "Train yourself to see and hear, whatever you are doing. . . . Go look for the birds, walk quietly through likely places, sit and watch. Birds' eyes and ears are sharp; they are shy but curious. Learn to move quietly and watch without seeming to. Learn to sit motionless yourself, but to be aware of every movement about you. Watch for color, also, and for every sound—whether chirp or rustle or song."[92] Baker suggested that when using binoculars and bird books, "Read the books and study pictures and descriptions. Acquire habit of noting certain details quickly and automatically, without removing glasses."[93] She encouraged the birder to note bird size, general color, details about the bill or head, placement of color, tail, and traits such as sociability and manner of flying. She advised that the best time of study in spring or summer was from dawn to 10 A.M. or before sunset. In winter, she recommended study from noon to 3 P.M., and she suggested that the best way to attract birds was to have adequate cover (undergrowth), a good food shelf and berry plants, and water. She posed the question "Why Study the Birds" and answered it: "We study birds for pleasure, and because all innocent experience is valuable. Incidentally, there are many indirect practical benefits from bird-study; but primarily, the reason we study birds is to add to our joy in life. The more innocent sources of happiness and excitement we have, the richer we are; and not only that, but the easier it is for us to avoid the harmful ones."[94] When she wrote bird notes in the field, she used very large script with only a few words to the line, following her own advice of writing notes and continuing to look through field glasses at the same time.[95]

Karle Wilson Baker's own lifestyle is characterized in the essay "Domesticity—With Wings." Like the birds she studied, she held within her a desire to be free and soaring while she balanced marriage, family, and children with her active life as a writer, public speaker, and teacher.[96] Baker had trained herself to become an authority on birdlife, and she recognized the close relationship between her own life and that of the birds she studied. The years when she had watched the birds most closely had also been the years when her own domestic concerns had been most absorbing. In the last essay in *Birds of Tanglewood,* she confesses, "Indeed, in looking back over the memories and written notes of more than twenty years of bird study, I have been lately struck by the comparative meagerness of my records of domestic life. Certainly this has not been due in any degree to lack of interest; for my own ideal has always been precisely that of the birds—domesticity with wings."[97]

The very week that Southwest Press published *The Birds of Tanglewood,* Baker spoke at the Central Library in Houston in recital of her own works. She gave two programs, an evening lecture and a story hour for children. The library staff had arranged that several Houston bookstores stock Baker's books in time for Book Week. Also, the Houston Public Library was generous, by Depression rates, paying seventy-five dollars for the two programs. The librarians requested that Baker read from her own works at both programs and asked her to bring some of Charlotte's original drawings used in *Birds of Tanglewood.*[98] At the children's hour, Baker read from her unpublished manuscript of children's stories, "The Reindeer's Shoe," and some poems written years earlier for her own children, "A Little Boy's Bath" and "Apple and Rose." About the poems she commented, "I don't dare read these when the children are around. . . . When they are older I do not think they will mind. But you know how children are in their teens."[99] During Baker's visit to the Houston Library, a reporter from the *Houston Post* asked how she had managed to balance a career, writing, and family life. Baker responded: "I just kept on working and managed to sandwich everything in some way." When asked about her method of work, she replied: "Poems just come, and usually at the most inconvenient times. A thought sticks in my mind and simply haunts me until I get it on paper. It isn't all inspiration by any means. The inspiration comes, then worries me until I get it expressed in just the right words."[100] Earlier, Baker had been quoted in a student interview: "Mrs. Baker frankly says that the routine of housekeeping does not appeal to her. She loves a home, but there is such a vast difference in home-making and mere housekeeping. 'I want a home, but I would like for it to run itself automatically.'"[101] Baker's program in Houston was mainly poetry. Throughout her career, the public continued to demand readings of her verse over anything else.

In addition to her public speaking engagements, an audience grew to know Baker's poetry through the more widely available medium of the radio. In the 1930s, radio stations broadcast Baker's poetry, and listeners wrote to her about such broadcasts. One of the first letters came from a fan in Houston who had heard poems from *Blue Smoke* read over a local station. Other examples occurred in 1932, when the Columbia Broadcasting System out of Charlotte, North Carolina, aired some of *Dreamers on Horseback*. Also, the minister of the Foundry Methodist Episcopal Church in Washington, D.C., incorporated the poem "Pronouns" in his sermon broadcast over CBS in 1932.[102] "Pronouns" became the front cover for the *Bulletin* of the Riverside Church in New York City.[103] Nationwide radio broadcasts of Baker's poetry continued through the 1940s.

Karle Wilson Baker felt all her life that she would become a novelist, but she had set this ambition aside when her children were small; now she determined that the time had come in her career to return to prose completely. Baker wrote about her frustrations:

> . . . A wise mentor said to me, "You can learn to work in spite of interruptions. It's hard, but it can be done. It's a matter of managing your own mind." I was incredulous for a long time afterward; but I went on trying because of a burning inner necessity, and I did learn to get short bits of writing done in spite of constant interruption, and without permanent nervous collapse. I think I could write a book on the subject of acquiring that trick. But, even after I had acquired it to the point of being able to do essays and poems as a matter of course, to write a novel still seemed to me quite another story. To produce a continuous work of a hundred thousand words or so, that must have a vital unity, must be all of a piece—where was I to get the strength for that much sustained effort? . . . Nevertheless . . . I buckled down one summer—while the thermometer ranged through the upper nineties and my husband was recovering from an appendicitis operation—and started my first. Don't ask me how I got through with it—I wonder, myself. All I know is what we all learn sooner or later; that we can always do whatever we become convinced that we must.[104]

The manuscript Karle Wilson Baker began in the summer of 1930 is titled "White Elephant."[105] This first attempt to write a novel had much in it of an autobiographical nature. *White Elephant* is set in Texas at the turn of the century in a small town not unlike Nacogdoches. The story relates the trials in a young woman's life of leaving school, helping a family member, delaying her own goals, marrying, having children, and finally finding her career. Encouraged by the acceptance of *The Birds of Tanglewood* by Southwest Press and by the book's success across the state, Baker sent the manuscript of "White Elephant" to P. L. Turner in September 1931. By that time the small press was under financial strains due to the Depression, and the editor turned the novel down. (Eventually Southwest Press became Turner Publishers.) Not to be defeated, Baker sent the manuscript to an agent, Edith Burrows, in New York. Burrows sent the manuscript to twelve large publishing companies, but all said "no" to "White Elephant."[106] The novel was never published. Nevertheless, putting together a full-length novel gave Baker experience in prose writing that proved valuable as she set out to write her next novel, and she was determined to continue writing on subjects set in Texas. When Baker left Yale University Press and the East Coast to publish *The Birds of Tanglewood* with the Southwest Press, she restricted her immediate publishing future to Texas. Her expressed desire to write about Texas history set her course for years to come. A writer for the *Texas Weekly* commented that "If Mrs. Baker has gone to Yale University for publication in previous years, it has undoubtedly been because there was no one South of the Mason and Dixon line who could or would compete with the Eastern publisher of her manuscripts. For a Texas house to issue this collection means that there is someone to compete, but more important still, that there is a Texas audience which demands this expatriate to gain her readers, unless our deduction is wrong that the Southwest Press would not print this book unless it had a demand for it."[107]

During the exciting months associated with the publication of *The Birds of Tanglewood,* Baker renewed experiments of the mind that she had begun some twelve years earlier. Her interest in extrasensory perception had never waned. She recorded an incident with ESP in her diary:

> I have always been interested in "auras," whatever they may be: or, rather, ever since I discovered that such things were supposed to exist, and to be visible to some people. That was some ten or twelve years ago. At that time I read everything I could get hold of on the subject, though that was not much; and I even tried to develop the power of seeing auras by practice in observing in a semi-dark room the rays that stream from the finger-tips. (This was described in a magazine article, and recommended by a book I read.)
>
> . . . It was this experience, however, that made me note carefully the very curious incident that happened, quite by accident, this morning. I was lying in bed, barely awake, with one eye (the one next to the window) closed, and the other one open. My attention was caught by the

> very curious and well-defined band (as of steam, or mist), streaming across the vision of the open eye. . . . I soon realized that the emanation (or part of it) was streaming off my own nose—almost, but not quite, at the tip! It was not colored, as all proper auras should be, but was like mist or steam, with only their slight luminosity. It was, I thought, clearly of the same sort as those I had been able to see streaming from my finger-tips, but more marked and well-defined. . . . It was not the mist of my breath; I tried that, but the air was not cold enough to condense it. The thing was absolute, clear-cut, definite; the fine, streaming lines had a wonderful suggestion of power.[108]

Her fascination with investigating what one might discover beyond the ordinary senses would grow in the coming years. Aberrations and auras became common for Baker in her experiments with ESP during the writing of her second novel, *Star of the Wilderness.* However, for the time being the routine life of the author took precedence over experimentation of the mind.

In the first three months of 1930, Baker met speaking engagements in Shreveport, Rusk, and Marshall, while simultaneously working on another book with Texas themes. She submitted a manuscript of her collected verse, which she called "Dreamers on Horseback," to P. L. Turner and Southwest Press for publication. The collection was made up of poems from her two previous books of poetry, *Blue Smoke* and *Burning Bush,* but she also included poems about Texas that she had written in the 1920s. Even though he had turned down *White Elephant* in 1929, Turner was eager to publish another book by this successful author who had quickly become one of the "stars" in his catalog. In December 1930, Baker signed a contract with Southwest Press for "Dreamers on Horseback."[109] Turner set the publication date for March 23, 1931; the actual release date was April 10.

Baker decided that *Dreamers on Horseback* would be her last book of verse. From this point on, she was determined to concentrate on prose. Any poetry that should come would come because it had to, not because she was setting aside any time for it. She confided her plans in a letter to Leonidas Payne: "I am determined to get some definite jobs of writing done . . . If all goes well, Southwest Press will bring out in February a new volume, called *Dreamers on Horseback,* which will be, in effect, my 'Collected Poems' and farewell to the Muse. (Not to prose—only verse) . . . Then, next fall, there may be a book of stories of the East Texas countryside and villages. But that is unofficial."[110] The book on East Texas that Baker referred to was a manuscript called "A Hundred Miles of Memories."

Karle Wilson Baker in February 1931, at the time of the Great Depression.
(Private Collection, Baker Estate)

Life continued at its usual pace; Baker was teaching at the college and meeting speaking engagements. She gave a lecture on Emily Dickinson in Dallas and at the University of Texas in February 1931. Leonidas Payne had very much wanted Baker to come to the University of Texas once again to speak. She was already committed to speak on Dickinson to the Craig Class in Dallas the last week in February, and she felt she could not take the time away from her classroom obligations and writing deadlines to prepare another lecture for Austin. When Payne wrote back that she could repeat the program on Dickinson at the University of Texas, Baker agreed to the engagement. Payne also mentioned that the Depression was cutting into the university's honorarium funds and the fifty dollars he could offer at that time would probably not be available later. He also suggested that a public lecture would be good advertisement for her upcoming book of collected poems.[111] In her reply, Baker reaffirmed her decision to stop writing verse: "So many people are writing graceful little verses—like mine—that I've lost all desire to write them. If I can't do something bigger, I can at least do something more distinctive."[112] Some of the poems that Baker thought of as her best are very Dickinsonian in style and subject. She called the poem "I Love the Friendly Faces of Old Sorrows" one of her best:[113]

> I love the friendly faces of old Sorrows;
> I have no secrets that they do not know.
> They are so old, I think they have forgotten
> What bitter words were spoken, long ago.
>
> I hate the cold, stern faces of new Sorrows
> Who stand and watch, and catch me all alone.
> I should be braver if I could remember
> How different the older ones have grown.

Baker also considered her group of six short lyrics, "Songs From a Still Place," to be among her best:

> VI. —Free:
> Upon God's window-sill
> Caroling high and shrill,
> Shaken with ecstasy,
> There clung my spirit—free!
>
> God showed His glorious Head—
> Singing, to Him she said,

"Who was it did me wrong?
Why was I caged so long,
Tangled in wires and strings,
Under the stars?"

"Birdling, I made the wings—
You made the bars."[114]

On February 24, 1931, Baker left Nacogdoches by train for Austin by way of Dallas. She spoke to the Craig Class on the twenty-sixth, and the next day she sat for professional photographs in Dallas. On the twenty-eighth she left at 8:48 A.M. on the MK&T train for Austin, arriving at 3:10 P.M. Payne and his wife met the train; Baker had supper in her room at the dormitory and lectured at 8 P.M. at Garrison Hall. After the lecture, the Paynes held a reception in her honor at their home.[115] The *Daily Texan* recorded some of Leonidas Payne's comments during Baker's visit: "I have long been an admirer of Mrs. Baker both as a poet and as a person. Her volumes of poetry, *Blue Smoke* and *Burning Bush,* two of the most distinguished lyrical volumes ever published by a Texan, have for some time been out of print. I am pleased to learn that there is to be published within the next few weeks by the Southwest Press a collected volume of Mrs. Baker's poetry. . . . *Dreamers on Horseback.*"[116]

The next day, Baker read her own poetry to Payne's English classes. The *Daily Texan* reported: "Dr. Payne introduced her as 'Domesticity—with Wings' an expression which he took from one of her books."[117] Following the lecture, she was a luncheon guest of the Dobies. J. Frank Dobie and Baker were not frequent correspondents nor did they meet together many times. Six years later, however, Dobie wrote Baker asking her to arrange a speaking engagement for him at Stephen F. Austin State Teachers College.[118] Two months after the Dickinson speech, Baker returned to Austin to speak by invitation at the Conference of College Teachers of English.[119]

The public response to *Dreamers on Horseback* was very favorable. Payne sent Baker glowing comments about the prepublication copy she had sent to him: "I should like to believe that this substantial volume will become a permanent landmark on the poetic highway of the great Southwest, and also take its honorable place in the poetical literature of the nation. In fact, I do believe it."[120] Dorothy Scarborough, who also received a prepublication copy of the book, wrote from New York, "The unaffected simplicity of it, the beauty of your concepts, the imaginative expression delight me. I am so glad to have this collected edition of your poems, which will be a collector's item."[121] Professor William Vann at Mary Hardin-Baylor College in Belton thanked the editors of the Southwest Press for his volume of the book: "Mrs. Baker is, beyond question, the finest artist among Texas poets."[122] Hilton Greer's review of the new book appeared in the *Dallas News:*

> Readers who know and treasure the work with which Karle Wilson Baker won high place among the contemporary poets of America will be first to welcome this offering of her "Collected Verse." It presents, with a full report of her stewardship to the art, an opportunity to trace her consistent growth. The new book includes, with most of the poems which were published in earlier volumes, those which Mrs. Baker has written in the last decade. These later poems complete a record of sustained artistry. They reveal, with no obtrusive effort at revealment, the sure craftsmanship, the inevitable wording, the concentrative power, the tense lyricism, the tangy philosophy, and, at times, the whimsical playfulness which prompted a distinguished critic [E. B. Reed] more than ten years ago to name her the writer of "the biggest little poems in America. . . ."[123]

In May 1931, John Rogers, an assistant editor at the Southwest Press, responded to a letter from Baker and concurred with her suggestion to promote *The Birds of Tanglewood* with Boy Scout and Camp Fire groups in Dallas. He also mentioned that he had suggested to Turner that the book would make a good supplementary reader in the schools. Responding to a question from Baker about how nominations were made for the Pulitzer Prize, Rogers also wrote, "It will give me great pleasure to arrange to have 'Dreamers on Horseback' offered, and I am very glad that you wrote about it at this time. The reason I happen to know about it is that just a few months ago, I wrote to Dorothy Scarborough for information regarding Dobie's book."[124] Perhaps Baker asked Rogers not to submit her name because he was already submitting J. Frank Dobie's name. John Rosser, editor at the World Book Company, wrote to Mrs. Baker on June 4, 1931, that he had sent off his nomination of *Dreamers on Horseback* for the Pulitzer Prize for Poetry.[125]

Two well-known ballads from *Dreamers on Horseback* helped to identify Baker as a Texan writing on Texas subjects: "Song of the Forerunners" and "Within the Alamo." "Song of the Forerunners," about the men and women who pioneered Texas, had been pivotal to her career and had received national attention when a committee selected it for first prize at a poetry contest sponsored by Southern Methodist University in 1922.[126] "Within the Alamo" opens with an explanation in prose:

The story goes that Travis, just before Santa Anna's final attack upon the Alamo, drew a line on the floor with his sword-point, and asked that every man who was ready to die with him cross over to his side. James Bowie, who was too ill to walk, asked his comrades to lift his cot across. Every other man but one stepped over. Whether the legend is true or not, it agrees well with all that is known of Travis, particularly with his letters from the Alamo, which are preserved among the archives of the state of Texas.

He drew a straight line
Across the dirt floor:
Within, it was death-still—
Without, was a roar

And a scream of the trumpets:
Within, was a Word—
And a line drawn clean
By the sweep of a sword.

No help was coming, now—
That hope was done.
No more the free air,
No more the sun

Bright on the blue leagues
Of buffalo-clover.
Travis drew a line
And they all crossed over.

Travis had a wife at home,
Travis was young;
Travis had a little boy
Whose tight arms clung,

But Travis saw a far light
Shining before:
Travis drew a sword-cut
Across the dirt floor.

* * * * *

And now past the Plaza
Other tides roar,

Since Travis wrote "Valor"
Across the sand floor,

And the guns they will rust,
And the captains will go,
And an end come at last
To the wars that we know,

But as long as there travails
A spirit in man,
In a war that was ancient
Before Time began,

Here will the brave come
To read a high Word—
Cut clean in the dust
By the stroke of a sword.

Professor W. H. Vann of Belton College wrote to Baker that he wanted to use "Within the Alamo" in an anthology, but he also wanted to make some changes in the poem. Baker's response helps us understand her creative process:

> I'm glad to give permission for the use of the Alamo poem without the introductory note. I can see that it would hardly be needed in a collection of this sort. —In regard to the other proposed change: The first line ought to set the time unequivocally, don't you think? Establish the beat unmistakable, I mean—so that subsequent deviations may have something to deviate from! Or, to speak seriously, so that the reader perceives at once the dominant or basic pattern. Later in the poem I have, "Travis had a wife at home"—but by that time the ear is tuned to the uncompromising underlying beat of
>
> "He drew a straight line
> Across the dirt floor—"
>
> and can make the extra syllabled line march with it. So, unless you still, most particularly don't want it, I'd rather leave the "he." I don't think it's weak or ambiguous, since *Alamo* means *Travis* to the youngest fifth-grade declaimer. If anything, it adds a hint of suspense, while we wait for the name.[127]

Baker's focus on Texas history also included a group of poems called "Some Towns in Texas." Using the Italian sonnet form, she paid special tribute to the city that was her home all her adult life. Baker understood the town's important geographical location in the development of early Texas. Nacogdoches was one of the largest towns in Texas in the 1830s. "Nacogdoches Speaks" was one of the group of poems:

> I was The Gateway. Here they came, and passed,
> The homespun centaurs with their arms of steel
> And taut heart-strings: wild wills, who thought to deal
> Bare-handed with jade Fortune, tracked at last
> Out of her silken lairs into the vast
> Of a man's world. They passed, but still I feel
> The dint of hoof, the print of booted heel,
> Like prick of spurs—the shadows that they cast.
> I do not vaunt their valors, or their crimes:
> I tell my secrets only to some lover,
> Some taster of spilled wine and scattered musk.
> But I have not forgotten; and, sometimes,
> The things that I remember rise, and hover.
> A sharper perfume in some April dusk.

Baker had a true affinity for her adopted Texas. Speaking through her poetry, she brought recognition to the state in a manner that had never occurred before. In "Texas Cowboy," she expresses her own puzzlement as to why she is so consumed with the cowboy myth:

> From garden-beds I tend, it is not far
> To those great ranges where he used to ride;
> . . . .
> He is a Thought; he is not flesh-and-bone
> He is immortal Youth astride a Dream:
> . . . .
> And I . . .
> A Woman with a bird, a book, a flower,
> Who sifting life, has kept the quiet part,
> Whose days like pearls are sorted, hour by hour—
> Why is it that he gallops through my heart?[128]

Early in the 1930s, writers, politicians, and educators across the state had begun to plan for the Texas Centennial in 1936. It was natural for Baker to express first through poetry the new spirit of the times in Texas. Poems in *Dreamers on Horseback* demonstrate her love of writing about historical figures, places, and events. But still determined to write prose, Baker set out to write a combination history/travelogue about famous places in East Texas. She was fascinated with where she lived and its deep historical connections to the founding of Texas. *El Camino Real* (The King's Highway), Sam Houston, Thomas J. Rusk, the early Spanish friars, and the historic sister city of Natchitoches, Louisiana, riveted her attention. For Baker, these were romantic notions as well as real places and people. She mentioned her writing scheme in letters and conversations with Leonidas Payne and Elinor Frost.[129] She knew she had the competence to write on such subjects; she just needed time for research. After she had written three articles for the project, she sent them to the editor of *Holland's Magazine* in Dallas. She was hopeful that the magazine would serialize the articles, which she would later incorporate into a book. She titled the project "A Hundred Miles of Memories" and included in the articles sights, people, and events along the historic El Camino Real. Even though Baker thought the project was perfect for the centennial celebrations, *Holland's Magazine* did not accept the proposal. Also about that time, Baker's attention shifted from Texas and its historical past to Texas in the present day. She saw the possibilities of a new novel on Texas in the drama playing out before her eyes in the East Texas oil field. Suddenly events in her own life in the early 1930s provided material that she felt would be timely in the centennial year. Her lifelong desire to write novels, her interest in Texas history, the fact that she lived in a town steeped in Texas history, the excitement of the oil boom, and the prospects of the Texas Centennial Celebrations in 1936 combined to provide Karle Wilson Baker further encouragement to concentrate on writing prose.

An event even more significant for East Texas than the centennial took place on October 3, 1930. This occurrence changed many lives in the area including that of Karle Wilson Baker. On that day, the Joiner Well (Daisy Bradford #3) blew in near Henderson and brought with it the discovery well of the great East Texas oil field. Baker, her husband Tom, daughter Charlotte, and nephew Junior Wright (Maurice Wright Jr.) witnessed this historic event. Baker found herself mesmerized by the excitement and exploration of the oil field. She postponed "A Hundred Miles of Memories" to focus on this contemporary event at her doorstep. Referring to that evening of October 3, 1930, she wrote:

> It was one of the most dramatic happenings that has ever come my way. I had never thought of writing about oil before, and I am not sure that the idea of *Family Style* was born that night. . . . I was incubating some-

> thing quite different ["A Hundred Miles of Memories"]. But as this living serial-story began to unfold, . . . I became more and more fascinated. Of course the excitement ran out like wildfire in every direction from the discovery well, and for about ten days we in Nacogdoches had a wild, illusory little boom of our own, with people knocking at every house to inquire if there were any rooms to rent, and standing-room was at a premium in the banks and hotel lobbies. There was supposed to be a "nose" of the Sabine Uplift that ran straight down from Joinerville to Nacogdoches—I think it was mapped to go right through the elm-thicket that is part of what I call the "wild garden" behind my house. . . . And the "outpost well" that was supposed to prove our prospects suddenly and devastatingly disproved them. The scouts and lease-hounds and boomers folded their tents like the Arabs and were gone. But my interest in the spectacle and the human drama remained and grew. Chances to visit the field were many, and for the next year [1931] I never missed one.[130]

Baker wrote the novel *Family Style* in thirteen months. She began on June 29, 1931, at nine o'clock in the evening, and when she stopped writing at midnight, she had the first two pages of what would later be chapter two of the novel.[131]

During the summer of 1931, Charlotte Baker taught in the art department at Stephen F. Austin State Teachers College. Karle Wilson Baker used the summer months to write. One project included a second public school reader, *Two Little Texans,* but her main writing focused on "Family Style." In September 1931, Baker returned to the college classroom. In October, she learned that because of a lack of funding, the state board of education would not adopt *Two Little Texans* for the public schools. Baker wrote to her friend Leonidas Payne that "adoptions are depressed out of existence this year." In the same letter, she referred to Payne's request for a copy of "The Seeker," a small booklet containing one of the essays for *Old Coins.* She wrote, "'The Seeker' is my husband's joy and pride; for some reason he boasts of it more than all of my other 'recognitions' put together! I have only one copy."[132] Seven months later, she noted in her diary that a few weeks before the end of the spring semester (the end of May 1932) she had finished the first fifteen chapters of "Family Style." By July 18, her typist, Sugene Spears, had completed the typing of these chapters.[133]

Between July 20 and August 15, 1932, Karle Wilson Baker, Charlotte, and Charlotte's friend Marian Ginter vacationed on Galveston Island. They had a small cabin where Baker slept at night; the girls slept on the beach. The summer was warm, and Baker wrote that she too slept outside the cabin one night. During the day Charlotte drove the family car onto the beach nearby where the girls were swimming, and Baker sat in the car (which they had nicknamed "The Seahorse") and wrote each day. She referred to this time in the beach cabin, which was hot and too small for three people, as a "depression vacation." At other times, Baker drove the car up the beach to a relatively deserted spot, opened all the doors for a breeze, and worked on her book.[134] Thomas E. Baker and Ben T. Wilson came for two of the weekends and brought Toncie, Ben's daughter, with them.[135] The vacation was cut short when a storm blew in, and the women left for home, but not before Baker had finished writing chapters sixteen through twenty-one. She wrote chapters twenty-two through twenty-five at West Windows in Nacogdoches between August 18 and August 24; Sugene Spears completed the first typing on September 8, 1932.[136] Five years would pass before Coward-McCann published *Family Style* in 1937.

Perhaps anticipating questions about why she wanted to write on a subject set in "a man's world," Baker posed the issue in a public address before a meeting of the College Women's Club and the Junior League in Houston:

> The idea seems to be that oil is a rough subject—the exclusive domain of the so-called He-Man. Why should a woman who had spent her time writing verses and essays about children and trees and birds want to touch it—and, anyway, how could she possibly know anything about it? A brief answer to the first question is, that even rough subjects have tender spots; and that life does not present itself in velvet and lace even to the poet. . . . The answer to the second—as to how I happened to know about it—is a long story; too long to tell here. I will say only that all my Texas life—and I came in my early twenties—has had oil, so to speak, just around the corner.
>
> The first oil-discovery in Texas was made in Nacogdoches County just eight years after the original discovery in Pennsylvania; it was made by a son [Amory Starr] of a Secretary of the Treasury of the Republic of Texas, and a son [Peyton Edwards] of the leader of the Fredonian Rebellion, who were out hunting together. Ever since, the county has been an unfailing magnet for wildcatters. I myself have poked a stick into the bottom of a famous spring and watched the oil-bubbles rise and spread in rainbows over the surface; I have cooked picnic bacon over a flame that you may get any day by touching a match to the casing of an aban-

> doned well in an old cotton field. My son has grown up to "talk oil" with his father and uncle who were talking it over his cradle. If a poet can not help looking for beauty, neither can a novelist—even a mere potential one—help listening for stories; and there can be few subjects in the world, surely, that so teem with stories as what is commonly and very accurately called "the oil-game."[137]

Baker learned oil field terms both firsthand at the well site and from the newspaper articles she collected.[138] Even though she introduced unfamiliar oil field terminology to many general readers, she received the criticism that her writing did not sufficiently reflect the perspective of a man in the field. The critics seemed to expect a coarser presentation. Charlotte Baker Montgomery defends the novel and points out that her mother's foremost interest in writing was always the characters and the interaction found in personal relationships.[139] Karle Wilson Baker always found her frequent visits to the oil field compelling:

> During these numberless trips of exploration, I talked with everybody, high and low, that I could come within range of. . . . We drove over mere twisted trails through miles of pine forests, and got stuck in mud-holes and quagmires. We ate—a few times—at the sort of oil-field restaurants where they say that your only safe order is a hard-boiled egg and a coconut. Above all, we watched that indescribable spectacle, a great oil-field at night. I have seen only two things that compare with it: the Grand Canyon and the lighted cliffs and pinnacles of New York. And of course it is like neither of them.[140]

In a letter to a study club in Temple, Texas, where she was scheduled to speak on *Family Style,* she commented on the importance of both accuracy in research and revision in writing: "I've been in frequent contact with oil "Wildcatting" for half a lifetime; and after I decided to write about it I spent actual years in studying every phase of it. The only boast I feel able to make is that I believe that there are very few inaccuracies in the technical background of the book. Besides the studying and investigation, I rewrote it several times."[141] To describe field operations, Baker collected oil field lingo, which she called "picturesque vernacular," from on-site visits and newspaper reports. She understood and used correctly terms such as "Christmas Tree," "Rat hole," "Kerry-joint," "lease-hounds," "tool-pushers," and the phrase, "Shut down for a fishing-job." She explained the term "slumber-jay," which her brother, Ben T. Wilson, had brought to her:

> "Now don't ask me how it's spelled," he said, "I haven't been able to find out. It sounds as if it were slumber and jay. It's an elaborate electrical test, made with a special, expensive machine; and so far as I know, has nothing to do either with slumber or jaybirds.". . . A few years later, I [KWB] had an opportunity to see the Schlumberger test made on a well. I found out where the Schlumberger got its name. It was invented by an Alsatian: a scientist with a German name living in what was then French territory. In the course of a generation or so, his German name, "Schlumberger," had acquired a partly French pronunciation, "Schlumberger." It is easy to see how that would flatten into "Slumberjay" in American oil-fields.[142]

Friends frequently sent Baker oil field stories about unusual or accidental discoveries. Referring to such anecdotes she wrote, "Of course I did not transplant any of this bodily to my story; for by this time my characters had taken hold and begun to arrange things to suit themselves; but I did want to be sure that every single incident and every technical detail was authentic: that if it didn't happen, it *could* have happened."[143] She related one anecdote passed on to her that was particularly amusing:

> A truck-load of rig-timbers was being sent over the featureless miles of West Texas, with instructions to unload at a point where the geologist of the company had driven down a large stake for a mark. But before the truck came along, a lone cowboy made camp there, and tied his pony to the stake. Now a good stake was a rarity in that country, so, in the morning, he simply pulled this one up and took it along, driving it down the next night to tether his pony. But when he broke camp in the morning, he innocently left it, since he would reach his destination by night. Trundling along some miles behind him, the truck-driver, of course, passed up the first location, and dutifully unloaded his derrick-timbers at a spot forty miles farther on. The error was not discovered; the wildcat was drilled and came in a gusher, the discovery well of a huge field. Of course the story goes on to say that the geologist's original "location" was later drilled, and proved to be the driest of dry holes. Other unconventional discoveries were made in the field by the "doodlebuggers" who claim to locate oil with a forked stick, or by consulting Madame Zenobia, the oil field palmist and fortuneteller.[144]

Baker's husband and brother were actively investing in oil field operations, and she learned much from them. She wrote to a friend about her husband's involvement: "There was drilling in different parts of the county, for months; and we always had some stake in them—often it was land that Tom or Ben already owned, or leases they'd had for twenty years. Duke's well, and Harlowe's well, [in *Family Style*] were intimate friends of mine: I merely changed their location a little. I visited them almost daily, and sat with them for hours, day and night. Nothing came of any of the wells in the county."[145] She attributes her knowledge of how she came to know the country people who make up the main characters in her novel to her husband, Tom, and the fact that he came into contact with country-folk every day as a banker in a small town. He often described to her the human events and dilemmas in the lives of people he helped through the bank.[146] She said she thought that the country banker was second only to the country doctor in playing a role in people's lives and getting to know and understand them. Baker states that the observations she made at the well sites and the drama she saw played out there in material gains and losses helped her to create realistic characters and taught her a new humility. There she witnessed unleashed excitement, devastating disappointment, courage, and dignity in failure along with many other human emotions. Having learned from these experiences, she wrote, "The technique that everybody should acquire who permits himself even a speaking-acquaintance with oil—[is] the trick of enjoying hope and refusing to suffer from disappointment."[147] Another way she learned about the country lives she vividly portrayed in the novel was through her exposure to the students she taught at the small Stephen F. Austin State Teachers College: "Without this experience [teaching] I doubt that I should ever have dared to write a book of any kind about farm-people. . . . The ideal novel, to my mind, portrays people largely through action, but it will have small value unless the people it portrays are real and living."[148]

Baker illustrates her knowledge of such people and her interest in character development through the personal relationships in the novel. The plot is dynamic, but the interaction of the characters is the most fascinating part of *Family Style*. In her written comments after the publication of the novel, Baker stated that character was her chief interest in a novel and mentioned the origin of some of the personalities in *Family Style:*

> A writer does not reproduce real people in characterizations because the characters themselves in a novel take on a sort of mysterious life of their own. They become so real to the writer that he often forgets where he got the original suggestion from which they sprang. . . . A mature writer prefers to take a mere suggestion as his starting-point—one striking

> trait of character, a single significant act as the nucleus of the book-person who is beginning to take shape in his imagination. . . . But it is likely to be someone you know very slightly, . . . or a total stranger whom you have merely seen. Or, you may take up a collection of features from friends, acquaintances, and newspaper photographs.
>
> The original Rose Anne, for instance, I saw only once, tripping around the edge of a slush-pit at a wildcat well deep in the pine-woods, in her dainty, high-heeled pumps; and I haven't the slightest idea whether she had a single one of the traits of the real Rose Anne who grew out of her image.
>
> Duke—one of my own favorite characters—started as a sort of composite of three or four people I have known. . . . All I ever saw of Henry was the "mouth neatly turned up and tucked in at the corners, and the deep cleft, oddly off center, in his pointed chin." They belonged to a small boy who never saw the oil-fields, with whom I once had a ten-minute conversation. . . . Fred himself grew out of one small, mean exploit that I happened to know—the transaction with Uncle Fin. Ella's started from her long, sad nose. Duke's mother, who seemed to spring complete from nowhere, was probably a composite of many old country mothers I have known . . . though in all that time I had never talked to her for fifteen minutes. And so it goes.[149]

The novel's heroine, Kathleen Priest, has definite autobiographical characteristics. Kathleen is hard working and determined. Like Karle Wilson Baker, she wants to make her own way and have an independent income.[150] Kathleen is different from the traditional housewife of her day, often surprising family members with her maverick entrepreneurship in the oil field. Likewise, Baker understood the role of the "modern woman" in the 1930s and saw it as an important element in her own life.

The year 1931 included many trips to the oil field with her husband and brother. Baker had opportunities to observe firsthand the range of life in the field—from derrick construction, everyday field operations, and oil well fires to lease-men and the local oil field cafes.[151] The first trips were made about once a week to the well at Joinerville. In February, they also drove to the Lathrop well near Longview and to the Driver well. In fact, the oil boom was so important to the bank that young Tom W. Baker (Tomby) left the University of Texas in his senior year to join his father in the bank because of the extra work and opportunity.[152] In the fall of the same year, the entire family made frequent trips to the Ginter well near Nacogdoches. Because the

Bakers knew the Ginter family personally, they were especially sad for them when a saltwater well came in instead of the real thing.[153] The drama that occurred in the every day life of the oil field, "that sharp, giddy drop from the pinnacle of hope to the very pit of disappointment" impressed Baker.[154] She saw this happen firsthand in the case of the Ginter family:

> The man had been a successful independent operator in an established field, who had suffered a series of misfortunes, and who had become convinced of the likelihood of finding deeper sands in our shallow field. He was attempting to recoup his losses by bringing in a well himself, supervising the actual work on the rig as a drilling contractor does when he drills a well for someone else. His health had partly failed, but he had inexhaustible energy and courage. There were two delightful daughters of the age of my family, and a fine mother. . . . The well-drilling, necessarily carried on on the most economical lines, dragged on through the whole summer, and we fell into the habit of driving down often on summer evenings, sometimes taking a picnic supper, the young people strolling and singing afterward in the moonlight. The indications grew more favorable and hope mounted; and when the time came to make the momentous attempt to bring in the well, we were almost as tense and anxious as our friends. The scene at the well was much like those I have described in *Family Style;* and this was one time that I was allowed to ask all the questions I wished, and to go as close as I liked—even to stand on the derrick-floor! Everything seemed right and they started swabbing in high spirits. And then—it went on and on.
>
> The high spirits began to flag. And, at last, after hours of slowly dwindling hope,—stoutly camouflaged—one of the men, following a sad suspicion, tasted the fluid that was coming from the well. And then—the worst happened—it was salt water! As the stoic wit of the oil fields puts it, "the sea-gulls were flying."
>
> And I shall never forget how our friend the wildcatter took it. Physically worn out, he had gone to sit in his car, strategically placed to command the scene at close range. When they brought him the sample, so that he could verify its indubitable saltiness, his only comment was a rueful smile. For the space of ten minutes or so he merely sat and watched, as before. Then, at last, he unfolded his long, thin body and climbed down out of the car. "Well," he remarked, cheerfully, starting toward the derrick where the useless swabbing was still in progress, "I guess it's time to stop doing that and begin doing something else."

> There was nothing else to do, as far as that well was concerned, except to dismantle it—the project into which had gone thousands of borrowed dollars, indestructible courage, and many months of vigilance, resourcefulness, and the hardest sort of hard work. That prompt and cheerful summing up of the whole matter made me feel queerly humble. How many actual years of my own life I could have salvaged for productive effort, how much sooner I would have overtaken my successive goals, if from the very beginning I had had the sense and determination to leave no gap between "stopping doing that" and "beginning something else!"[155]

A tireless researcher, Baker sought background information on the oil field from a variety of resources. She found the *Dallas News* and the *Houston Post* important sources for listing current oil field activity and providing maps of drilling sites. In addition to official oil field maps, she drew her own maps detailing locations of small drilling operations in the back roads of East Texas that were sometimes left off the larger maps. These smaller locations were often important to her novel. Also, she compiled several large scrapbooks of news clippings to use as resource material. Even today when one reads the news clippings from the 1930s, the excitement of the times is evident. Some of the stories of actual events are so extraordinary that they seem fictional. Some of the characters that Baker developed in the novel came from descriptions of actual people mentioned in the news articles.[156] Along with the scrapbooks, Baker created large charts about two and a half feet square to track simultaneous facts, collating the research material both chronologically and by subject matter for ready reference. (She used a similar method for organizing chronology and events when she researched a later novel, *Star of the Wilderness.*)[157]

Charlotte Baker's teaching position at Stephen F. Austin State Teachers College in 1931 had been for the summer only. During the Depression, members of the same family could not teach at the same time at a state school. Charlotte had graduated in 1930 from Berkeley but because of the Depression had not been able to find a job. Baker was growing more concerned over her daughter's plight. At her request, A. W. Birdwell wrote to state schools where he had contacts. In the spring of 1932, Baker wrote long letters to her friends A. J. Armstrong at Baylor[158] and Leonidas Payne at the University of Texas[159] for help or suggestions in the search for employment for Charlotte, but they could offer no leads. Times were hard, and jobs were not forthcoming. Meanwhile, Baker gave much thought to the mother-daughter relationship. She analyzed her bond with her own mother, reflecting on both satisfactory and unsatisfactory aspects, and concluded that she intended to have a good, strong relationship with her own children. She wrote, "Above all, I will adopt, and try to keep, an attitude of inspired responsiveness. My love must never insist, never intrude; and to this end I will be busy about my own concerns, instead of dependent for my interests upon those of my children. But the children shall know that it is always there, always ready—my uttermost love and care."[160]

Charlotte found employment and started teaching in the public schools in Kilgore, Texas, in September 1932. Kilgore was a boomtown in the center of activity of the East Texas oil field. The small town expanded overnight and became dense with traffic serving the field. Landlords threw up shanties for housing, and the influx of population meant more children attended the public schools. This appointment had special ramifications for Charlotte because she found herself absorbed in the development of the East Texas oil field as she lived in this hub city of petroleum activity. She sketched many scenes of all aspects of oil production just as her mother was soaking up the atmosphere of the boomtown and incorporating it into her novel. Though they were working independently and in different mediums, both mother and daughter recorded lasting impressions of one of the most important events in the history of the country. One of Charlotte's oil field drawings became the dust jacket for *Family Style.*[161]

Baker had visited Mexico years earlier, but in October 1932, she wrote to the dean of the summer school at the University of Guadalajara, Mexico, hoping to teach there the following summer. She wrote that she had "a violent case of Mexicomania" but that she could not afford a pure vacation to Mexico during the Depression. She thought perhaps she could support herself while she was there, suggesting that she teach a course in verse writing. Unfortunately the university could offer no positions, so she had to postpone her travel to Mexico.[162] Baker's record books document her thrift and her dedication to earn money through writing. She detailed income received through royalties, honoraria, and teaching. (The college paid her one hundred dollars each month.)[163]

Karle Wilson Baker had a group of close friends who met on alternate Thursdays to discuss books. The group called themselves "The Philosophers" or, less formally, "The Pseudo-Philosophers" or "The Cheese-eaters" (because one member was a vegetarian and the others complied by serving only vegetarian refreshments). The members of the group, who met for many years and formed lifelong friendships, were all connected with

Stephen F. Austin State Teachers College and were Baker's closest friends outside her family. Tommy (Mary) Thomson was the dean of women and taught Spanish, Loulein Harris and Mildred Wyatt were college librarians, Mary Jane White taught dance (and was the vegetarian), Elizabeth Tucker taught home economics, and Lois Foster Blount taught history.[164] When "Family Style" was completed and awaiting a publisher, Baker took the unusual step of sharing some of the novel with the group at one of their reading sessions. Also, she trusted the judgment of Dorothy Scarborough, a fellow Texan, who was teaching at Columbia University. She wrote to Scarborough asking her to suggest the name of a literary agent in New York. Scarborough responded with several suggestions.[165]

Earlier in 1932, Baker read an article in the *Dallas News* about Melrose Plantation near Natchitoches, Louisiana, and how its owner, Cammie Henry, used it as a writers' colony. When Baker wrote to the author of the article, W. B. Goolsby, asking how to obtain entrance to Melrose, he responded to her and also posted a letter to Henry recommending that she invite Baker for a visit.[166] Henry wrote immediately to Baker to set a time when she and Charlotte could come and stay at Melrose Plantation.[167] Baker sent Henry an autographed copy of *The Birds of Tanglewood,* and the illustrator of the book, Charlotte, autographed it as well.[168] Cammie Henry saw her role at Melrose as that of a matriarch offering a retreat of solitude and quiet where, uninterrupted, writers could create. Melrose, an antebellum plantation on the Cane River, had various outbuildings for guest lodging, and the main plantation house provided the dining room. The setting was secluded, remote, and conducive to writing and painting. When Baker first went to Melrose in November 1932, her husband drove her to Natchitoches. On that visit she stayed in the log slave cabin, which was the writer's cabin. Charlotte joined her later for a weekend.[169] During the visit, Baker gave Henry three more autographed books: *Dreamers on Horseback, Old Coins,* and *Two Little Texans.*[170] A barrage of correspondence from "Aunt Cammie," as guests informally referred to Henry, followed, with multiple requests that the Bakers return.[171] Henry was a gracious and generous hostess, but she also wanted to build Melrose's reputation as a place where important literary figures and artists had visited and, perhaps, had created during their stay.

Also in November 1932, Karle Wilson Baker had an important speaking engagement that she had looked forward to for some time. The program required travel by train to Memphis, Tennessee, to speak before the National Council of Teachers of English, an event that took place over the Thanksgiving holiday, when Stephen F. Austin was not in session. Baker spoke at one

A photograph of the Writer's Cabin at Melrose Plantation in Louisiana. Karle Wilson Baker stayed in this cabin on the plantation grounds when she visited Melrose Plantation at Cammie Henry's invitation. (Courtesy Steen Library, Stephen F. Austin State University)

of the main luncheon meetings held in the Peabody Hotel. The planning committee had asked her to read four of her poems at the tea: "I Love the Friendly Faces," "Morning Song," "Let Me Grow Lovely," and "Good Company."[172] The American Association of University Women had invited Baker to speak in Little Rock on the way to Memphis, but she declined; there was not enough time on this trip. Throughout 1932, women's clubs in Texas asked her to speak. Among others, she spoke in Fort Worth, Houston, Mt. Vernon, Paris, Lufkin, and Abilene.[173]

Another significant speaking engagement occurred in December 1932. Baker accepted an invitation from A. J. Armstrong to read selections from *Dreamers on Horseback* and *The Birds of Tanglewood* at Baylor University. The trip to Waco took seven hours by bus; Baker arrived just in time for a party in her honor at the Armstrongs' home. Her presentation the next day was planned to last an hour and a half. Armstrong had ordered a large number of Baker's books from Southwest Press for her to autograph and sell after the lecture. He also asked her to stay an extra day in Waco to have her photograph made with a group of Sigma Tau Delta English fraternity members to include in the *Round-Up*, the Baylor yearbook. Baker responded favorably to all of his requests.[174]

The day after Christmas, Baker wrote to Elinor Frost in preparation for Robert Frost's upcoming lecture tour to six colleges in Texas.[175] Earlier that year, Baker had worked with Armstrong, Leonidas Payne, and Earl Huffor at Sam Houston State Teachers College to arrange an eleven-day lecture tour with Frost giving public readings of his poetry at Baylor University, Southern Methodist University, the University of Texas, Stephen F. Austin, Sam Houston, and Texas State College for Women. Baker was the initiator and driving force behind the famous poet's visit to Nacogdoches. Only a person of her literary stature could have attracted a two-time Pulitzer Prize-winning poet to a fledgling college in a rural East Texas community. By 1933, Baker's own reputation was widespread; along with other recognition, she was listed in *Who's Who Among North American Authors*. Many requests for her biographical information and selected poems came from handbooks and directories such as *Women of the South, Women of Arkansas, Texas Women Writers, Southern Literature*, and even the British publication *Town and Country Life*. Although she was unsure whether he would remember her, Baker had met Frost a few years earlier when he lectured at SMU. She arranged for the Frosts to stay in her home while they were in Nacogdoches.[176]

The year 1933 was also a time of business anxiety for her husband and a time of financial disaster for most of the country. A national bank crisis occurred in March when President Franklin Roosevelt closed all banks on March 6. Naturally, Thomas E. Baker, along with his brother-in-law, I. L. Sturdevant (who was the president of the Stone Fort Bank), and other local bankers, had many concerns. Baker attended bank meetings in Shreveport and Dallas about the problem. On March 12, the Bakers listened on the radio to the president's speech about the bank shutdown. The next day, Baker and a vice president from his bank went to Dallas, going and returning on the same day. The Dallas banks reopened on March 13; the Nacogdoches banks reopened on March 15.[177] However, even in the face of national disaster, East Texas was fortunate. The newly discovered oil field did much to buffer the effects of the Depression in the area.

Robert Frost's rigorous lecture tour of Texas began at Baylor University on April 18, 1933, and continued at Southern Methodist University the next day. He returned to speak again in Waco and then left for Austin and the University of Texas.[178] On Wednesday, April 26, the Frosts left Austin by train for Jacksonville, where at four o'clock in the afternoon Karle Wilson Baker and her brother, Ben T. Wilson, met them and drove to Nacogdoches. Elinor Frost described the journey: "The drive from there to Nacogdoches was through beautiful scenery, but two thirds of the way the road was under construction, and extremely bumpy and slow. However, we finally reached Nacogdoches. Mrs. Baker's home is very charming. Behind the house it is real woods and fields, with low hills in the distance, and the wood thrush was singing his best."[179]

Frost delivered his address at Stephen F. Austin at eight o'clock that evening. A reception followed at the home of Eugene Blount, which was located just across from the school campus on the original Thomas J. Rusk land grant. Elinor Frost did not attend either the lecture or the reception because of fatigue from the journey.[180] However, she mentions an account of the evening in a letter: "There was a fine audience there—over a thousand persons—some of them driving 75 miles to hear Robert. The college gave the money for the lecture, so those who came didn't have to pay. I thought it was very touching that people should be interested enough to drive such distances. Mrs. Baker is a charming woman."[181]

Charlotte Montgomery remembers the Frost visit very well. She attended the lecture at Aikman Gym that evening. She and a group of friends drove from Kilgore to Nacogdoches for the occasion. Charlotte stopped by her parents' home before going to the lecture. Once inside, she was shocked to see an unknown woman at the top of the stairs. It was Elinor Frost. Feeling discomfort at the situation, the shy Charlotte made hurried excuses and left right away. Looking back on that evening, Charlotte recalls that Frost's reading of "The Death of the Hired Man" had impressed her more than any other part of the program. She also confirmed that the audience was large and that her mother's efforts were responsible for bringing such an important person to a young, little-known college to speak.[182] The *Pine Log* reported on the program the next day. Frost had read "The Death of the Hired Man" by request of the audience (probably made by Karle Wilson Baker since she often used it in her classes). Prior to Frost's arrival on campus, Baker had written a short biography of him for the campus newspaper. The article emphasized that Frost was a farmer as well as a poet and teacher, which was perhaps intended to impress the rural community.[183] On April 27, Baker and her brother took the Frosts by car to Huntsville where Frost continued his successful lecture tour at Sam Houston college.[184]

Elinor Frost had been so impressed with Baker as a poet as well as a person that less than a year after the visit she wrote to Baker requesting some of her poetry to present in a program for her study club in Amherst, Massachusetts. She also commented that a photograph showing the Stephen F. Austin campus with its tall pine trees would interest the club. Baker responded by sending Elinor Frost a book of her poems and some original sketches by Charlotte. Robert Frost sent a book of his poems to Baker in thanks for the visit.[185]

Shortly after the SFA commencement exercises at the end of May, Baker returned to Melrose Plantation for two weeks. While she was there, she sent the manuscript of "Family Style" to the Simon and Schuster Publishing Company; it was rejected and returned in July. At Melrose, "Aunt Cammie" entertained Baker along with Lyle Saxon and Daniel Rosenbaum. Saxon was a tall, handsome, genial man with a great deal of charm. He had achieved his literary reputation as a historian. His first novel, *Children of Strangers,* is a story of mulattoes living along the Cane River. Baker recorded that she visited interesting sites along the Cane River and enjoyed long, cool morning walks with the other guests during her stay.[186]

Baker spent most of the summer trying to place "Family Style" with a publisher. Even this successful author knew all too well the heartache and disappointment of the rejected manuscript, but she was determined to use a nationally known publishing house for the book in spite of its Texas setting. The difficulty of finding a publisher for the novel was beginning to weigh on her. Even shorter writing projects became trying and involved much more than merely having an idea and writing about it. She tried to minimize the wasted time, postage costs, and expended effort by sending query letters to editors of smaller publications for her short stories and essays. She had a plan or "turnaround" policy: whenever a story came back rejected, she had it in the mail almost immediately to the next potential publisher on her list. Because she was such a prolific writer, she often mailed different stories to several different publishers at the same time, improving the odds that something would be accepted for publication.[187] She had used the "turnaround policy" for years. In the years when she was writing so much poetry, the method had been effective. For example, a lyric poem, "The Window," went to ten different magazines before it was accepted for publication. Each time the poem came back, Baker faithfully posted it to another publication the very next day.[188] Her persistence usually brought success.

The profusion of Karle Wilson Baker's output during the decade at SFA is staggering. Recognizing her drive to write, she had confessed in an early diary, "I am convinced that I am just a writing person—a person with a passion and a gift for putting into writing the things I see, hear, and feel."[189] In addition to major publishing goals, which took much of her time, she frequently wrote smaller pieces that took much less time. Charlotte Baker Montgomery has referred to these as "pot-boilers."[190] Baker wrote articles for religious publications (such as the *Torchbearer)* and youth magazines on a variety of subjects ranging from historical personages to lighthouses, bells, and kites. Charlotte illustrated many of these articles with ink drawings.[191] The mother-daughter team shared common interests and supported each other. Baker frequently suggested to her magazine publishers that Charlotte illustrate her articles. In one letter to Una Smith at the *Torchbearer,* Baker wrote that writing such articles was "a sort of rest and comfort in the midst of the ardors and disappointments of the more ambitious struggle." She was waiting for the publication of "Family Style." Then she added, "I want to help Charlotte to an outlet for her work, and this is a very good one for a beginner. When I am ready to stop, she can step into my shoes—only she can do both writing and pictures. She is clever at both."[192]

The fall semester of 1933 began at the end of September with the annual lawn party at the Birdwells' house; it would be Baker's last year at Stephen F. Austin. Teaching that fall was fairly uneventful, but requests to speak to organizations and clubs across the state continued. In October alone, she received letters from groups in Dallas, Marshall, Gilmer, and College Station.[193] The Texas Federation of Women's Clubs made persistent overtures to Baker in 1932 and 1933 asking permission to reprint her poems, asking her to write about the "Pioneers of the Texas Federation," and even declaring that they wanted to make her the "Poet Laureate" of the Third District of the Federation.[194] It was not possible for her to meet all of these requests.

In February 1934, Baker sent "Family Style" to a literary agent, Mathilde Weil, in New York City. On February 17, she left alone by train for New York. When she arrived two days later, the city was undergoing its worst blizzard since 1888. She met with Weil on February 22, and again on March 2. Also on March 2, Baker met with Jane Manner, an instructor of "professional lectures," for lessons in public speaking.[195] Personal appointments with literary agents or publishers were expensive and rare for Baker. Most often she relied on the U.S. Postal Service to handle her business. Unfortunately, the trip to New York did not yield a contract for "Family Style." Publishers who turned the novel down usually stated the Depression as the reason, but when the manuscript came back from the literary agent, Baker wrote that the moment "marked an all-time low in the history of the book."[196] By March 7, 1934, having been away just over two weeks, she returned by train from New York to Nacogdoches. After she taught classes on March 12, she left by bus for Dallas to speak to the Craig Class. The next day she gave a poetry reading on KRLD radio, sponsored by Southern Methodist University and arranged by the chairman of the Department of English, John O. Beaty. Beaty wrote afterward to Baker, "The reading of your poetry was an important factor in the great success of the broadcasts."[197] By March 16, she was back on campus, teaching classes. Requests from clubs and organizations continued and increased in 1934. In addition to other appeals, she received requests from Atlanta, Clifton, Marlin, College Station, Center, Wortham, and Fort Worth (Texas Christian University and the Daughters of the Republic.)[198] By far the majority of requests were for Baker to speak as a poet rather than as a writer of prose. Sometimes she declined, stating she could not be away from her teaching responsibilities; sometimes the smaller groups could not meet the fifty dollar fee, which had been a fixed charge for her speaking engagements since 1922. Nevertheless, writing and speaking engagements were demanding more and more time away from teaching responsibilities. By the end of the spring semester, at the age of fifty-six, she chose to retire from teaching.

In May, the regents for Stephen F. Austin State Teachers College nominated teachers for the 1934 summer school sessions and named Charlotte Baker acting head of the Art Department for the next three months.[199] While Charlotte was back in Nacogdoches, she encouraged her mother to send off "Family Style" once again: "Mother," she said, "the magazines are full of things about oil, and everybody seems to be interested. Why don't you start

Family Style out again?"[200] Baker noted that in the next few days she sent queries to a score of publishers about her book. One young woman, Jessica Tower at Appleton-Century, wrote back that she would be interested in seeing the manuscript because when she was a junior in high school, she had memorized some of Baker's verses. Baker sent the manuscript to her.[201]

Baker wrote in her diary about the frustrations she felt waiting to hear from the Appleton-Century Company:

> I have been trying lately to get into a writing vein again, and finding it very difficult. The obvious reasons seem to be the ones with which I have long been familiar, the chief of them the need of some success to lift the invisible barriers that hem me in. (The manuscript of *Family Style* has been in the hands of the Appleton-Century Company almost exactly two months.). . . I have resolved to write at least 350 words on every one of my five working days in each week. Two days, Saturday and Sunday, I have long given up altogether, as a general thing, to family concerns and miscellaneous tasks. . . . So this is the beginning of the practice of this new device. I shall write *something;* when I cannot work at the task I have set myself, I shall turn to this record. Anything counts, except letters. I shall at least have practice in the attempt to express my meaning exactly, in clear words.[202]

In July, Jessica Tower wrote Baker that her company would take another look at "Family Style" if she would be interested in reworking certain parts: "The consensus of opinion seems to be that it is excellently written, authentic in feeling, and rather complete, but that it moves slowly."[203] Baker recorded her reaction in her diary:

> I was filled with joy, and hope soared. . . . I have said since I finished the book that I wouldn't rework it further except in collaboration with someone who definitely considered publication. . . . When I talked it over with Tom, who was greatly interested, he suggested that I write and offer to go to New York, to consider it face to face. "I'd love to go, I said, Can we spare the money?" "Well, I've been gambling on oil wells. I might as well gamble on a novel," was the reply.[204]

When Baker learned that Tower would be away from New York all summer, she delayed her trip until October. On October 19, accompanied by her husband and daughter, Baker took the train to New York City. After a week her husband and daughter returned home. Baker did not return to Nacogdoches until November 17. She was well traveled in the United States and had often traveled to distant cities alone, including a trip to New York City the previous February. While her children were in school in California, she had found herself traveling to the West, but during the worst years of the Depression, she, like most other people, had traveled shorter distances, if at all. She had felt comfortable in New York City ever since she had attended Columbia University in the summer of 1919; she liked city life and the opportunities only a city could offer.

After she saw her husband and daughter off at Grand Central Station on October 27, Baker moved into Beekman Tower. A few days later she called on the editor at Appleton-Century. After the appointment, she immediately began revisions on the manuscript of "Family Style."[205] Baker described her writing process:

> That two weeks stands out as one of the high spots of my writing life. I was quite alone; I had a little tower-room overlooking that world's wonder, midtown Manhattan; and I sat by the one big window and worked with pencil and typewriter until the scant floor-space was covered some inches deep with a speckled snow of pages. Whenever I got too hungry I would go out and eat, and whenever my eyes went out I would take a ride on a bus, or prowl around the fascinating streets and byways of that inexhaustible city.[206]

An exclusive literary group in New York, The Poet's Club, had solicited Baker's membership as early as 1923.[207] The club offered lunch, tea, and dinner and had limited overnight accommodations for out-of-town guests. William Rose Benet served as president, and such luminaries as T. S. Eliot, Sara Teasdale, E. A. Robinson, Louis Untermeyer, Padraic Colum, Sherwood Anderson, and Amy Lowell were members. The object of the club was to provide a gathering place in New York City where members could meet and exchange ideas. While she was in New York, Baker attended a party at the Barbizon Plaza held by The Poet's Club. On that occasion she met Gertrude Stein. The Poet's Club offered a watercolor by the German artist George Grosz as the door prize, and Baker was the lucky winner of the signed picture.[208]

More interviews with Jessica Tower followed, and then on November 13, Baker left New York by bus for Washington, D.C. After a day of sight-seeing, she resumed her train travel to St. Louis, where she stayed overnight with her half-sister, Bess Wright. Tom and Charlotte met her train in Longview on November 17.[209] To Baker's disappointment, she received a letter from Appleton-Century declining publication of "Family Style." The letter stated that "in view of the depression" they were afraid to take a chance on the sales.[210] Baker had sent a manuscript copy of "Family Style" to her friend Anna McCaleb Sheets in Oregon, Illinois. Later she sent a copy of Tower's rejection letter to Sheets. Infuriated that Appleton-Century had declined publishing the book, the loyal Sheets wrote a long letter to Baker. Referring to Tower, she commented, "If she's as poor a reader as she is a letter-writer, I shouldn't want her to accept my book. . . . I don't like her, but I should like to know how old she is." Anna's seventeen-page letter includes many suggestions regarding character development for all the major characters in the story. She saw characteristics of Tom E. Baker in the fictional character Duke. Anna wrote that Duke was so much like TEB that she "kept waiting from the beginning for her [Kathleen] to call him 'Gibraltar,' and at last she did." "Old Gibraltar" was a term Baker sometimes used to Sheets to describe Tom Baker as a rock of support. In other comments, Sheets wrote, "I like Family Style thoroughly, and as my impressions simmer down and 'sugar off,' I like it better and better. Its outstanding charm to me lies in its contrasts—the renching [*sic*] headiness of the boom against the soft, gentle East Texas landscape. . . . The delicate writing against the 'crudeness' and blackness and stickiness of the oil."[211]

Charlotte Baker Montgomery believes that New York publishers in 1934 did not connect with a novel set in East Texas until the area gained national attention through tragedy. The 1937 explosion and catastrophe at the New London School made publishers in the East more aware of the human dimensions of the East Texas oil field. Montgomery thinks that the national media coverage of this tragic event that killed nearly three hundred children and adults actually helped bring about the publication of *Family Style*.[212] Baker would have to wait three more years before she would see the publication of *Family Style*, which Coward-McCann finally published on September 20, 1937.[213]

In 1914, Baker had written her ideas about the "so-called woman's movement," which she found to be "the most thrilling thing in the present age," to send to her former teacher, Robert Herrick, at the University of Chicago. In the letter to Herrick, she stated that for ten years she had been dreaming of writing about the new American woman who had changed attitudes about life, sex, and the family. But she never mailed the letter.[214] Baker's "greedy contemplation" of the opportunities afforded women in the woman's movement saw fruition in her own life in the decade 1924–34. She seized every opportunity that came her way to "fill her place" (as she had stated in the poem

Dust Jacket for Karle Wilson Baker's novel, Family Style *(Coward-McCann 1937). Drawing by Charlotte Baker made in 1936. Charlotte Baker accompanied her mother to many well sites and made drawings of the East Texas Oil Field. (Private Collection, Baker Estate)*

"The Tree"), further her career, and reach her goal of being an independent woman. She benefited personally, but she was also an example for young college women and other women across the state who asked her to speak to their organizations. The new woman's movement, coupled with her own determination, provided the liberated lifestyle she desired. The end of her teaching career at Stephen F. Austin State Teachers College meant the beginning of many new opportunities: more writing, more publications, more speeches, more travel, and more diary notes of self-analysis and exploration into her creative process.

"I had always expected to write novels."

CHAPTER 4

The State and the Writer Come of Age

In 1935, "Family Style" was still unpublished, but as she waited for a publisher, Karle Wilson Baker continued to write about Texas. With more time for writing after she left teaching, Baker returned to the project "A Hundred Miles of Memories," which she had abandoned to write about the East Texas oil field. On September 25, Henry Smith, a new editor for the *Southwest Review,* wrote to Baker asking her to contribute to a proposed special Texas Centennial edition of the journal. Her research for "A Hundred Miles of Memories" resulted in a series of three articles for the *Southwest Review.*

Smith sent a proposed table of contents listing the writers he hoped to include in the special issue. The list was impressive: Baker would be among such luminaries as Marquis James, Eugene C. Barker, Herbert P. Gambrell, Walter P. Webb, J. Frank Dobie, Sam Acheson, and John A. Lomax. Smith proposed that Baker write an article about Nacogdoches during the French and Spanish periods. The terms included a word length of 3,500 words and a compensation of seventy-five dollars.[1] In addition, the table of contents included artists the *Review* intended to use as illustrators in the centennial issue. Smith had named the type of illustrations he wanted to use, noting that there would be other artists not yet selected to contribute to the issue. Baker showed the letter to her daughter, Charlotte. Baker had starred the section suggesting that other artists might be considered and added a handwritten notation: "If you'd made studies during all that time I was picking at you, you'd have something!! Maybe you have!!!"[2] She was eager to include Charlotte in this important project. Smith wrote a month later and thanked Baker for sending some of Charlotte's drawings of the East Texas oil field, but he said that the budget for artwork was limited and that the *Review* was already committed to other artists for pictures of the field. On the other hand, he encouraged Baker to think about illustrations for her article.[3] Three days later, Baker sent Smith a progress report:

> . . . I've been having a grand time—even though a most painful one, in spots!—working on the Nacogdoches article. I now have the first draft done; I'll get it off to you in a few more days—within a week, at most. The struggle (as is usual, with this sort of material) is due to the effort to keep it within bounds. It was good of you to remove any definite word-limit, but I don't want to take advantage of your indulgence. I'm going to reduce it as much as I can bring myself to, unaided, and then I'm going to ask you to return it to me with stern instruction, if it's still too long. Or even, if there's not time for that, to slash it yourself![4]

On November 22, Smith wrote that everyone at the *Review* was delighted with the article on Nacogdoches and thanked Baker for sending Charlotte's pictures as suggested illustrations to accompany the article. One of Charlotte's drawings was titled *Paradise of the Shepherds*, and the other had a large letter *T* surrounded by two Indians, a conquistador, and a padre.[5] Both drawings seem especially well suited to the article, but in the end the published piece did not have any illustrations, probably because of the cutbacks in expenses the *Review* had to make.

On January 27 of the next year, Smith sent the disappointing word to Baker that the State Commission of Control of the Centennial had turned down the *Southwest Review's* subsidy request for the centennial issue. The *Review's* modified plans meant that the editors could continue with the issue, but they now could offer the contributors only thirty-five dollars for an essay instead of the proposed seventy-five dollars. Also, the *Review* would have to print Baker's article in a "belated issue."[6] In the same letter, Smith requested that Baker continue to write about Nacogdoches and to send the articles to the *Review*.[7] She responded,

> It's too bad that the centennial commission didn't see things our way. I had surmised as much, when I didn't hear from you earlier in the month.
>
> If you can use the second installment of the Nacogdoches material at

Pen and ink drawing by Charlotte Baker, ca. 1934. The Spanish Conquistador suppresses the native Indian, while the Spanish Friar ministers to him. The drawing was intended for use with Karle Wilson Baker's article, "Nacogdoches: The Indian and Spanish Town," that appeared in the October 1935 issue of the Southwest Review. *The* Review *did not use the drawing. (Private Collection, Baker Estate)*

> the same price, I shall be glad to let this go to the *Review* for thirty-five dollars. I'd rather have it appear there than almost anywhere. And I'm anxious to complete it; I have much of the material already on hand.
>
> However, just now I have undertaken some other things that will have to come first. [KWB was looking at galley proofs of *Family Style.*] I suppose there would be no hurry about it. If you decide to use Part II on these terms, can you give me any idea of how much time I would have to get it to you?[8]

Between 1935 and 1937, Baker wrote three articles for the *Southwest Review:* "Nacogdoches: Indian and Spanish Town" (October 1935), "Nacogdoches: The Gateway of the Pioneers" (January 1936), and "Trailing the New Orleans Greys" (April 1937). An unsigned review praising the first article appeared in the *Pine Log* on April 10, 1936:

> . . . With charming simplicity Mrs. Baker portrays the sleepy Indian village, "sprinkled with conical huts arranged after a prevailing fashion" and inhabited by civilized Indians, successors to the historic Mound builders. Such a settlement was found by Captain Alonzo de Leon, who, spurred by the fear of the intrusion of the French, came to plant a Spanish settlement in East Texas some forty miles west of Nacogdoches. But some twenty years later the young Chevalier de St. Denis, who probably visited Nacogdoches, laid out the "Camino Real." Henceforth the village flourished with its position near the eastern end of the Royal Road. So does the author describe Nacogdoches in its days with the Indians and with their Spanish conquerors. From a drowsy Indian village to a thriving trade center that was to echo the footsteps of a revolutionary Texas we follow our own town in an article that reveals authentic facts written in an alluring style.[9]

Baker had already completed extensive research for her study on Texas history when she prepared the manuscript, "The Story of Texas," but her investigations went even deeper for the articles for the *Southwest Review.* Her "Notes on Texas History" notebook cites many sources and is evidence of her lengthy research. Baker was well aware of Reverend G. L. Crocket's highly informative book, *Two Centuries in East Texas* (1932), which she listed in her research notes for "Nacogdoches: Indian and Spanish Town."[10] Baker included information about original land grants in the territory and wrote about early settlers in East Texas such as Antonio Gil Y'Barbo, a rich trader and rancher situated on El Camino Real. The Karle Wilson Baker Papers contain extensive notes taken from various published books on Texas history that she consulted in her research. In small, personal notebooks, she wrote handwritten summaries of Texas history from textbooks by Rev. Homer S. Thrall and Mrs. Pennybacker, Sam Houston's *Letters*, and S. L. Knapp's *History of America*.[11] In addition to the notebooks, she compiled extensive note cards on historical sources.[12] Descriptive details in the article illustrate her careful research. For instance, she comments on the social culture as well as the politics of the day:

> . . . The house of Don Samuel on the plaza was always open. Friends from Natchitoches and New Orleans, American officers from Fort Jessup, and important travelers up and down the Camino Real joined the Barr and Davenport circle in the balls, dinners, horse races, and riding-parties that were arranged to help occupy the leisure of the Spanish officers. In the end, war was averted through Herrera's diplomacy, which unmasked the far-spreading schemes of Aaron Burr.[13]

When Jay Hubbell wrote Baker in 1925 asking her to help set the requirements for contributors to the *Southwest Review*, he had stated that he wanted to attract the best writers, but he also wanted to get away from the very academic format of the *Texas Review*, the journal his was replacing. This may be a reason why Baker did not footnote her sources but instead documented them in the text of the article.

The second article for the *Southwest Review*, "Nacogdoches: The Gateway of the Pioneers" (January 1936), did much to inform the public about men who had influenced the development of the town, including Y'Barbo, an agent among the Indians who rose to the position of lieutenant governor of Nacogdoches; Stephen F. Austin; Lt. Augustus W. Magee and Don Bernardo Gutierrez of the Magee-Gutierrez Expedition (1812); Hayden and Benjamin Edwards, organizers of the Fredonia Rebellion (1826); and Sam Houston. Some of the other early citizens of the town mentioned in the article were Col. Frost Thorn, a large landowner and Nacogdoches's first millionaire; Adolphus Sterne, a wealthy citizen of the town who helped to finance the Texas Revolution; Col. Jose de las Piedras, the commandant at Nacogdoches; Sam Davenport, an Indian trader in the early 1800s; and John Durst, a wealthy landowner and businessman. Some of these men were little known to readers outside of the Nacogdoches area. Baker would later base fictional characters on them. The article contains bibliographic information, but as with the first article, does not use formal footnotes. Instead, Baker once again credits her sources within the text of the narrative. Her ledger notes on

Texas history indicate that she likely got the idea for the title of her second article from S. L. Knapp's *History of America* (1875): "Nacogdoches was the gateway, the Old Stone Fort the guidepost, and the King's Highway the road by which Anglo-American energy and ambition was to reach the golden west."[14] Early in the article she refers to Crocket's "patient and sympathetic studies of Spanish East Texas," and she again cites Reverend Crocket specifically when she discusses Col. Jose de las Piedras in Nacogdoches.[15] She makes informal references about consulting the Texas historian Eugene C. Barker's *Life of Stephen F. Austin* when she writes about Austin "in his letters about Fredonian difficulties" and when she comments, "Dr. Barker sums up the situation." The letters she includes from Hayden Edwards to Stephen F. Austin and from Victor Blanco to Benjamin Edwards come from Barker's book also.[16] Baker noted that she found much information about the McGee-Gutierrez Expedition in the six volumes of the Lamar Papers.[17] From writings by R. B. Blake, she learned about many forgotten landmarks in East Texas. Also, an old inventory of the William G. Logan estate was especially useful. She acknowledged that these important sources were both helpful and frustrating:

> This document [the Logan Estate inventory], along with Colonel Gray's diary, Ehrenberg's autobiography, Dr. Starr's unpublished memoir, the journal of Adolphus Sterne, and certain choice finds among the recently accessible Raguet papers, fill the soul of a modern chronicler with despair. Its treasure of vivid detail is richer than a pirate's chest. How choose from these documents the spoils to pack a few tight pages?[18]

When Baker wrote, "[Hayden] Edwards had put a fortune into his enterprise," she had found in her research that "Edwards had spent $50,000.00 on his colony." She also wrote that "the most influential people in Nacogdoches did not want a war for independence. . . . They were making money too fast."[19]

Writing about the Battle of Nacogdoches, she refers again to Dr. Crocket and the historian Thrall as sources. She used *The Raven*, Marquis James's Pulitzer Prize-winning biography of Sam Houston published in 1929, and James's work also aided her when she wrote about some of the more important residents of Nacogdoches.[20] Information found in "A Narrative Sketch of the Panic of Eastern Texas During the Month of April, 1836" from the Raguet Papers was crucial to her article, and she noted the importance of having access to these papers: "Nothing I have seen gives so vivid a picture of Nacogdoches in war-time as a certain document in the Raguet papers."[21]

The newspaper account in 1845 about a movement toward higher education in Nacogdoches led by James Starr came from Starr's unpublished memoirs mentioned in the *Southwest Review* article.[22] In addition to consulting written documents, Baker interviewed an elderly lady born in 1829 on El Camino Real near Nacogdoches. The lady, unnamed in the article, was a Mrs. Peevy who provided an eyewitness account of many important events in Nacogdoches's history. She had been a personal acquaintance of Gen. Sam Houston, and at the time of the Baker interview, Peevy was the town's oldest citizen.[23] After the *Southwest Review* published "Nacogdoches: The Gateway of the Pioneers" (January 1936), Baker made plans to print the article as a pamphlet, at her own expense, to help the local Nacogdoches Historical Society raise money for local centennial efforts. The intended cover of the pamphlet was Charlotte's drawing, *Paradise of the Shepherds*. Even though the *Review's* editor, Henry Smith, reassigned copyright to her, the pamphlet never materialized.[24] Baker's third article for the *Southwest Review* would not appear for another eighteen months.

Baker continued to participate in a variety of organizations and helped to arrange their meetings in Texas. S. G. Knott, the director of the National Folk Festival, wrote to Baker in March 1936, in response to her invitation to have a meeting in Nacogdoches, that he was making preparations to hold a meeting there.[25] The next month, when the English honorary fraternity, Sigma Tau Delta, held its annual meeting in April at Mary Hardin-Baylor College in Belton, Baker took part in an event that would lead to the formation of the most important literary organization in Texas. Baker, along with other leading Texas writers and scholars, attended a program devoted to Texas literature, and at that time, the group decided to form an organization that would honor Texas writers. Baker was part of a select committee including L. W. Payne Jr., Hilton Greer, John O. Beaty, Claud Howard, Rebecca Smith, and W. H. Vann that made plans to meet in Dallas in November to organize what would become the Texas Institute of Letters. When Baker wrote to Vann on April 13 congratulating him on the successful conference, she also expressed her intent to be a conscientious participant in the newly proposed organization: "I shall be most interested to hear from the Centennial organization plans as they develop. Like everybody else, I suppose, I should have been glad to escape the responsibility (and something of mild odium, probably) that will fall upon those who take the lead in the enterprise; but I *am* anxious to do what I can, and since I didn't escape, I'll try to make the best of the 'bad eminence.'"[26] As a member of the planning committee, she offered the name of a speaker for the first meeting: "The name of

Robert Frost comes into my mind as a possibility for a speaker, because I admire him so very much and find him most delightful personally. I don't know whether he could be secured, or whether he would be the best. If I have further ideas I will pass them on."[27]

Many Texas writers saw the formation of the organization as an important part of the Texas centennial observance, but not everyone felt that way. Initially, both J. Frank Dobie and Walter Prescott Webb expressed serious reservations. Dobie wrote a skeptical letter to Vann and criticized a person he thought should be excluded from the governing body:

> I doubt seriously if anything that could be done by any commission would do anything towards producing first rate literature in Texas or elsewhere. If such a commission were appointed, I should hope that the smug, hypocritical, although well-mannered Beaty [John O. Beaty] of Southern Methodist University would not be appointed on it. In the first place he doesn't know anything about Texas literature, and in the second place his mind is so small that anything he fostered would be valueless.[28]

Webb wrote to Vann that he did not like the idea of an exclusive group or formal organization. He suggested that, instead, all those interested in writing should meet yearly as they had done in Belton.[29] Of the original fifty charter members, Dobie and Webb (along with Eugene C. Barker, Karle Wilson Baker, John A. Lomax, Hilton Greer, and Grace Noll Crowell) received the most votes from their fellow writers to become members of the organization.[30]

In May, Baker wrote Vann that she would leave on July 1 for a six- to eight-week trip to Mexico. Charlotte and the Bakers' niece, Floy Lewis, accompanied her; Thomas E. Baker joined them before the end of the trip. While in Mexico, Baker gathered important information that she would use later in her historical writings.[31] In September, Vann received responses to his letter asking Texas writers to nominate ten from their circle whom they would consider "fellows" of the institute. The writer's national reputation was a major consideration. Karle Wilson Baker's name was often the first on the nominator's list.[32] Dobie wrote again to Vann expressing his concerns: "I am not going to nominate anybody for the fellowships. I don't see the use trying to have this band of elect. The reason I am joining the organization is not because of any honor I should feel in belonging to it, although I appreciate the esteem of my fellows, but because I think it has a chance to do some good for the culture of Texas."[33] Two weeks later, Dobie wrote again to Vann with his list of ten nominees, including himself, but Karle Wilson Baker (spelled "Carl") headed the list.[34] Throughout the entire process, Dobie expressed a desire to replace nominees who were scholars and intellectuals with men who published Texas writers.[35] Webb also was among the many who nominated Baker to be a fellow. On October 27, 1936, Baker acknowledged Vann's letter announcing that members of the institute had selected her to become a fellow: "Of course I was deeply gratified that I should have been selected as one of the Fellows. My own difficulty in making my choices gave me quite a lively appreciation of the honor involved in being chosen by any considerable proportion of the group."[36] In actual fact, fellows for the institute were not awarded until years later; Baker was named the third fellow of the institute in 1952, following Dobie and Webb.[37] Also in October 1936, as part of the city's centennial observance, Nacogdoches dedicated the reconstructed Old Stone Fort on the Stephen F. Austin campus; Baker read "Song of the Forerunners."[38] The next month, on November 9, Baker attended the inaugural meeting of the Texas Institute of Letters in Dallas in the lecture room of the Hall of State at the Centennial Exposition; Dobie and Webb were also present. The temporary officers named were L. W. Payne Jr. of the University of Texas, chairman, and Rebecca Smith from Texas Christian University, secretary.[39]

The next month, Baker took part in the rebirth of another important organization in Texas. Herbert Gambrell, who had served as the historical director of the Texas Centennial that year, and his wife, Virginia, were the organizing forces behind the revived Philosophical Society of Texas that had been founded in 1837. On December 5, Baker attended the renewed society's first meeting at the Melrose Hotel in Dallas. She was one of three women invited to join and was elected a director.[40] Typically, Baker was the only woman or one of the few to play a major role in such societies in Texas.

Three months later, in March 1937, Baker received a rare letter of request from Dobie:

> I's [*sic*] like to visit East Texas pretty soon and Mrs. Dobie wants me to drive in that direction so that she can see the flowers. I don't want you to bother yourself about the matter, but if there is some convenient department or organization that handles public speakers, I'd appreciate it if you would convey thither my ambition to talk in Nacogdoches. I might talk on Mexico, but maybe I'd do better on animals and their lore: "what the Cricket Said to the Coyote down in the Thicket—while the Rattlesnake Listened"—or something like that.
>
> I'd like to come by April 1. My price if [*sic*] $50.

Robert Frost spoke here Saturday night. He mentioned three Texas writers, one of them a poet, yourself—mentioned them in a complimentary way.[41]

Dobie wrote again to Baker that he had heard from T. E. Ferguson, professor and chair of the English department of that college, that he could not bring him to speak because Rachael Field was already scheduled for March 15.[42] Baker had arranged the speaking engagement some months earlier for Field.[43] Baker too, received many requests to speak at colleges in Texas between 1936 and 1940. Invitations came from Texas A&M at College Station, Trinity University in Waxahachie, Southwestern University in Georgetown, the University of Texas, Hockaday Junior College in Dallas, Our Lady of the Lake in San Antonio, and others. Requests for copies of her poems came from universities in Maryland, Colorado, Tennessee, Utah, and Texas.[44]

Nevertheless, during these busy months, Baker continued the writing project for the *Southwest Review.* The third and last article, "Trailing the New Orleans Greys," completed the series intended for the *Review*'s special Texas centennial issue. Baker wrote to the editors that she would have the article for them by May 1, 1937.[45] But in July, Baker wrote again to editor Henry Smith that she was finally sending him the New Orleans Greys article: "The more I worked with the material the more I wanted to present it as the personal experience it had turned out to be —a sort of detective-adventure in tracking down the Greys, rather than a mere sober collection of facts about them."[46] She added that the tale of the New Orleans Greys was an "incomparable" story, but she feared the article was too long for the *Review.* Also, she changed the spelling to "Greys" in the published work from the "Grays" spelling in her notes and drafts.[47] On July 17, Henry Smith acknowledged the arrival of the article: "The essay on the Greys arrived yesterday, and I have glanced through it with immense pleasure. Thank you very much for sending it. . . . We do not know whether it will be better to publish the essay in one installment or two. I think there is no question of cutting it—we want to use it all. . . . The *Review* has fallen behind its schedule, but we plan to bring out several issues within the next two or three months."[48]

For this final article, Baker relied heavily on information she found in diaries written by William Fairfax Gray and Herman Ehrenberg, both of which are contemporary eyewitness accounts of Texas in 1835 and 1836. Gray, years older than Ehrenberg, wrote an account of his travels across Texas, "From Virginia to Texas 1835: Diary of William F. Gray." He relates details of his journey to Texas and return to Virginia (1835–36); he later writes about a second journey to Texas in 1837.[49] Since Gray was in New Orleans when volunteers were recruited to aid in the Texas campaign and was present at other crucial events, such as the meeting of the Texas Convention at Washington-on-the-Brazos, his diary offers important primary information. Ehrenberg, a volunteer with the New Orleans Greys in the war for independence from Mexico, presents an invaluable firsthand account of the forming of the Greys by Adolphus Sterne and the Committee for Texas and a knowledgeable account of the Battle of the Alamo. Baker found Ehrenberg's diary to be not only colorful and well expressed but also factually important. His account of the Greys' stop in Nacogdoches at "Squire" Sterne's house and the banquet the town provided the troops offers interesting insights into the attitudes and customs of the times.[50] Ehrenberg and Gray had different perspectives on the events—one was a young soldier, the other a shrewd land purchaser—but both accounts offered important supportive information to Baker's research. Her papers show that she researched many other sources as well.[51]

Baker begins the article with an account of her visit to the National Museum in Mexico City to see the flag of the New Orleans Greys that had been at the Alamo: "The flag of the Grays has been mended and re-mended, sewn to a canvas base. But it is made of what appears to be a not very heavy quality of pure silk. Hardly a trace of the blue color remains—a faint cast on what looks to be white. The fringe is about an inch wide and is heavy and well-preserved—about 4 x 6 ft., originally."[52] She wrote that her visit to see the flag inspired her to research the Greys. Traveling later to Austin, Baker reviewed the muster roll in the General Land Office of the men at the Alamo. She compared these names with the list supplied in Ehrenberg's diary to determine how many of the Greys were in the Battle of the Alamo.[53] She related Ehrenberg's moving account of the fatal march on the morning of Palm Sunday after the Battle of Goliad. He had taken part in the battle and had survived the massacre by sheer luck. Baker wrote of his good fortune, "Ehrenberg, untouched by the bullets, grappled with a pursuing soldier, was slightly wounded in the encounter, but escaped under cover of the smoke. As he swam the river, he lost his diary. . . . After much suffering and a narrow escape from death, the young soldier reached the Texas army and was honorably discharged."[54]

Baker also explains that Ehrenberg, having lost his original diary, rewrote the story of his experiences from memory, in German, and published the book in Leipzig in 1843. It was reprinted twice in the two years following. At the time Baker was writing her article about the Greys, there was no complete translation of Ehrenberg's diary, so she had it translated for her own use.[55]

Baker continued to squeeze in speaking engagements while she prepared the New Orleans Greys article. The Philosophical Society of Texas asked her to speak at their meeting at Liendo Plantation. Baker read her 100-line dramatic monologue about the sculptress Elisabet Ney, who lived at Liendo Plantation.[56] She introduced the poem with a brief biographical sketch about Ney:

> The poem I am about to read was written for this occasion—only, I didn't know it then, for that was at least fifteen years ago. The unique story of Elisabet Ney and Dr. Montgomery had fascinated me, and for some years I seized every opportunity and followed every clue that promised any light on their history and personalities. . . . Mrs. Taylor, the biographer of Miss Ney, says of Liendo, "The setting up of this home marked for Elisabet Ney an entirely new phase of her life. The break with her brilliant past was complete. A totally new interest engrossed her. . . . At the time of their coming to Liendo, their elder child. . . . was a year and a half old; the other, Lorne, was an infant. . . . The coming of her children filled Elisabet Ney with a hitherto undreamed-of enthusiasm. She forgot her art; she forgot her overwhelming ambition and pride—or, rather, she transferred all that ambition and pride to her children. . . . Many years later, in Austin, someone expressed amazement that an artist with such a record of success behind her could have so completely given up the pursuit of art for all those years. "I was busy with a more important art," she replied, "the art of moulding flesh and blood."[57]

In her own case as both mother and artist, Karle Wilson Baker was devoted to her two children, but she never gave up the pursuit of her art as had Elisabet Ney.

During her research for the series for the *Southwest Review*, Baker had uncovered material that drew her to the personality of James Grant, a soldier in the Texas Revolution. Grant became the main motivation in her research for her next novel, *Star of the Wilderness*. She shared her enthusiasm with Henry Smith:

> Just now I'm haunted by Grant, and can't rest until I've finished assembling and digesting all I can find out about him. So far as I know, there is actually no connected account, or study, of him, strange as it seems. I

find, from the Sterne diary, that he was at Nacogdoches for a time. You knew, of course, that he was part-owner of an immense tract between Saltillo and Parras. If what I find turns out to be enough for an article, would you be interested in one called "The Beloved Scot?" One reason I am obsessed by Grant just now is that he seems to be determined to be in my next novel; and if so, I must know more about him. Another is, that though I have never found time to get much excited about genealogy, I ran across the fact not long ago that my own Highland ancestors, the McCoys and Sutherlands were neighbors of the Grant clan.[58]

In August 1937, she wrote to Smith: "I am unearthing a perfect mine of original documentary material about my Beloved Scot! It will take the rest of my natural life to dispose of it. 'Woe worth the day' when I first indulged my latent appetite for research!"[59]

That same month Baker wrote W. H. Vann that she would not be able to attend the meeting of the Texas Institute of Letters in Dallas that year. She informed him that Coward-McCann was bringing out her first novel, *Family Style,* in September and that the publisher wanted her to go to Chicago for the launching of the book. Her daughter, Charlotte, was living in Chicago, and Baker planned to stay for several weeks.[60] Also during the summer of 1937, Baker tried to place the manuscript of the children's book "The Reindeer's Shoe" with a publisher. Charlotte had illustrated the text with charming silhouettes of the characters and scenes. The New York publishers Coward-McCann, Viking, Doubleday, and the Thomas Crowell Company all turned the manuscript down.[61] The success of one novel did not serve as a guarantee for future publications. Baker had to practice the advice she had given other writers: patience and persistence.

September 20, 1937, was a day for celebration in the Baker household. *Family Style* was at last in the bookstores. It was the first fictional story published nationally about the East Texas oil field. Kilgore, Texas, the setting for the novel, was the quintessential boomtown. Baker describes the town in *Family Style* as a place of congested population, tangled traffic, overrun facilities, and inadequate housing made up of small, recently thrown-up tentlike houses along the busy highway coming into town. In the novel, she relates the excitement of the local townspeople the day the big well was expected to blow in:

As Marie drove down into the business part of town, threading her way through the tangled traffic . . . she decided that Fred had been wrong in saying the whole town would be out at the well. The whole town was

> obviously standing on the side-walks, packed together out of the drip, so thickly that you could hardly push your way through. . . . Yet the number and variety and queerness of all these strange people did surprise her. Undeniably, many of them were "tough" . . . four-fifths of them were men. To be sure, many of the cars wedged about the office-buildings and hotels were big and expensive-looking; . . . "I guess it's too wet out at the well," she said to the salesman, "rain's driven them all in to town."
>
> "Don't you believe it, Mrs. Priest. The boss just got back from there; he says there's 5000 of 'em, at least. Just sitting there in their cars, determined not to miss the show." . . .
>
> A shout had rung out in the street outside: then two or three. . . . And then the wildest clamor broke loose. Automobile horns tooted, sirens shrieked, people cheered, and yelled and laughed . . . Marie found herself standing in the doorway of the store, salespeople and customers all wedged in together, all laughing and shouting and shaking hands. "It's the Lathrop! She's come in like a house afire! They say she'll make 40,000! She's the biggest one yet."[62]

Baker's prose style is never mundane. Poetic phrasings penetrate the descriptions in the novel. She describes a derrick and well site as observed through the eyes of a lover of language:

> Now, before Kathleen realized that they were near it, they found themselves almost at the foot of the new derrick. A clearing had been made on the brink of a small ravine in the very heart of the pinewoods; tall pines stood all about it, and from the derrick-floor the workmen looked down upon a sloping green floor of brushy tops. The slender steel derrick soared past the treetops with an air of fragile strength; great clouds of silvery steam blew sifting patterns across it, and the ruddy flames under the boilers glowed across the gray day like huge, rude hearth-fires.[63]

The entire East Texas area was rich in oil field imagery. On visits to the oil field, Baker had the opportunity to observe firsthand the gamut of life there, from derrick construction, everyday field operations, sludge-pits, roughnecks, and lease-men to oil well fires and makeshift oil field cafes. In the novel, Kathleen Priest runs just such a café. Her husband, Duke, refers to the people who frequent it: "Well," said Duke, unconsciously growing rather grand himself, "I'm tired of entertaining company in a restaurant. All these people that keep dropping in to see us, like that woman that's writing a book."[64]

Perhaps this is an oblique reference to Baker herself.

Duke Priest, a small-time farmer, hopes to find oil on his land, but at the beginning of the novel, he gets a job working as a supervisor for a trucking company:

> Kathleen did not make good her threat to go to Kilgore, now the center of the thirty-mile field. But Duke did.
>
> A trucking contractor had just been killed in a wreck on the highway, leaving his widow to manage his business or lose it. Duke found her, hollow-eyed, gray-lipped and grim, standing outside a shack marked "office" in a pouring rain. She was hardly shoulder-high to a disgusted-looking truck driver who was arguing about the order she was giving him. Duke . . . intervened in the discussion before he realized that he was "butting in."
>
> "Excuse me, ma'am, but I reckon I know what he means. That make of truck just won't do what the heavier ones will. Now, when the roads get in this condition—"
>
> "Sure, that's just what I been a-tellin'her," put in the driver, aggrievedly, but with marked relief. "Mr. Bramlett, he knowed that-there truck was a crip. He was aimin' to replace it just as soon as he could make a good trade. Now that-there International"—By the time the man had gone his way, mollified, Duke found himself practically employed.[65]

Baker describes the colorful scene at the site as the well came in:

> Suddenly, without *any* warning, *any* break in the monotonous, clanking sound, a hoarse shout went up from the derrick-floor. At the same instant the lights were snapped off, leaving only one flood-light which had been set from a distance upon the well. A deepening roar came swelling up from the bowels of the earth.
>
> "Look out! Stand back! She's coming!" Excited voices took up the cry of the workmen, who had thrown down their tools and were running away from the derrick. "Look out! Put out your cigarettes! There she comes!"
>
> She came indeed. A great cloudy column shot to the top of the derrick, then sprayed out and lost itself in the dim light. The crowd, the wilder for its instantaneous change of mood, sent up a hoarse, jubilant,

> many-throated roar. They were laughing, slapping each other on the back, throwing their hats into the air and stumbling over each other as they tried to recover them in the darkness.[66]

Just before the publication of *Family Style,* Baker received a letter from C. M. "Dad" Joiner, who had drilled the discovery well in the East Texas oil field:

> I have just read a notice of the publication of your new book on East Texas. I am pleased to note that someone with real ability has taken up this work and I am sure that your book will be warmly received.
>
> It would please me very much to have the first autographed copy and if you will mail one to me at the above address, 4745 East Third St., Long Beach, California, inclosing [*sic*] bill for same I will remit promptly. In addition to this I will probably want several volumes when I ascertain the price at which the first edition may be offered.[67]

The discovery of the East Texas oil field ushered in the largest oil find the world had ever seen, and Karle Wilson Baker stepped forward to offer a dramatic account to the reading public. Because her early recognition as a writer had come first from her poetry and then from her essays, it is somewhat ironic that she always saw herself as a novelist. A month before the publication of *Family Style,* Baker sent a fifteen-page philosophical and biographical letter to John McGinnis, who was to review the book for the *Dallas News.* This lengthy and important letter reveals her feelings about art and life:

> I have been told repeatedly by people who ought to know, or who were trying to help me, that the essay was my true *forte.* But, while I want to write essays, just as I have written verses, something in me vehemently rejects being disposed of as a poet, or as an essayist. . . . There is in me something practical and constructive, something urgently aware that life works by embodying itself; something that craves the heft and solidity, the sharp edges, of concreteness, even while it remembers that Life is more intense at the core. . . . These are some of the things that will probably keep a writer who isn't a "born story teller" trying to tell stories to her dying day.
>
> . . . My high-water mark [in publishing short stories] was reached just a month or two before my marriage: a rather long story, called "An Accidental Saint," was accepted by Norman Hapgood . . . of *Collier's.* He sent me an enthusiastic letter of acceptance, and a check for three hundred dollars—good pay, for those days. I thought I was well on the way.

Photograph of men on the derrick floor of the oil well Crantill-Germany #1, two miles east of Rusk, Texas. Karle Wilson Baker describes both the wooden derrick and the oil field workers in her novel Family Style. *She likely took this photograph as well. (Courtesy Steen Library, Stephen F. Austin State University)*

> I informed my intimates that I was going to have my babies as the Indian squaws do, on the march. I thought women made much too much of an ado about the difficulty of combining a career and marriage. If you had a gift, you needed only to add a little intelligence and spirit. I saw myself quite easily managing Life with one hand and Art with the other. . . . the sum of my achievement is that I am still married, and still writing. . . . anyone would see that I am the sort of woman who stays married; and my husband—though you hardly saw enough of him to discover it, is an exceptional man. I have done better with Life than with Art. But I'm not through: I haven't "finished the course." And I've never deluded myself with the belief that success with the one excuses failure with the other. For Art *is* life; . . . I've never done my best; I've only tried to. And whenever the finish does come, it will find me still trying.[68]

She also comments that during the writing of the letter her husband received a telephone message from Joaquin, Texas, (about fifty miles away) that they had "drilled a plug" and the callers believed it was a successful oil well. Since Tom had a few small holdings near this wildcat, he, Charlotte, and Ben T. Wilson decided to leave for the well early that afternoon. Baker told them she would not go, but later when Tom called from the office to tell Charlotte to be ready, he added, "Tell your mother to remember the oil-man who went to Heaven; she'd better change her mind!" In her letter to McGinnis, Baker wrote, "This time I didn't; I had the house to myself to finish this [the letter]. But *Family Style* grew out of just such expeditions—hundreds of them, spread over thirty years. And then, when the big field really did come in, the drama of it gripped me so that I had to settle down and write the story."[69]

Family Style was so popular that countless study clubs and organizations asked Baker to make public appearances and discuss the novel. She went all around the state giving talks, but she still had time for the small towns in Nacogdoches County, too. The hostess for a club in the village of Alto, Texas, wrote, "My husband and I'd like for you and Mr. Baker to come by our house and go on to the club house with us. Probably you'd like to freshen up a bit after your drive over. As you no doubt know, Alto has neither street names nor house numbers, but almost anyone here can direct you to our place."[70] Responding to a clubwoman in Temple, Texas, who was interested in reviewing *Family Style* for her organization, Baker sent her assessment of a "good novel":

> It should enrich him just as life itself does—not by teaching and explaining, but by making him feel values that he cannot express—

meanings and significances in common human experience. And it should rest and refresh and strengthen him by picking him up out of the confusion and perplexity of his own life and letting him live the lives of other people, for whom he has no responsibility—only fellow-feeling and curiosity. Therefore, character and atmosphere are as important in a novel as plot, though for different reasons.[71]

In her public speeches about *Family Style,* Baker frequently concluded with comments about its contribution to the East Texas community:

> . . . I wanted it to be a living picture of one little corner of the world and one absorbing sort of human activity—of East Texas, and of an oil-boom. . . . An oil-boom is a dazzlingly American phenomenon; and, in many ways besides size, this one was the most thrilling, the most earth-shattering and world-building in history. A more striking fact, still, the suggestion has been made more than once by thoughtful and informed observers, that it may prove to be, on any important scale, the last. I like to think that I may have been successful in preserving a true picture of something so dramatic and so typical in our national life.[72]

Enthusiastic reviews of the new novel appeared across the state.[73]

John McGinnis wrote, in a review originally published in the September 19, 1937, *Dallas News* and reprinted in the next day's Nacogdoches *Daily Sentinel:*

> Just about all of the characteristic oil field people with their customary stage properties appear in Karle Wilson Baker's *Family Style,* a novel which presents a sustained study of the East Texas oil "play." Here are to be found the serried lines of geometric derricks; highways cut into canyon-like ruts by innumerable trucks loaded with casing, trails that lead to new "locations" through endless sloughs of boggy mire; mysterious scouts, leathercoated drilling contractors, big-company officials stepping from unexpected airplanes, lease hounds accumulating right to share in the profits by sharp practice and fraud; great crowds of the desperately interested and the merely curious, waiting for wells to be brought in; . . .
>
> More than in any other Texas fiction I have come across, the setting is successfully pictured as distinct from all other lands. The novel is true to its locale. . . . The people, with their everyday affairs and their funerals and their weddings, belong in those houses, under those pines, and nowhere else.

All in all, *Family Style* is a good oil novel—although some men who read it may think Mrs. Baker didn't make the oil field quite the he-man jungle they have found it. It is also a good East Texas novel, and finally, it is simply—a good novel.

Rebecca W. Smith, a member of the Department of English at Texas Christian University, reviewed the novel in the November 1937 issue of *Texas Outlook:*

> . . . The biggest theme in contemporary Texas is the impact of prosperity upon the native, rooted stock who live in small towns and on farms. . . . Mrs. Baker has struck out boldly in her first novel to seize upon this theme, locating her action in the East Texas field . . .
>
> *Family Style* is well written, and rich in the manners and lore of the oil fields. The descriptions of the countryside and of the dramatic fires and catastrophes around the derricks and refineries show how much Mrs. Baker remains a poet in her prose writing. Despite the lack of struggle in the character of the heroine and, consequently, the lack of climax in the plot, this novel is interesting and sound. It deserves to be widely read and appreciated.

The *Houston Post*'s December 5, 1937, review also commented on the poetic qualities of Baker's novel:

> As exciting as the bringing in of the discovery well is this novel of the world's largest oil field. . . . We see the turmoil and traffic, we hear the noise and clamor, we feel the ceaseless grind and struggle of a new field met with almost superhuman hardihood and endurance. . . .
>
> The book is vivid, moves swiftly, and is bright with contrast. When the reader has gone just so far with stark realism, he sees a woodland strip or the crescent moon through the eyes of a poet. This is not surprising as Mrs. Baker is one of the outstanding poets of Texas. . . . *Family Style* should hold a place of distinction among regional novels. The people with their rustic speech, the scenes, the action, everything that makes up the book is Texas. Texas readers cannot afford to miss this book.

The private collection of papers in the Baker estate houses summaries of reviews of *Family Style*. The *El Paso Times* called *Family Style* "a delightfully readable book." The reviewer for the *Dallas Times-Herald* wrote: "There is not an unnecessary character nor an unbelievable situation in the well-knit plot." Praise appeared in the *Dallas Journal:* "The heart of East Texas is in this story." The *Saturday Review of Literature* in New York wrote, "Mrs. Baker's story of a Texas oil field is well-conceived and well thought-out, full of drama and knowledge of human beings." The *New York Times-Herald* commented that "Mrs. Baker has limned her characters clearly and her portrait of Kathleen, bright, forthright and innately honest, is especially refreshing."[74]

The highly favorable reviews and Baker's continued public exposure in the state prompted members of the Texas State Historical Association to invite Baker to join their organization.[75] With the publication of *Family Style,* Baker felt affirmed as a novelist and encouraged to continue plans for a second novel. Throughout her career, she had written essays and short stories, but those writings had never brought the national recognition that her poetry had. She did not publicly express her feelings about her deliberate transition to writing prose until she spoke to the Poetry Society of Texas in Dallas in December 1938. She felt some obligation to the society because she had been a founding member and was its first vice president. In the speech she admitted, "It began to come to me as a curious surprise that whatever recognition I had managed to achieve was as a poet. I had gone on writing poetry because life had to be expressed; but I had hardly aspired to the name. On the other hand, I had always expected to write novels."[76] Surely the members of the Poetry Society found her comments surprising. Baker also said that she saw this change as a "natural evolution," that the ability to write novels came with "maturity and life experiences." She added that she never felt very comfortable being called a poet: "I have always felt a little like a masquerader in the crimson velvet mantle of the poet. I rattle around in it; it is too big for me, and too rich." She compared her role as a poet to that of an orchestra member, insisting that she played only the flute (the personal lyric) and that writing a novel is like playing the piano because of its many parts. Baker emphasized that she did not consider shifting from poetry to novels a "descent," but neither did she consider it necessarily an "ascent": "Poetry is not a form, but a spirit: it is life; it is an intensity of realization of life. A noble novel is pervaded by it: in a different way, perhaps to a different degree, but just as truly and as life-givingly as a noble poem."[77] Having publicly pronounced her intention to pursue the expectation she had always had—to write novels—Baker was poised to continue the writing of her next book.

With her determined shift to prose writing, Karle Wilson Baker may have underestimated her contribution to American literature as a poet and risked endangering her position in American literary history; time, however, proved that the risk and the shift worked in her favor. Baker's centennial articles provide factual, carefully researched narratives that shed light on events from Texas history that had not been fully explained in other sources. With the publication of these articles, she became a respected writer of nonfiction in the state. *Family Style* became a national best-seller. Her skillfully portrayed characters in *Family Style* describe realistically the people who lived in rural East Texas in the 1930s. The nation and the world recognized the East Texas oil field as the largest discovery of its kind, and in her novel, Baker captured the excitement of the times and interpreted the region for future generations. First driven by the excitement of the Texas centennial celebration, Baker found herself absorbed by Texas history. In the coming years, she pursued this interest and wrote another best-seller.

"I am convinced that I am just a writing person—a person with a passion and a gift for putting into writing the things I see, hear, and feel."

CHAPTER 5
The Creative Process

In January 1938, Karle Wilson Baker wrote in her diary about serious backaches and rheumatism, but by February, she noted that she was working on her second novel, "A Letter from Jamie" (later titled *Star of the Wilderness.*)[1] February also looked like a promising month for "The Reindeer's Shoe." The Henry Holt Company was looking at the manuscript, and Karle Wilson Baker's literary agent, Sydney Sanders, was trying to get motion picture rights for the book. The recent success of animated cartoons and of Walt Disney's *Snow White and the Seven Dwarfs* had prompted Baker to contact the literary agent to look into movie rights for "Reindeer." Sanders referred her to the Swanson Agency in Hollywood, but the agents there replied that Disney had its own staff writers and did not accept outside work.[2] In March, Baker entered the manuscript in a children's book contest sponsored by the Henry Holt Company, but that was unsuccessful as well.[3] She tried to place "Reindeer" with at least six other publishers in New York, but they all declined.[4] About that time, Baker got an unexpected invitation on the recommendation of Oveta Culp Hobby to serve on the 1939 New York World's Fair Committee. Hobby, of Houston, was the Texas chair of the Advisory Committee on Women's Participation for the World's Fair. Baker considered serving on the Texas committee an honor.[5]

The year progressed as others had with travel and speeches. Baker delivered "Literary Wildcatting," a talk about the development of *Family Style,* to the Craig Class in Dallas in April. Later that month, the city of Nacogdoches celebrated San Jacinto Day and dedicated the nine flags of the state of Texas at the Old Stone Fort in a special program. The College Choral Club under the direction of Ida Pritchett performed "The Pine Tree Hymn."[6] In May and June, Baker made several research trips by bus to the library in Natchitoches, Louisiana, in preparation for her new novel. Her husband drove over on the weekends to join her at the hotel in the small town. Later that summer, she and Charlotte spent five days in Natchez, Mississippi, gathering more information for *Star of the Wilderness.*[7] Baker recorded that when she spent a week in Natchitoches in May 1938, she brought the story of the new novel "up to arrival at Nacogdoches" and added that "certain chapters had been written at Natchez on week-ends."[8]

Even though she was very involved in researching *Star of the Wilderness,* Baker took on the mantle of president of the Texas Institute of Letters. At the fall 1938 meeting in Dallas, the membership elected Baker the second president of the organization, following Patrick D. Moreland.[9] In later years when W. H. Vann wrote the history of the institute, he referred to the 1938 meeting: "This meeting was not only one of the best, but also one of peculiar significance. Mrs. Karle Wilson Baker, an outstanding literary figure, was elected president."[10] The *Pine Log* reported Baker's election: "Mrs. Karle Wilson Baker, . . . was elected president of the Texas Institute of Letters which met Saturday in Dallas. . . . James H. Parke, chairman of the new drama department at the University of Texas, . . . named vice-president of the Institute, and William H. Vann of the Mary Hardin-Baylor College at Belton, is the new secretary-treasurer. Councillors are Dr. Walter P. Webb, professor of history at the University of Texas . . . and Whitney Montgomery, Dallas poet."[11] When Baker held a council meeting of the institute on May 12, 1939, in Austin, the council nominated new members, proposed an increase in dues, and scheduled the annual fall meeting for the third weekend in October in Dallas in cooperation with the Cokesbury Bookstore. Also, council members voted to ask Stark Young to be the principal speaker, but he declined.[12] Later, the council asked Marquis James to speak and invited Katherine Ann Porter to attend the meeting as a special guest.[13] Neither James nor Porter could attend; the committee finally found a speaker from the institute's own membership.[14] In 1939, under Baker's presidency, the institute formed a book award committee that presented the Best Texas Book of the Year Award to J. Frank Dobie at the 1939 fall meeting in Dallas.[15]

In August, Baker must have been surprised and a little amused to receive a letter from the publisher E. P. Dutton and Company requesting to see her latest novel. She had waited years to successfully publish *Family Style;* now

Photograph of Thomas Ellis Baker with his car on the chalon at Gaines Ferry Crossing, a ferry crossing of the Sabine River, August 1934. The Bakers visited places, such as the Gaines Ferry Crossing, which Karle describes in Star of the Wilderness. *(Courtesy Steen Library, Stephen F. Austin State University)*

she seemed to be "in demand." (Her friend, Hilton Greer, had written Dutton's about her preliminary work on *Star of the Wilderness.*) On August 25, Baker replied to Percy Johnson at the Dutton Company, thanking him for his letter but stating that she expected to publish the new novel with Coward-McCann, who had published *Family Style.* She wrote that the novel was not yet completed and that she was about to leave on another trip to Mexico for further research "to verify some matters of fact and atmosphere."[16]

As president of the Texas Institute of Letters, Baker relied on the efficiency and organizational skills of Secretary Vann. She wrote to him in November 1939 in response to a letter of his that had outlined several considerations for the upcoming meeting, including plans for the program for the next year: "I agree with you about the *ideal* program, but think you have accomplished quite a feat, in the circumstances. It is very nice of both Mr. Lomax and Mr. Dobie to 'come to the aid of the party.' We must all let them know that we appreciate it."[17] Later that month, Vann wrote a letter of appreciation for Baker's service to the institute: "Let me say very simply that I appreciate your intelligent interest during the year. You have given time that might well have been spent otherwise; your ideas have always been valuable; and your conduct of the various sessions at Dallas was altogether happy."[18]

Serving as president of the institute did not keep Baker from her writing projects. By May 1940, she had a draft of her new novel in Sanders's hands. He wrote to her on May 23 saying that he not only wanted to help place the novel with a book publisher but had also made preliminary plans to have it made into a motion picture.[19] In a letter to Sanders in August, Baker, who was sixty-two at the time, refers to her unflagging urge to write: "As to novels, I have more planned than I have time left to write, two or three quite definitely. Mexico and Texas have conducted their affairs for the past four centuries with the novelist primarily in view. I shall come back in another incarnation and do the Border."[20] Her declared expectations added further validity to her longstanding claim that she "was just a writing person." In September Baker traveled to New York City for a few weeks to see Sanders and to work on her manuscript. She was always exhilarated by city life. Tom Baker planned to join his wife in New York when the American Bankers Association convention met there later. Her work on the book over the next two years resulted in the publication of her second novel, *Star of the Wilderness,* which became a Book-of-the-Month Club selection, but the movie rights were never sold.

The Nacogdoches, Texas, location of *Star of the Wilderness* gave Baker the opportunity to recount the Spanish and Indian influences as well as Anglo life in the frontier town. Baker skillfully wove famous conflicts from the 1830s such as the battles of Nacogdoches, Bexar, Goliad, and San Jacinto into the compelling fictional story of a young family's successes and failures as they sought a new life in the Texas territory. The reader learns about Spanish/Mexican politics of the time and the difficulties of traveling across the expansive Texas frontier. A major figure in the novel, Dr. James Grant, the Texas revolutionary, was an important landowner in the Coahuila territory. Baker wrote a short synopsis for the novel to use in advertising the book:

> In *Star of the Wilderness* Karle Wilson Baker has written a fascinating story of the years preceding the war with Mexico. The central figures are Jessie, gently bred, who finds herself in "the Spanish Country," her husband Paul, a charming man, but an adventurer and gambler, and Paul's kinsman, the great Dr. Grant, who figures so largely in the early struggle for the independence of Texas. Grant was known to young soldiers who crowded at his heels as "the Beloved Scot." Why Houston hated and Austin trusted him, concerns the reader hardly so much as the part he played in Jessie's and others' lives, occupied with matters important chiefly to themselves. Yet each took his place in the larger pattern when the hour struck.
>
> The action of *Star of the Wilderness* moves from Cincinnati to the Heights of Chapultapec, pausing to look down the Texas Trace from the bluffs of Natchez, and to climb a balcony in Monclova, the crumbling capital of Mexican Texas. But the heart of the story is in The Redlands, one of the "settled places" that Jessie longed for, already proud of its social graces in 1830. There the dances went on and the teacups tinkled, right up to the moment when Santa Anna led his young officers across the Rio Grande to "flush their maiden swords."[21]

Star of the Wilderness begins with the young McAlpine family's boat trip down the Mississippi River on their way to the new Texas territory in search of fortune. Paul McAlpine had received a letter from his cousin, Dr. James Grant, touting the many opportunities awaiting the adventurous in this new frontier. On this already difficult journey, the family faced further complications when Jesse McAlpine gave birth prematurely. Baker describes the harrowing passage from Louisiana through the untamed land en route to Nacogdoches:

> The word "Nacogdoches," constantly recurring, was one of the few things she remembered of that time. Another was reaching the Attoyac

River and finding that it was wide as the Sabine, with no *chalan*.[22] . . . They were once more in the heart of a deluge. . . . They had doubled back on their steaming tracks and turned off somewhere; and then in the utter blackness that had fallen, struggled on and on through the night. The next thing was a low bulk of intenser shadow ahead, whinnyings, shouts exchanged, and the light of a smoky lantern. They were inside a low log hut with a dirt floor. A man who had no face, only eyes and beard beneath his matted hair, was standing in the middle, holding the lantern and pointing out the heap of blankets and pine boughs on which they laid her. In the opposite corner was a horse. . . . She heard the man mumbling miserably as he let it out into the rain. But it did not seem strange to her at the time that the horse should be there; her only concern was not to let it step on the baby. Otherwise, she would have been much more afraid of the man, at first, than of the horse. He was so hairy and unkempt, and being surprised by guests with a horse in the best and only room of his house evidently made him look wilder than ever. . . . He took a shovel out of the corner and cleaned up after the horse, going far out into the rain each time to empty his shovel. His fierce movements as he worked seemed to betray agonies of humiliation and protest.

> . . . He stayed with them till they got across the Attoyac. She didn't know how long that took, either; but the carriage had vanished, and they were in a covered wagon. She could remember the hairy man, riding bareback, swimming his own horse and holding the rein of one of the plunging creatures that drew the wagon. She remembered that the water had crept into the wagon bed, and that everything in it was wet. She herself was sitting on the seat, holding the baby. . . . Again she recalled swaying along after dark and hearing Paul and Sylvan saying "Nacogdoches," over and over.

> . . . She heard Sylvan cry, "The lights, *senor*! The town!" Still holding the baby tight at her breast, she peered out of the opening in the wagon cover. She could feel the horses bracing themselves and hold back as they started down the treacherous, slippery hill. And there, in the blackness below—very far down, it seemed to her—she could see lights, blurred and faint through the rain on her lashes and the streaming curtain of rain that flapped beyond. That was the last thing she remembered.[23]

In the novel, Baker draws vivid portraits of frontier people in the 1830s and the passageway to the new territory, Nacogdoches, in particular. According to Charlotte Montgomery, her mother based the fictional character Colonel Bardeen on the factual Nacogdochan John Durst. Baker describes the active little frontier town:

> They rode on into the plaza, passing Colonel Bardeen's store. Beyond the store was the two-roomed building which Mac's father rented from Colonel Bardeen for his law-office. It was painted white and had a little front porch supported by *colonettes,* like the ones in Lawyer's Row in Natchitoches, or in a hundred towns in the Old States.
>
> . . . The plaza was full of horses and men and wagons; it was always full, nowadays, Colonel Bardeen said. People were coming in faster than they had done since the rush from the States began, when the first colonization law was passed. In the center of the plaza there was a well of the sort to be seen in any Mexican village, with a thick curb built up into a heavy arch, from which the buckets were suspended. It was made of the same rough, yellowish stone as the Old Stone House, which stood on a corner across the way. Around the well was a solid, restless mass of wagons and beasts and people. The wagons were of every description, from the Mexican *carretas* with wheels sliced in one piece from the trunk of some great tree, to fine American Conastogas, with canvas still clean and red spokes still shiny, which had made their first trip over from Natchitoches. The beasts were goats, oxen, mules, burros, and horses. And as for the people (aside from a few gentlemen in their familiar silk hats, which the old settlers here called 'bee-gums'), they seemed to Mac the most unusual assortment he had ever seen. Looking down on them from the vantage of his pony, he thought that the peaked sombreros and coonskin caps predominated; but there were a few broad-brimmed gray beavers from the States, and many Indian head-dresses. He had seen Indians all his life back in Ohio; but he had not got used to seeing them in such numbers.[24]

Much of the success of her two novels, *Family Style* and *Star of the Wilderness,* was due to Baker's careful research. Her process for creating *Star of the Wilderness* is particularly fascinating because she employed both conventional and unconventional methods in her research. Printed sources, archives, diaries, and personal interviews were all part of her traditional research, but her interest in extrasensory perception led her to use less conventional methods as well. A conscientious scholar, Baker depended upon countless documents to support her work. The bibliography she compiled in researching *Star of the Wilderness* cites books on the history of Texas that were acknowledged as the most valuable sources at the time. She had already consulted some of these sources a few years earlier when she wrote the articles for the *Southwest Review.* Also, Baker often wrote interesting comments in the margins of the bibliography she compiled in her research.[25] She had borrowed an important source, *Texas and Texans,* vol. 1, by Frank W. Johnson (edited and updated by Eugene C. Barker in 1914) from her friend Lois Foster Blount. Baker commented that Almonte, one of the contributors to the volume, "has much very interesting material." She noted from that source the population of several towns in 1835: "Bexar 2400, Goliad 700, Victoria 300, Nacogdoches 3500, and San Augustine 2500." Also she heeded Almonte's account of the economic climate on the frontier:

> Money is very scarce; not one in ten sales is made for cash. Purchases are made on credit, or by barter; which gives the country, in its trading relations, the appearance of a continual fair. Trade is daily increasing, owning to the large crops of cotton, and the internal consumption, caused by the constant influx of emigrants from the U.S.

Baker recorded that *Memoirs* by Antonio Menchaca (1937) was "extremely valuable, offering some new facts and a wealth of picturesque and dramatic detail." In the San Antonio library, she consulted *Story of the Alamo* by Pearson Newcomb, noting that it contained "many useful, good small pictures" and *Combats and Conquests of Immortal Heroes* by C. M. Barnes, observing that it was a "rare and very useful book about San Antonio." Baker labeled William Corner's *San Antonio de Bexar* (1880) "valuable and unique." *The Heroes of San Jacinto* by Sam Houston Dixon (1932), *Waterways of Westward Expansion: The Ohio River and Its Tributaries* by Archer B. Hulbert (1903), William Gray's diary, *From Virginia to Texas* (about the Redlands), and Lockhart's *U.S. and Mexico* are also listed in her bibliographic notes. Baker took a special interest in Eugene Barker's *Austin in Mexico,* remarking that it contained "much quotation from Austin's letters," and in particular, she noted Barker's comments on Mexican authority and the break with authority in Nacogdoches. Barker had written, "Small as these things are in themselves, they are fair and true instances of the feelings indulged toward the Anglo-Americans by the Mexican authority. They first took alarm at the rising at Nacogdoches in 1826 under the lead of Edwards, which may be said to be the germ seed of their subsequent troubles, and the war of independence."

Other notes in Baker's bibliography indicated that *Grace Plantation* by Ola Beanhein (1938) influenced Baker's description of the fictional plantation "Retiro Verde" in *Star of the Wilderness.* She left a bibliographic note that she had borrowed a copy of Elizabeth Brooks's *Prominent Women of Texas* (1896) from R. B. Blake. D. B. Edwards's *The History of Texas* (1836) provided useful information about weather conditions in 1835. Frank Adams's *The Clans, Sects, and Regiments of the Scottish Highlands* (1924) contained interesting information about the Scots. She revisited sources she had used for the centennial articles such as *With Milam and Fannin: Adventures of a German Boy in Texas' Revolution,* Herman Ehrenberg's diary of a first-hand account of the formation and activities of the New Orleans Greys. In addition, Baker again consulted papers belonging to early Texas families such as the Blakes, the Raguets, and the Lamars. She used the Blake papers to authenticate facts regarding the Battle of Nacogdoches. In her notes, she summarized Blake's writings, calling her account a "Strategy of Battle of Nacogdoches." The excerpt following is from her notes about the Battle of Nacogdoches and demonstrates her interest in point by point detail:

> Evening of July 21, men are gathering at Pine Hill, east of town. Early morning of Aug. 1, Piedras draws up his men east of town to defend Eastern suburbs. In the level, wooded creek bottom, on eastern bank.
>
> About 9 o'clock Americans arrive from their camp to parley with Mexicans. Piedras defies them: announces he is ready. Americans attack and a furious battle commences "in the eastern suburbs about eleven o'clock." About noon Mexicans retreat across Lanana to business part of town and entrench themselves in the Old Stone House, the church and church plaza.
>
> Americans, instead of crossing creek go farther up stream and cross at Spanish Graveyard (H. S. campus) they go over and come down North Street, in rear of Mexicans.
>
> Soon after the main body of Americans pass, a belated company of Redlanders, who had come into town at the southeast corner, stops at Adolphus Sterne's and is instructed how to follow them (Blake)
>
> As they begin the march down North Street they hear a French horn (Blake) They continue, and when about opposite the Stone House, they (on North Street, about where the Catholic Church was at that time) are met by a furious charge. Encarnacion Chirino fell at the first, and others were wounded. The Americans wavered at first, but then rallied and stood firm. Their answering volley killed a number of the Mexicans and turned them back to their fort. A furious fight followed, in which the Americans broke up and fought from behind houses, etc. Mexicans

> made several attempts to renew the charge, but were driven back. They finally fell back from the church and church plaza and concentrated on the Stone House.
>
> About mid-afternoon they were driven out of the Stone House, and the main body of the army was concentrated in the Cuartel, or Red House, the older part of which was built of adobe. Had advantage of dormer windows on the second floor. The fight continued with unabated fury until night separated the combatants.
>
> During the night of August 2 the citizens built breastworks between them and the Cuartel, in preparation for a closer combat on the morrow."[26]

Baker relied on such comprehensive notes to reconstruct the battle in her novel. In her account, she related how Colonel Piedras slipped out of town in the night. At one point, her notes combine fact with fiction when she interjects fictional names beside the historic ones: "When the evacuation is discovered, James Carter with 17 volunteers (including Col. Bardeen) starts out in pursuit. Captain Hillmer serves as guide and scout."[27] *Bardeen* and *Hillmer* are fictional names in the novel for Durst and Sterne. In her account of the "Runaway Scrape" in *Star of the Wilderness,* Baker relied on the Raguet papers, which offered an accurate historical description of the East Texans' flight to Louisiana in the final days of the war with Mexico.[28] Baker likely used other sources that are not mentioned in the bibliographical list, including Eugene C. Barker's *Life of Stephen F. Austin* (1925) based on the Moses and Stephen F. Austin papers housed in the University of Texas Library and Marquis James's biography of Sam Houston, *The Raven* (1929). She had used Barker and James in articles for the *Southwest Review.*

Sketchy notes from her papers include a section labeled "Developments that might involve Paul [Paul McAlpine]" and "Items about Nacogdoches," which she incorporated into the novel. She made other notes on the political climate in 1822, including the Fredonia Rebellion in Nacogdoches led by Haden Edwards. Other interesting facts about Nacogdoches include her notes explaining that Stephen F. Austin used the phrase "the Nacogdoches madmen" more than once in relation to the granting of land titles. In spring 1827, Austin appointed land commissioners to provide a regular and permanent method of keeping land title records because forgery was "easy and frequent" around Nacogdoches.[29]

In addition to these written works, Baker consulted primary sources at libraries in Austin, San Antonio, Houston, and even Mexico. In her earlier article, "Trailing the New Orleans Greys," Baker used information from the National Museum in Mexico City. She recorded that the flag at the museum had impressed her greatly: "It was not the 'Flag of the Alamo,' but it was captured there; and I am inclined to believe that my novel of the Revolution would never have got written had I not seen with my own eyes that tattered banner. For it was the boys who followed Morris and Grant who carried that bit of faded silk, and there it was, as real as the clothes I had on. And it was through their eyes that I first really saw their 'Beloved Scot' [James Grant]."[30] Baker felt that the role Grant had played in Texas history had never received the recognition it deserved. Traveling in Mexico by car with her husband, Charlotte, and Charlotte's husband, Roger Montgomery, she combed Saltillo and Parras trying to find traces of James Grant.[31] Whereas she used fictional names for many of the characters in the *Star* novel, she used Grant's actual name, as she did for Sam Houston, Stephen F. Austin, and other famous Texans of the period. (Mixing authentic names with fictional ones added credibility to her story.) She became fixated on the character of Grant and focused on him over all other characters in the novel.[32] Baker describes "Jamie" in her elegant, poetic style:

> His hair was fine and soft, and curled a little; but it was very thick, and stood away from his forehead like a bird's feathers blown backward. It was reddish in strong light—"like an Irish setter's," Paul said. . . . She saw that his handsome mane was full of white threads that had not been there when she saw him last, but one did not suspect them at first. They blended with its reddish darkness, softening it toward ashen, sunburnt blond. . . . His silver-studded leather wristlets above the long brown hands seemed somehow the most characteristic item of his apparel: one never saw him without them.[33]

While the Bakers were traveling in Mexico, Karle Wilson Baker located Grant's will and used information from it in *Star of the Wilderness.* Again looking for concrete evidence from Grant's life, she visited a century-old winery that may have been the one Grant established and which she describes in *Star of the Wilderness.* In Monterrey, she tried to find relatives of Dona Guadalupa, Grant's wife. Baker traveled to New Orleans to locate and interview great-grandchildren of James Grant's brother, Hugh,[34] and she discovered little-known facts about Grant's ancestry by writing many letters of inquiry to Scotland. She also made trips to Victoria, Texas, exploring the locale and talking with the relatives of Don Placido Benavides upon whom another character in *Star of the Wilderness* is based.[35]

Again using a conventional approach to research, she sought help from resource persons such as Harbert Davenport of the Texas Historical Society; Harriet Smither, the state librarian; and her friend and professor of history at the University of Texas, George P. Garrison. But the Rev. George L. Crocket became one of her most valued resources. A famous East Texas minister, historian, scholar, and craftsman, Crocket reputedly knew more about the history of East Texas than anyone else. In 1932, Reverend Crocket had published what has become a landmark study, *Two Centuries in East Texas.* His local reputation made him a logical consultant for Baker's writing projects. Since they were both on the faculty of Stephen F. Austin State Teachers College, the two had many opportunities to talk together. Baker had gotten advice from Rev. Crocket when she was writing "A Hundred Miles of Memories":

> Will you read this paper and make a note of any errors of fact that you may find? What I have in mind is a series of articles pointing out the interesting *places* in Texas, and giving briefly the historical and traditional associations that make them interesting. It is addressed to the general reader, and frankly stresses the human and picturesque side of the subject; I am trying to gather up and present in connected, readable form all the scattered and drifting local lore that I can find, and make it easily accessible. Nevertheless, I am most anxious that no statements involving ascertainable historic fact shall be either false or careless. That is why I am asking you, if you will be kind enough, to check it for me. You will see that I have made liberal use of your own book![36]

Filed among the Baker papers, Crocket's response explained Spanish terms, such as differences between *hacienda* and *rancho,* and the origin of the Y'Barbo name, and discussed the significance of the names *Gaines* and *Gutierrez.* Also, he commented on the six Spanish missions Baker refers to in "A Hundred Miles of Memories." Crocket recommended that she consult the historian Henderson Yoakum as a source on Nacogdoches social life in the early 1800s.[37] The letter to Crocket is revealing because even though Baker used librarians and other resource people for research, she took the rare step of sharing the unpublished manuscript of "A Hundred Miles of Memories" with Crocket and asking him for critical suggestions. This information became useful again when she wrote *Star of the Wilderness.*

While primary sources and resource people were important, Baker went even further in her creative efforts to achieve realism and accuracy for *Star of the Wilderness* by constructing detailed charts, graphics, and time lines to organize her material. Since she often worked on several projects at the same time, she found this method helpful for keeping facts in order. She knew also that a detailed chronology was essential for a unified composition. The Baker papers contain at least sixty pages of chronology of Mexican and American history contemporary to the time of the setting of *Star of the Wilderness.* Baker noted most major historic events that occurred in the early 1800s in the United States, Texas, Spain, and Mexico.[38] She made hundreds of notes on index cards she had cut in half. Many of these cards attribute information to Louis J. Wortham's *A History of Texas: From Wilderness to Commonwealth,* which Garrison had recommended earlier. After she organized the chronology, Baker laid out the information on oversized paper to form a large chart that included not only events in the lives of the fictional characters at a given time but also paralleled state and world events contemporary to the fictional circumstances.[39]

Hand-drawn maps of the story's location also played an important role in her creative process. Baker may have gotten the idea of making plats of a downtown area or sketching maps of portions of the state from articles she had seen on writing methods used by the popular American novelist Sinclair Lewis. Baker's scrapbook from the early 1930s contains clippings from various magazines about famous American writers. An article about Lewis included a hand-drawn map of a part of Pony River Valley, North Dakota, the setting of one of his stories. The author of the article explained Lewis's method:

> To sharpen the focus of his vision, he then draws detailed maps of the section of the country, with its hills, rivers, railroads, and roads. There will be maps of the streets and the suburbs of Zenith for *Babbit,* for instance; a diagram of his office building and of his house, with floor plans of each story, and the arrangement of the furniture. In his notes for *Arrowsmith,* there are at least twenty such maps. After this is done, and he can see his characters, he sets them into their proper environment and has them live their lives.[40]

Baker's hand-drawn map of towns along the Mississippi River details stops made by the "Star of the Wilderness" river packet on her maiden voyage. Her maps of Louisiana and East Texas illustrate the young fictional family's difficult inland journey from Natchez to Natchitoches and their passage into the untamed interior. Fort Jessup, Gaines Ferry, El Lobanillo, the Attoyac River, and Nacogdoches are among the sites painstakingly rendered. She marked distances that were relevant to the accuracy of the novel:

"Natchez to the mouth of the Red River: 80 miles by water and 60+ by land. Distances between Alexandria and Natchitoches: 80 miles by water, 60+ by land; Gaines Ferry to Milam: 7 miles; Milam to El Lobanillo rancho: 8 miles; Attoyac to Chireno: 3 miles; and Chireno to Nacogdoches: 20 miles."[41] Such concrete geographical information and her use of actual place names in the novel adds realism to her work. Gaines Ferry, an existing place on the banks of the Sabine River, provided the weary little family in *Star of the Wilderness* a way to cross into Texas. From William F. Gray's diary, *From Virginia to Texas*, Baker had read of Gray's ordeal at the Gaines Ferry Crossing. She incorporates a similar scene in *Star of the Wilderness*, where she describes the river as far out of its banks, which made the crossing hazardous. The blast of a cow horn was the signal to Gaines that someone needed the ferry: "From a sapling beside the road he took a cow's horn hanging there by a leather thong. . . . He raised it with a flourish, adjusted his lips to its mouth, and blew. Far over the water, under the dark trees, shivered the long, eerie note: penetrating, yet soft; plaintive, yet gravely happy—a wildwood note such as Robin Hood himself might have blown. As long as they lived the two children remembered it."[42]

Baker described El Lobanillo in the novel; she had designated it on her map as an important early settlement: "This is Gil Y Barbo's country," answered Sylvan. "It was near here that he had his principal *rancho*, El Lobanillo, sixty years ago. And it was there he left a few of his kin when all the Spanish people in these parts were ordered back to Mexico. . . . And it was to this country that he led them back at last."[43]

One of Baker's hand-drawn plats gives a detailed account of the fictional Bardeen homesite, "Retiro Verde," and its environs. The Retiro Verde plat shows a large plantation complete with outbuildings, including a plantation store, guest house, quarters for the house servants, orchards, vegetable gardens, poultry yard, and Don Luis's (Col. Louis Bardeen's) ferry landing on the Angelina River just as Baker described it in the novel:[44]

> As they emerged at last from the forest and came out upon the ancient clearing which surrounded the new house like a visible peace, the name seemed very fitting . . . the ferry, the mill, the blacksmith shops, the stables—all those would be his.[45]

In addition, Baker made maps illustrating how she visualized downtown Nacogdoches in 1716 and in 1802. The earlier map was probably drawn for a project on Spanish Nacogdoches, but there is no proof of this. The drawing for 1802 shows the town nestled between the Lanana and Banita Creeks, designating in particular the King's Highway and Pilar Street in Nacogdoches. She indicated the church square and the public square and marked the locations of residences with an *X*. The Adolphus Sterne and Robert Barr residences are the only houses she noted by name. Baker refers to these landmarks frequently in *Star of the Wilderness*, and her map of 1802 offers a concrete picture of what she thought the town must have looked like in 1829, the date when the novel begins. Most likely she consulted this map again for her third novel, *It Blows from the Spanish Country* (unpublished), about the McGee-Gutierrez Expedition of 1812.

The wealthy fictional characters Col. Louis and Madame Antoinette Bardeen play important roles in the novel. As stated earlier, Baker based the character of Colonel Bardeen on the historic figure John Durst of Nacogdoches. Baker learned about Durst from the Oligivy-Sterne diary and from a folder of material given to her by Lois Blount.[46] Rudolph Hillmer is another fictional character based on a prominent Nacogdochan, Adolphus Sterne. Baker used W. B. Zuber's book, *Captain Adolphus Sterne*, for information to develop the character. Zuber had conducted personal interviews with Sterne's son, Charles Adolphus Sterne, and Sterne's daughter, Rosine Ryan. In addition, Baker learned facts about Sterne's life from an article by Rabbi Henry Cohen in the centennial edition of the *Houston Post* titled "Jewish Leaders in Texas."[47] She gave Herman Ehrenberg, the young diarist and German volunteer in the New Orleans Greys, the name of Ludwig Oberstadt.[48]

In 1939, while she was writing *Star of the Wilderness*, Baker, her husband, Tom, and daughter, Charlotte Baker Montgomery visited a descendant of Antonio Gil Y'Barbo, the Nacogdoches leader who had designed the early city plan in the Spanish style. Baker's sketches depicting downtown Nacogdoches in 1716 and 1802 were likely influenced by this interview with the eighty-nine-year-old John Y'Barbo. He described the locations of the Stone Fort, the church, and the Gil Y'Barbo house—information he had learned from his family's history. Baker recorded notes from the visit: "He spoke with a becoming pride of his well-known ancestor, 'They tell you now that Gil Ybarvo [this was his preferred pronunciation] didn't have any sense . . . because he built the Old Stone Fort and put his house right there beside it. But Gil Ybarvo was smart; he put his house on one side of the Stone Fort and the church was on the other. If the Indians attacked, he could hurry all his family into the fort at any time; if they attacked while the people were at church, it would take only a minute to get from the church to the fort.'"[49]

Charlotte Baker Montgomery had made two ink drawings intended to accompany either her mother's new novel or the Texas centennial articles in the *Southwest Review.* In both, Nacogdoches is referred to as "A Paradise of Shepherds," and one of Charlotte's drawings has this title. The other drawing portrays a dance scene similar to those described in *Star of the Wilderness.*[50] Quite likely, Baker requested these sketches from Charlotte because she wanted her publishers to use Charlotte's illustrations to accompany her writings. Plotting her stories on graphs and charts and using Charlotte's drawings enriched Baker's creative process.

As Baker researched the historical period for *Star of the Wilderness,* she became very interested in the social customs of the day. By studying histories of the time, she learned particulars of the frontier culture to incorporate into her story. In her notes, Baker cites from Wortham's history of Texas about social life in the colonies: "All visiting is done on horseback, and they will go fifty miles to a ball, with their silk dresses, made perhaps in Phil. or N. O. in their saddlebags. Sunday was a day of visiting, and to ride five or ten miles on horseback, take dinner and spend the day with families, was the custom."[51] Such frontier "balls" are mentioned more than once in the novel. In one instance, Madame Bardeen offers dancing lessons to the heroine, Jessie McAlpine. When Jessie asks why such lessons are necessary, Madame Bardeen's reply reveals a philosophy that citizens of the little frontier village of Nacogdoches share about the importance of maintaining some form of civilization: "Because you'll need it. Because, out here on the edges of the world, we cherish everything that keeps us civilized. The best people here, as you see for yourself, are used to good society. We take great pains to keep things going, so that our children won't grow up barbarians—and so that we won't lapse into barbarism ourselves, for that matter."[52]

Even though Baker clearly conducted most of her research using traditional methods, the most fascinating aspect of her creative process in writing *Star of the Wilderness* came from an unconventional method: her use of ESP and her reliance on voices from the spirit world to advise and direct her writing. For a writer to seek a muse is not unusual; since the days of Homer, writers have sought such inspiration. In modern times, however, the search for a muse was sometimes interpreted as extrasensory perception, a psychic phenomenon. Baker's interest in psychic phenomena began early in her writing career and continued until her death. The "spirits" of William Vaughn Moody (her mentor at the University of Chicago), her mother, and the historical figure James Grant became major players in her search for psychic awareness. Since 1920, "automatic writing" had been her method of reaching the world beyond. She had described in her journal her first encounter with automatic writing, how within a few minutes of beginning the experi-

Pen and ink drawing by Charlotte Baker, ca. 1935. Intended for use with Karle Wilson Baker's article, "Nacogdoches: The Gateway of the Pioneers," that appeared in the January 1936 issue of the Southwest Review. *The* Review *did not use the drawing. The drawing is also representative of a scene in Karle Wilson Baker's novel* The Star of the Wilderness, *in which the author describes a typical ball in Nacogdoches in the 1830s. (Private Collection, Baker Estate)*

ment, she had a curious sense of life in her right hand and arm—a sensation like a light charge of electricity: "In a very short time, I should say within ten minutes, the faint movements which resulted in the vague, wavy lines moving up toward the top of the paper. . . . At this time there was no sense of an identifiable individual presence: only of some strange force, unmistakable, supernormal as far as my own perception could tell, focussed at the point of the pencil. It was almost overwhelming, and my heart pounded almost unbearably in my breast. . . . The sensation was exactly as though some force were trying to learn to use my hand to form letters."[53] Baker stressed that she felt not the presence of a person but a "force," even though the word "Mother" appeared on the page: "The directing force seemed *inside* the hand and arm, instead of outside. . . . From the time the first word was written—the first "Mother"—I began to be troubled by the fact of foreseeing—or guessing—the rest of the word . . . even so, I am scrupulously careful to let the force applied to the pencil finish the word slowly."[54] She wrote that she would show this experiment to her brother, Ben T. Wilson; she felt he would agree that the resemblance to their mother's handwriting was "very remarkable." During all of her experiments with ESP, Baker insisted that intellectual curiosity took precedence over any desire to have a simple act of communication with relatives who had died. However, she felt that if she did make contact, it would be through her dead mother.[55] Her son, Thomas W. Baker (Tomby), firmly believed that his mother had psychic powers and related several examples. In particular, and timely to her journal entry of 1920, he told of an incident when his mother was out of town, and he fell and almost broke his nose. He remembered that she called that very night to ask, unforewarned, about his nose. He was ten years old at the time of this first manifestation of what he felt were his mother's psychic powers. Another example occurred when Tomby and his friends Stephen and Henry Tucker went as boys to fish at the juncture of the Angelina and Attoyac Rivers. He said that he became sick while there, and his mother knew he was ill through ESP and made her husband drive her there by car to get him, even though the roads were not easily accessible.[56] Baker's diary includes a note written during World War II that details how she asked her psychic connections about her son's military service and whether he would suffer much from the war.[57]

Almost twenty years after writing Moody's biography, "William Vaughn Moody: An Informal Study," which she never published, Baker again found herself using automatic writing to connect with voices she believed were speaking to her from the afterlife. As earlier, the primary speakers/writers were her mother and William Vaughn Moody. This time, they acted as agents for her to communicate with James Grant. By March 1941, Grant's shade became her chief adviser on the revisions for *Star of the Wilderness.* Genealogical research into her own family had led her to historical information about Grant, but Grant's character assumed a "life of its own" even after the novel was completed by directing her revisions as perceived through his "spirit's" instructions. In her psychic communications, Baker asked general questions regarding the novel and specific questions about Grant in particular. Needing to fill in parts of the novel with clearer descriptions, she asked Grant to describe himself as he looked in the 1830s. She claimed that the spirit's response differed from the description she had already given of Grant in the novel; the spirit told her to leave much that she had done as it was but to "change the few things that we shall give you. . . . Calmly work and wait in great anticipation and faith. You are to win a great success with our help. Your good friends and fellow-workers are delighted with the progress." The letter, "dictated" by the spirit, is signed both *Mother* and *James Grant.*[58]

Baker continued to rely on cowriters from the spirit world for revisions to *Star of the Wilderness,* making changes and adding information as they instructed. In one encounter, Baker said that Grant suggested that she look to World War II, then in progress, to help her understand the Mexican War in her novel:

> The difference between your interpretation and what I want to get to you is in emotional verve and singleheartedness. . . . I was swept on by a sort of blind passion for liberty and an ambition to be a beneficent force in Mexican affairs. I was not ambitious to play a great role except as a means to an end—that of expulsion of tyranny. You write in cold blood . . . after the fact. I was *in* it—a burning part of it. Imagine yourself in the very thick of this war against Hitler and his wolf-pack. We felt like that. . . . Think about that fact. It will ripen your mind, and give you the excitement you need to get into your picture. Do not be discouraged—we will help.[59]

Such communications made Baker feel that her historical novel actually had a "timeliness" about it.[60] Reassured by the advice from the automatic writings, she asked Grant about her contract with the publishers, Coward-McCann, who had not quite committed to the project; he advised that all was well and would soon be completed. Convinced of the role Grant played in settling the contract, she wrote in her journal, "Dear Dr. Grant, I thank you and all our helpers from the bottom of my heart. At last the 'connection' seems to have been made for me, for Mr. Coward's letter is dated 'March 26' the day on which you told me he would write 'almost at once.'"[61] Another journal entry in April 1941 indicates that Baker was still seeking descriptive advice from the spirit world: "I wish I could get some sort of mental picture—some sort of clear visualization . . . of Dr. Grant." Baker noted Grant's response: "It will come sometime unexpectedly. Try to be prepared at all times." According to Baker's notes, Grant suggested that they stay in contact even after the completion of the novel.[62] By this time, Baker thought of her spiritual contact with Grant as a natural, common occurrence. The next time they communicated, Grant told her that their psychic connection would provide her with new creative powers: "We are doing something that has a new slant on the question of inspiration for the writer. We do not claim credit for ourselves, but for you. We want to show you what you are capable of. . . . When you have finished this book you will be ready to start on a new course of action."[63] Shortly after that experience, Baker felt that the spirit of Grant came to reassure her while she was in New York at the Gramercy Park Hotel working on revisions of *Star of the Wilderness:* "You can go ahead with your revisions. The suggestions and help you will need from us will reach you in time. You will grow clearer about it all as you proceed."[64] Again, Baker asked Grant for even more details to use in her characterization of him. "Give me something about Dr. Grant—appearance, traits, anything characteristic, no matter how small." Two days later she felt Grant's presence and asked about a picture in her hotel room. "Is the picture on my wall like Dr. Grant? It has the handsome features, the refinement and charm, but lacks the force, dash and fire I would expect."[65] The hotel picture was a copy of a Holbein drawing. When Baker revised the novel, she added a reference to the Holbein portrait: "He was a 'black Scot,' with the stature and hardihood of the Highlander, offset at first glance by his slenderness. Something in his bearing, or his meditative gray eye, suggested a gallant in a Holbein drawing—some friend of Erasmus or Sir Thomas More, who could indite a sonnet with one hand and wield a rapier with the other."[66]

At this time, Baker perceived that Grant's spirit suggested she contact his great niece, Mrs. Wallace McPherson, who lived in New Orleans. It suggested that to understand Grant's personality better, Baker must go and see the many family relics in the house. The communicant also directed her toward Hugh Grant, Dr. James Grant's brother, in her genealogical search.[67] In May 1941, Baker spoke to the spirit world once again about her revisions: "I've got to the point now, with the book, where I need more light. Can you help me, Dr. Grant?" A response came: "Yes, indeed. Listen at the doors of your heart and mind. We are always bringing you our gifts. . . . See me in the very flesh that rides across the wilderness. . . . When you fully feel the living ardor, you will strike your stride."[68] Grant's spirit continued to encourage her: "The book will succeed—never doubt it. We see its happy future." Baker asked, "Are the changes I have made sufficient? Do they satisfy Dr. Grant?—or is there still more to be done?" The response came: "The work is substantially done. . . . The picture at the hotel in New York was the crux of it. . . . You are growing in power and insight." It was signed *James Grant.*[69]

Baker's notebooks in the Baker private collection are filled with experiments in psychic phenomena devoted to directing the subconscious mind. Still, the creative process that produced *Star of the Wilderness* was a combination of forces: traditional research, the use of innovative graphics and visual aids, and experimentation in the world of psychic phenomena. Such diverse methods are indicative of Baker's complex personality and talent. Though the reader may wonder whether Baker was completely out of touch with reality while revising *Star of the Wilderness,* a study of her papers proves quite the opposite. On letterhead stationery from the Gramercy Park Hotel in New York, she prepared copious notes for her typist back in Nacogdoches, Sugene Spears, noting specific revisions not found in her "Psychic Notes on Automatic Writing" that she intended to make in the novel. Ultimately her psychic fascination centered on James Grant and apparently helped her create his character more effectively. Upon completion of the first draft, the competent Spears wrote to Baker, "I found Jamie's story so enchanting that it wasn't work at all."[70] In the very last stages of proofing the book, Baker turned to her trusted family for help. Charlotte undoubtedly had seen a final copy already, but a handwritten note from Baker's papers indicates she wanted her husband and son to offer advice:

> To Father and Tomby
> Dear Advisors:
> This peculiar format is due to the fact that this is the final copy, that goes to Mr. Coward; so be as careful with it as you can, in handling. Also to reasons of convenience in any further re-arrangement or revision. When it is finally sent, the paper-clips and protecting yellow sheets will be removed, and the pages numbered, straight through.
> Thank you!
> Munny[71]

On August 10, 1941, Baker left from Nacogdoches for Mexico City; "A Letter from Jamie" was with the editors at Coward-McCann. On August 15, she met Charlotte and their friend Elizabeth Tucker in Guadalajara. Baker's adventuresome temperament led her and Charlotte to hire a taxi to take them to Chapala, Guanajuato, and Queretaro. The antiquated Mexican taxi ran out of gas before they returned to Guadalajara, which merely heightened the experience for them. According to Charlotte Montgomery, the travelers were back in Nacogdoches by September 1.[72]

In November, Thomas Coward sent Baker a telegram asking her to suggest alternative titles for "A Letter From Jamie." He wrote, "Present title commercially impossible." Baker replied with a list of ten suggested titles; the first on her list was "Star of the Wilderness." She wrote to Coward at the end of the month, "Here is the description for the catalogue. . . . I'm curious to know how the search for a title progresses. Here's another candidate—a rather wild-eyed and comet-haired one: *The Spur in the Sky.* The symbolism may not be obvious: perhaps spurs are not star-shaped except in Mexico and Texas? Or perhaps that doesn't matter, if it's pictorial and attractive? Or perhaps it's too much like "Pie in the sky"!!![73] Baker wrote on the author information sheet submitted to Coward-McCann, "The writing of *Jamie,* and the uncounted re-writings, took two years and a half. After that came the cutting—which meant still another re-writing, even more harrowing."[74]

In February 1942, anticipating the public success of *Star of the Wilderness,* Coward wrote to Baker asking her to make time for autographing parties at stores in Dallas and Fort Worth in April.[75] Coward-McCann arranged book sales and signings in Dallas at the Cokesbury Bookstore, the Baptist Bookstore, Sanger's, McMurray's, and the Baker Hotel Bookshop. In Fort Worth, the publisher arranged signings at The Fair, W. C. Stripling Co., and Monning's.[76] Cokesbury produced a circular advertising the book:

> . . . Karle Wilson Baker has done more than re-create a vivid era—she has told the story of a family facing and participating in frontier life. . . . The main part of this fine story takes place in the Redlands and is crammed with superb descriptions of fighting at the Alamo, and of the Americans, Scots, Mexicans, Spaniards, Germans, who gave their lives that Texas might be. . . . It is a novel you will not soon forget, a masterpiece of detail woven together to capture the fire that burned in the hearts of Texans as their great State was born.[77]

Star of the Wilderness came out on April 20, 1942. A week before the publication date, Baker expressed apprehension about the book's potential reception in a letter to George B. Dealey, editor of the *Dallas News:*

> I had planned to write you, before this, about my new book, which will come out on April 20. It is a novel of Texas in the 1830's, with the action centered at Nacogdoches as it was in those days. I haven't been sitting at my desk writing it for forty years, but I have been getting ready to write it almost that long! That's a terrible fact for one mere book to have to measure itself against, even though it's a fairly long book. But at least you'll understand that I'm quite fond of it, and happy that it's out: in spite of the qualms and the dreadfully vulnerable feeling that the first days of publication always bring. In the case of an historical novel, in a state practically populated by historians, that inescapable feeling is particularly acute.[78]

Almost six years after the publication of *Star of the Wilderness,* on New Year's Eve 1948, Karle Wilson Baker returned to the spirit world and recorded a "vision" (rather than the usual automatic writing) from Grant. In the intervening six years, her interest in psychic phenomena had evolved beyond automatic writing. For the remainder of her life, she pursued an interest in psychical research and viewed her experiments as contributing to that research. She wrote in her journal in 1954:

> My aim is general psychic experience, but the visions are the only type of it I am specifying. . . . I took up a new book about directing one's life by impressing one's aim and desires upon the subconscious mind. . . . I speak of it here because of its present connection with a new phase it has precipitated in my study of parapsychology, and the question of deliberately attempting to increase my own very modest endowment of psychic sensitiveness, and rapport with the psychic world. . . . At the same time that I am feeding my own longings, I shall be contributing, no matter how slightly, to the central problem of modern psychical research: how to produce a thing consciously, which is now only unconsciously produced.[79]

Baker was seventy-six when she wrote this journal entry. When the Philosophical Society of Texas held its meeting in Nacogdoches the next year, Baker expressed her desire to the program chairman, Jesse Andrews, that they invite Dr. Rhine of Duke University to speak on extrasensory perception. But she quickly modified her suggestion: "However, I'll admit that a peaceful little town nestling in the heart of the 'Garden-spot of the Universe' (quoted from the Founding Fathers), is not the place to plant quite such a bomb! It's just a general suggestion. Perhaps, sometime, Houston might take it on!"[80]

After the publication of *Star of the Wilderness*, Baker spoke to many different organizations. She prepared a script for such occasions that she called "The Story of The Story," which explained that the narrative that finally emerged to form the novel grew from three main sources. First, she pointed out that she had based some of the characters on family members from generations ago as she recalled them from stories her grandmother had told her. She was especially influenced by the personality of her grandfather, John Montgomery, who had been something of a rake like Paul McAlpine. Secondly, she acknowledged that the town and surroundings of Nacogdoches and her interest in Sam Houston and the Texas Revolution had inspired her to pursue historical research. She had started with the idea of combining the theme of a fictional family with historic facts about Houston. However, she soon realized that she was more intrigued with the dashing figure of Dr. James Grant, who became the central figure in the novel even though he was less well known historically. The third influence on the development of the novel came from work she had prepared for the articles for the *Southwest Review* in 1936.[81]

At public readings, she also discussed how the editors had insisted that the book was too long and how she had had to reduce it by one-fourth, leaving out interesting sections on San Augustine and the Battle of Nacogdoches. A folder among the Baker papers contains loose bits and pieces of notes Baker wrote to herself when she was reducing the size of the novel. One instruction reads, "Take a 'large tuck' in trip to Texas/in Battle of Nacogdoches."[82] Baker felt that reducing the manuscript added a timelessness to the material and noted another benefit of cutting the length of the novel: "The other consolation is that the enforced cutting has provided me with the perfect alibi. If somebody misses something that ought to be there, I can say, 'Oh, I had that in the first version, but I was obliged to leave it out.'"[83] One omitted part, "Epilogue: A Letter from the Redlands," is about Texas joining the Union.[84] The epilogue suggests that Baker was leaving the door open for a sequel. Emphasizing her role as novelist rather than historian, Baker often concluded her speech: "After all, my aim was to write, not a history, but a story of life in Texas in the 1830's. Both the novelist and the historian must deal conscientiously with their material; but the rules by which they are bound are not quite the same. So you mustn't look for all my landmarks and old houses, all my race-tracks and twin-chimneys. Some of them exist only in that world where memory and imagination meet and where everything interesting and delightful in the vanished Past is gathered and treasured up."[85]

In addition to invitations to speak about *Star of the Wilderness*, Baker received letters from people who intended to review the novel for their study clubs. She often responded to such letters with a pamphlet she had prepared about her publications, and sometimes she enclosed a booklet on the history of Nacogdoches. One such request came from Pauline Burke of the Washington Club in Washington, D.C., in February 1943. Baker's lengthy reply to Burke offers an explanation of the novel and reveals insights about Baker, her pride in both Charlotte's and Tomby's achievements, and her generosity and graciousness in sharing information with others:

> I am greatly pleased to have your letter telling of your plan to review *Star of the Wilderness.* I am mailing you today a booklet that may perhaps be useful in filling in the background of the book. The Old Stone Fort shown in the illustration is of course the "Old Stone House," as the early settlers called it, which played such an important part in the doings of those days.
>
> Some of the drawings are the early work of my daughter, Charlotte, who has since published three books of her own, under her maiden name, Charlotte Baker. Two of them were adventure-mystery novels, published by Dutton's and the other a Mexican story for young people, published in 1942 by Crowell's.
>
> As you will see from the enclosed slip giving biographical data, I am not a native Texan, though two of my uncles were engaged in Texas ranching in its hey day. I came to Nacogdoches in my early twenties, straight from college, and this has been my home ever since, though of course I haven't been here all the time. At that time it was a quaint, unique little town, such as you might expect from *Star of the Wilderness,* and in spite of its gradual growth through the years, it still keeps something of its early character. I was fascinated from the first by its history, which has been a study and a favorite diversion from that day to this. In writing about it, I find myself going steadily backward into the past, instead of forward. I am now hard at work on a novel [*It Blows from the Spanish Country*] about one of the so-called "Filibustering Expeditions," the one of 1812–13, which used Nacogdoches as its base. When I have finished that, I want to do one about the life of the picturesque old Spanish "patron" who founded the town and built the Old Stone House, Antonio Gil Y Barbo.
>
> So, you see, in a sense I've been writing *Star of the Wilderness* ever since I came to live in Texas, and was told by the old-timers how "Old

Sam" used to sit on a whiskey-keg in the Old Stone Fort and declaim Pope's "Iliad" for hours on end. . . .

The little family who form the nucleus of the story started from my own grandmother's memories. Her pioneering adventures did not happen in Texas; but the Scottish background was hers, and it gave me my life-long interest in everything Scottish. She must have been much like Jessie—and I'm afraid my grandfather must have been a good deal like Paul! The two children started from my mother's stories of herself and the young brother who died before I was born, but who left me my masculine name. In the end they turned out to be nobody but themselves—Jessie particularly, who is as real to me as anybody I know, and as distinctly individual. This is the way most novelists work, I think.

. . . I shall feel honored to have my book presented before the club, and shall be glad to have any further help I can. It is to be reviewed in Houston in April, too, and I am going down. My son is there now, a flying instructor to the Women's Ferry Command. My daughter is now in Indianapolis; her husband is a captain in the 365th Infantry, stationed at Camp Attenbury. I have two *only* children, you see, and have to talk about them a bit. . . .[86]

Charlotte Baker Montgomery was in New York when *Star of the Wilderness* came out. She had just published her third children's book. Baker wrote to Charlotte asking her to get a copy of *Star* to Wendell Wilkie:

Belovedest,

You may think I'm "goofy" on this subject, but I'm decidedly moved to do what I've been dallying with so long, and get a copy of the *Star* to Mr. Wilkie. I don't know how you can get the address, but there are ways to do it in New York and will you find one for me? I am having a copy sent to him by Coward-McCann. My urgency is that he will be leaving in a week or two for the Middle East. . . . With a heart full of love, and well-wishings,

Marmer[87]

Personal friends and critics alike warmly praised the new novel. George B. Dealey, the editor of the *Dallas News*, wrote to Baker after he finished reading the book, "I take off my hat to you, Mrs. Baker, in admiration for the fine job you performed. You must have worked at it a long time and worked hard. I am sure you have received many, many complimentary letters and reviews.

I want to add my mite to all of them."[88] Floy Lewis, Baker's niece, who had traveled with the family in Mexico in 1936, wrote an especially enthusiastic letter:

> Dear Tia,
>
> I think you are perfectly wonderful to write *Star of the Wilderness!* It covers such a sweep of territory and so many threads of history. You must have done a great deal of study and research. Of course, I was thrilled to read so much about (and learn so much about) Nacogdoches. . . . The citizens of Nacogdoches must want to cover you with glory for putting its history into a real work of literature. . . . I loved the Mexico references. Remember that night we stood on the heights of Chapultapec, Tia, and looked down on the city in the moonlight? Did you have this book in mind when we were there?
>
> . . . I thought Jessie was very lovely, possessing a beautiful spirit. She reminded me of you in her tower with her books of poetry. . . .
>
> Lots and lots of love,
>
> Floy[89]

A fellow novelist and member of the Texas Institute of Letters, Laura Krey, wrote to Baker from St. Paul, Minnesota, "I have just had the pleasure of writing the editor of the S. W. Review's issue dealing with Texas literature that I do not know any better novel than yours on the Republic."[90] The noted Texas historian Eugene C. Barker wrote, ". . . I read it with real pleasure. . . . I think you have given us a real contribution in your picture of men, women, manners and conditions. This seems so little to say in particularization of a book that I thoroughly like. It deserves many readers, and I hope that they will all like it as well as I do."[91] Herbert P. Gambrell, another Texas historian and fellow member of the Philosophical Society, wrote from Dallas, ". . . I think it is superb—easily the best historical fiction on Texas I have ever read. And how beautifully it proves that an author does not need to distort the record to write a story! The real truth is that whenever I read a book like this, I am convinced that it is people like you who make history worthwhile, and not the professional historians."[92] One of Baker's most treasured letters about the new novel came from her daughter, Charlotte, who wrote, "I received the book yesterday and it looks most impressive—I am not swept off my feet by the jacket . . . but it does give an agreeable impression and should show up well in a display. I think we can be relieved. The book itself is quite good looking. . . . I have lent my copy to Miss Alexander. Everyone is anxious to see it."[93]

Barker made his favorable impression public in his review for the *Southwestern Historical Quarterly* in July 1942: "If all that Mrs. Baker tells us about Grant is true, she has a more intimate and extensive knowledge of the historical character than has ever appeared in history. Mrs. Baker has saturated herself in the atmosphere of her period. She lives intimately with her characters and enables her readers to live with them. She has long been known as a writer of graceful poetry; her prose is equally smooth and pleasing. The book is certainly good history, not too much idealized; I think it is also good literature."

Sam Acheson, who reviewed *Star of the Wilderness* for the *Saturday Review of Literature*'s May 16, 1942, edition also praised Baker's skill:

> . . . In the concluding part of the book Mrs. Baker achieves a most difficult feat, the satisfactory integration of real battles and campaigns in the larger framework of her romance. The more familiar and therefore somewhat stereotyped events of the fall of the Alamo and the Battle of San Jacinto are brought in only by indirection. Instead, the novelist places in sharp new focus such turning points as the capture of San Antonio by the Texans late in 1835, the wiping out of the Texan outpost at Refugio, the panic-stricken flight of the colonists after the fall of the Alamo, and the massacre at Goliad.
>
> Mrs. Baker does belated historical justice to Dr. James Grant, the misunderstood Scot whose connection with both Coahuila and Texas long caused him to be suspect in the eyes of the Texas revolutionists. . . . This is the best fictional account of the Texas revolution that has yet appeared.

Vann, Baker's longtime associate, reviewed the novel for the *Houston Post's* May 10, 1942, edition: "Like Mrs. Baker's other volumes, this is the work of a conscious artist. Into it has gone much of her best talent. And the accurate and detailed background, sympathetic portrayal of character, and beauty and finish of style make it the best novel on Texas history yet written."

The novel also garnered a notice in the *New York Times Book Review* on April 26, 1942. Reviewer Louise M. Field described the novel as "very entertaining" and continued, "The novel is rich in contrasts, moving as it does from such scenes as that of the farewell ball in the big house at Nacogdoches to the ambush at Agua Dulce. The novel is very long, but it has a good deal of ground to cover and its characters are interesting."[94]

Karle Wilson Baker realized the achievement of bringing two important novels about East Texas before a national audience. Few other writers in the state attained the recognition she did for herself and for Texas. General enthusiasm over the new book resulted in letters from magazine publishers and literary agents soliciting Baker's work.[95] The path that lay ahead was filled with opportunity. With the publications of *Family Style* and *Star of the Wilderness,* Baker finally fulfilled her writing goal: "I always expected to write novels."[96]

"I discovered that I liked appealing directly to people—who were almost overwhelmingly responsive."

CHAPTER 6
Full Circle

After the publication of *Star of the Wilderness,* Karle Wilson Baker wrote a note to herself about an interesting find she had made among some old records. She titled it "One Piece Dove-Colour'd Velvet":

> I ran across that item yesterday in an old inventory of a Texas trading-post, made out nearly a hundred and fifty years ago, "One Piece Dove-Colour'd Velvet, $35.00." It was dropped in casually among entries of hatchets, deer-hides, pecans and ten-penny nails. A piece of dove-colored velvet in Mexican Texas, where travellers were frequently offered nothing to eat except dried venison dipped in honey, and were expected to cut it (if at all) with their Bowie knives! *Star of the Wilderness* was already written and published, but while I was writing it, and before, I had pored over many old records like this one.[1]

Baker knew that at some point the writer must draw a final line, plan a final period, and end a work, but the researcher always finds one more piece of information to add, one piece that he finds, perhaps regrettably, too late. Discovering new material might have been the driving force that pushed Baker to write yet another novel at the age of sixty-four. She briefly described that work in a letter to a reviewer at the Cokesbury Bookstore: "It Blows from the Spanish Country. Novel of the Magee-Gutierrez period in Texas. Scene from Philadelphia to 'Bexar.' Action takes place in Natchez, New Orleans, Natchitoches, Nacogdoches, Goliad and S. A. [San Antonio]."[2] Once again the tireless writer-researcher was off on another adventure. In creating the historical novel, "It Blows from the Spanish Country" (originally titled "High Winds on the King's Highway"), Baker applied the same rigorous methods of research she had used for *Family Style* and *Star of the Wilderness.*[3] The novel focuses on the historic Magee-Gutierrez expedition in Texas in 1812. When Baker began her research for the novel in June 1942, librarians at Stephen F. Austin State Teachers College directed her to a new resource person, Sister Agatha at the Incarnate Word Academy in Houston. Sister Agatha had completed a study of four Texas novels, including one celebrated as the first Texas novel in English, Timothy Flint's *Frances Berrian,* published in 1826.[4]

When Baker and her husband drove to Houston on a fact-finding trip, Sister Agatha was away from the academy, but by July, Baker had made contact with the nun and entered into a correspondence that developed into a long friendship. In her first letter, Baker explained that war shortages prevented her from getting to Houston very often. She said that her novel was about the Magee-Gutierrez expedition "when Don Samuel Davenport was the great man of Nacogdoches." In addition, Baker wrote that she had seen a copy of Flint's book only briefly when she visited Melrose Plantation, the home of Cammie Henry near Natchitoches, Louisiana, and had been trying to purchase her own copy. Baker added that she would be interested in purchasing a copy of Sister Agatha's thesis, "Four Texas Novels." "I look forward to seeing the Texas Collection at the Convent, and especially of talking to someone who knows the field of Texana as you do. . . . ," Baker wrote. "Indeed I shall come back at the earliest opportunity; and in the meantime I shall probably be appealing to you by letter on some of the tantalizing points that are always arising."[5] Sister Agatha proved to be a wonderful resource and sent Baker a copy of "Four Texas Novels," which had the added bonus of illustrations. When Baker discovered that the nun had an interest in old pictures, she asked her for additional help:

> Also, while you were working on Francis Berrian, did you run across any notable ones [pictures] anywhere of the actors in the Magee-Gutierrez expedition? My friend Mrs. Lois F. Blount, curator of the Stone Fort Museum on the college campus, has just lately run down and borrowed a whole set of pictures of the Davenport-Durst families. There are copies of two beautiful oil portraits of Don Samuel Davenport, an enchanting daguerreotype of his son, (Juan Bernardo Benigno Davenport) and a splendid characterful one of Harriet Jamieson Durst,

> the original of Madame Bardeen in *Star of the Wilderness.* I'd never seen a picture of her—and how delighted I was to find that she looked as she should. Now I particularly want to see likenesses of Magee, Gutierrez, Toledo, Herrero, Condero, the two Salcedos—or anybody else of the exact period, for that matter.[6]

Sister Agatha replied that she knew of few pictures from the period and that those she had seen were oil paintings, but she offered to help anyway. She volunteered to contact the Houston Public Library and recommended that Baker contact Carlos Castaneda, who specialized in Mexico-Texas history at the University of Texas; Marcelle Hamer, the librarian of Texana at the University of Texas; and a source that she felt would be the most helpful of all, her friend Adina de Zavala in San Antonio, who might have family pictures of the period. She also advised Baker to write the Texas State Library in Austin or the public library in San Antonio since they were depositories for Flint's book.[7] Baker wrote back thanking her and praising Sister Agatha's scholarly work: "I can't tell you how interesting and how useful I have found it. Even an amateur historian, like me, can see what a thorough and excellent piece of work it is; and the writer in me appreciates equally the clarity with which it is presented, and the skill that makes it scholarly without being pedantic."[8]

In addition to Sister Agatha's suggestions, Baker pursued her usual method of compiling an extensive bibliography. She accessed many sources from the Rare Book Room at the Stephen F. Austin library: the Lamar Papers, Chabot's *Texas in 1811* (where she found a letter from Ignacio Elisondo to Bernardo Gutierrez), and the *Quarterly of the Texas State Historical Association,* which contained many useful articles. In the *American Historical Review,* she found a translation of Jose Bernardo Gutierrez de Lara's diary that had been taken from the original diary in the Texas State Library. Also in the Nacogdoches archives she found a letter from Joseph de Tovar to Salcedo. She listed in the bibliography Carlos Castaneda's *The Six Flags of Texas,* Louis Wortham's text *The History of Texas,* and D. B. Edwards's book published in 1835 about Colonel Jose de las Piedras. Many more notes of bibliography are filed in the Karle Wilson Baker Papers.[9] Baker wrote some of her bibliographical notes on stationery from the Hotel Nakatosa in Natchitoches, where she stayed when she used the library there. She also received valuable assistance from Lois Foster Blount, her good friend and the curator at the Stone Fort Museum, to whom she dedicated the novel.[10]

In August 1944, Baker informed the editors at Coward-McCann of her next novel, and they encouraged her to send it to them upon its completion. But three years later, when she sent the manuscript to Thomas Coward, he replied that the market was flooded with historical novels and that they could not publish this one. In addition, he criticized the manuscript: "Your story has no sensational love interest, and what there is, in my opinion, is too slow. While you present a good picture of a little known phase in American history, the material does not seem to me exciting enough for the historical novel fan."[11] After Baker made revisions, Charlotte took up the cause in 1948 from her home in Portland, Oregon, submitting the manuscript to Farrar, Straus, and Company in New York. The editors there also felt that the book was too long and needed too much editorial revision for them to publish it.[12] In June 1949, Charlotte sent the manuscript to Little, Brown and Company in Boston, but the editors there did not make a publishing offer.[13] That year Charlotte appealed to the *Southwest Review* to see if they might serialize "It Blows from the Spanish Country," but the reviewing committee, though impressed with the book, turned it down:

> . . . Mrs. Baker has made excellent use of her material, and shows a historian's respect for chronological accuracy, so often lacking in historical fiction. The plot is interesting and well developed, and the action swift. As a matter of fact it is these very qualities that militate against our using a chapter from it as a story in the *Review.* The story is so well integrated, with the plot moving forward with each chapter, that it was impossible to find any part which would stand alone in separate publication.[14]

Charlotte sent "It Blows from the Spanish Country" to at least ten more publishers, but her efforts were unsuccessful.[15] In April 1952, after further revising the manuscript, Baker sent it to Jacques Chambrun, a literary agent in New York. By September, after trying three different publishers and failing to place the manuscript, he returned it to Baker. The major criticism had been that it was too long and rambling.[16] "It Blows from the Spanish Country" was never published.

During her years as a developing novelist, Baker had remained faithful to the Poetry Society of Texas, serving as its vice president for many years, and in 1942, had been made a lifetime member.[17] Baker had continued her involvement in a number of organizations, including the Southern Organization of Women of the National Democratic Organization in New York. When Winifred Kittredge, president of the organization, wrote to Baker in

December 1942 that the group would not have its annual luncheon in New York that year because of the war, she added that Baker would have been the chosen speaker.[18]

Over the course of her career, Baker overcame the discomfort she had felt as a young writer when she spoke in public. Because she was frequently asked for advice about writing and for an explanation of her success as a writer, Baker prepared a speech titled, "If You Want To Write." She had written in her diary, "I discovered that I liked appealing directly to people—who were almost overwhelmingly responsive."[19] Baker's words inspired countless aspiring writers in the years that followed her successful career as a novelist. She counseled the would-be author: "To be a writer is to sustain a state of mind—and *that* is the most complex and difficult thing in the world." Addressing the "business" of writing, she advised: "Wordsworth did not write his poems for money; he *published* them for money. . . . No writer worth the name writes *primarily* for money." She offered a test to the young writer to ascertain if he really wanted to pursue writing: "What would you do if you should inherit a million dollars? Would you hail it as a dispensation of Providence that set you free to write, or would you thank Heaven that you need never try to write again?" She added, "The people who are tormented with a desire to write and yet are actually devoid of all talent, have simply failed to analyze themselves correctly: have misinterpreted their own desires."[20]

Defining discouragement as the "mortal enemy" of the writer, she emphasized the importance and necessity of "staying power" because of the many obstacles the artist must overcome: "Persistence is eternally preached, from every side, to the aspiring writer; but I know from experience that what such writers need is not to be convinced that persistence is necessary, but to be shown where to find the courage that will make it possible for them to persist."[21] Baker's own "Manuscript Record Books" are a testimony to courage, especially during the early years when she sent poems, short stories, and essays alike to magazine publishers. At times she had to try seven or eight publishers before she found one to accept her work. Later, as a mature, professional writer, if she experienced a rejected manuscript, it usually was because her work did not meet the needs of the publishing house.[22] She was always convinced that a publisher was out there for her work; she just had to connect with the right one. She often wrote encouraging remarks such as "pleasant rejection" or "encouraging note" beside the entry of a returned work.[23]

She offered sound advice when she encouraged young writers to find a mentor like the one she had known in William Vaughn Moody: "Find a friend among those who have travelled the way before you, to companion you and help you to speak your own mind to yourself; and let him be of as great a power and prestige as you can manage, in order that he may help you to develop in yourself a taste for what is fine, to make you exacting in your demands upon yourself, and, finally, to keep you as much as possible in the great main stream of literature, and out of the contemporary eddies." When she offered advice to the writer who lived away from New York City, the Mecca of the art world, she was also thinking of herself:

> What about the ambitious writer who longs to go to New York but is "tied" in Texas—for instance? Well, I ought to know all about that writer. I could write a book for her benefit. But at this juncture I would only say, Don't think of yourself as "tied." Realize that the stuff of life, which seems so hard and stubborn, is fluid and plastic; and that each of us can, ultimately, be, have, and do whatever we want with all our souls to be, have, and do. Determine to use your present environment to the full, while you have it; know that beauty and power and opportunity are everywhere, just as sky and grass are everywhere, and sunlight and rain. . . . Write of what you, yourself know; and of what you know with your whole self, not merely with your head. No one can tell you what to say but yourself.[24]

Baker may have prepared "If You Want to Write" for the annual Southwest Writer's Conference held in Corpus Christi, Texas, which she attended for ten years, from 1944 to 1954. The conference awarded a Karle Wilson Baker Writing Prize at their literary contest in 1949. She was also a frequent guest at writers' workshops in other places.[25]

Baker wrote a personal and philosophical essay, "Full Circle," in the winter of 1944 at West Windows. In this private document, she describes an epiphany she experienced as a young girl of eight or ten while playing alone in her Grandmother Montgomery's garden at Linden Grange. The lesson she learned that day became her philosophy for art and life; it explains her mysticism: ". . . It was an assurance of the power, lovely and innocent, to be a part of all I could desire or imagine. To be, to do, to realize. The immense beatitude of existence: receive it, claim it, mold it. You can. To what end you will mold it you do not know, now. But remember, when the time comes, you can. Do not forget this moment: the azure sky, the boundless sea of gold. You are it, it is you, and in the burning reality behind it is treasure and your home. Do not forget."[26]

In October 1945, the *Dallas Times Herald* printed a special section in its

October 7 edition that responded to requests from all over the state for a special Texas issue of *Book News*. The *Dallas Times Herald* called it "A Roundup of the Most Interesting Texas Books of all time."[27] The *Herald* staff, along with guest editors from the *Southwest Review*, had compiled the articles for the special issue of *Book News*, which consumed seventeen pages. Baker received significant recognition when five of the editors included her contributions to Texas literature. The novelist Laura Krey wrote that among writers who had written novels set in East Texas during the days of the Republic, the major praise must go to Baker and *Star of the Wilderness*. Another contributor, Ernest E. Leisy of SMU, acclaimed *Star of the Wilderness* as "a novel [that has] the poetry and simplicity of saga literature." David Russell, the poet laureate of Texas at that time, wrote, "Karle Wilson Baker still stands, with her *Dreamers on Horseback*, as perhaps the most lyric voice yet to emerge from the state." Mabel Major cited Baker's *Dreamers on Horseback* in a list of "Fifty Books of Texas That Are Permanently Valuable." Ima H. Herron, a professor of English at SMU, listed Baker among authors from the Southwest that had written the best short stories.[28] The publication in the *Dallas Times Herald* reaffirmed Baker's importance to literature in Texas.

The next year, the University of Texas produced a special radio broadcast, "The Texas Destiny," celebrating the Texas centennial of statehood, which included a reading of Baker's poem "Song of the Forerunners."[29]

Each year, the Roberts Contest of the Sons of the Republic of Texas awarded a prize for the best book of the year on Texas. Herbert Gambrell wrote to Baker in November 1951 that he was sorry that *Star of the Wilderness* and Eugene Barker's *Life of Stephen F. Austin* were contenders in the same year for the prize. The award went to Barker for his work of nonfiction. In his letter, Gambrell praised Baker's book, "I think you have captured better than anyone has in fiction the spirit of the times and the people, and that the work richly merits a very special award."[30] Gratified by his remarks, Baker sent a letter of reply: "I want to tell you that for you to say that *Star of the Wilderness* "really merits a very special award" is an award, to me. And you'll be amused when I add, honestly, that I'm glad that you "put it in writing," so that I can take it out now and then and reassure myself that you really said it."[31]

A more rewarding triumph for Baker came eight years before her death. In 1952, she was named a fellow in the Texas Institute of Letters; it was the most cherished accolade of her life. After J. Frank Dobie and Walter Prescott Webb, she was the third fellow, and only woman, named by the institute. Baker had been one of the founders of the Texas Institute of Letters in 1936 and a charter member.[32] Her old friend, the secretary of the institute William H. Vann, informed her of the selection:

> It gives me a very special satisfaction to inform you that at a meeting of the committee appointed for that purpose, you were unanimously recommended to be named Fellow of the Institute, and this recommendation has been approved by the council. . . . Dr. Sampley [President of the Texas Institute of Letters] agrees with the recommendation of the program committee, that you also be invited to speak. . . . You are aware, of course, that we have only two other fellows—J. Frank Dobie and Walter Prescott Webb. I think your selection will add just the proper balance; and, I might add, in my opinion we need feel no obligation to recommend another any time soon. Let me assure you again, by the way, that we were all most heartily agreed on your nomination; and your presence on the occasion will give pleasure to your many friends.[33]

For her acceptance address, Baker appropriately chose to read two poems to follow a short expression of gratitude. At the awards dinner in Dallas on November 14, 1952, the Texas laureate, accompanied by her husband Tom, received the honor she so richly deserved. She responded in part:

> I want to thank you from my heart for the honor of being made a fellow of the Institute. . . . It was a lonely and innocent thing to be a so-called "Texas writer" when some of us began. The dew was not so heavy upon us in 1936, but we would have gasped at the signs and portents erupting every day upon the Texas Literary Front in 1952. I can see us all in my mind's eye, in those sessions; I wish I could see all the others sitting among you tonight. And I feel sure that the later comers, from the outposts you have won and the heady successes that have put strength into your writing hearts and iron into your literary nerves, will be glad to look back with me for the briefest of moments to pay a debt of memory to those forerunners. For myself, thinking of these things, of old friends present and absent, of the kindness you have shown to me and of the future, I am offering you my final word in a sort of gift package, which you may open at your leisure. Not having much valor, I am giving you the better part of it. With the permission of the Powers-That-Be, I am reading you two brief lyrics—companion pieces in a way.[34]

She then read the poems "Pause of the Year," which had won the Critics prize of the Poetry Society of Texas in 1950, and "High Summer."[35]

PAUSE OF THE YEAR

It grows late early
These wine-bright days
When flowers are leaving
And frost delays.

When I pass by the hedges
Bright clouds rise—
A startled silence
Of butterflies.

Their wings are yellow.
They always are
When winter is nearing
And spring is far.

The sun is careful
These windless days.
The last fruit mellows
In tempered rays.

The birds speak briefly,
When the berries turn red
There is much to be thought of,
Not much to be said.

They are quiet as angels,
These days that wait
While dark comes early
And love burns late.

"High Summer," written only a few months earlier in the summer of 1952, is about her longtime friend the thrush and the free spirit they share.

HIGH SUMMER

Through the thicket down the hill
The bell-bird thrush is singing still.
Surely as summer splendor burned
Has that sky-haunted call returned.

I am old, but he is new,
His span at best a year or two.
Mine—now an inch of ribbon furled—
Seemed sometime stretched to belt a world.

I am weighted, he is free—
As any bodied thing can be—
A song, a wing, small spider-feet
Weightless as dust-tracks in the street.

All too visible am I
Since Time stared at me, passing by.
His but a lyric's shape, agrees,
And leafy tune, high-hung, unseen.

Perhaps I saw, for all I know,
His fledgling sire, a year ago,
Teetering on his slighted nest,
Bright-eyed above his spotted vest,

But that, it seems, was yesterday
And I was free to stroll that way.
Today I keep to firmer ground.
Tomorrow, I'll be terrace-bound.

But after that—ah, we shall see!
No clay molds will straiten me
And I'll be back where I belong.
A wing—a throb of Love—a song.

Becoming a fellow of the Institute was a sober occasion for Baker, but a humorous anecdote comes from the 1952 meeting, which Vann recorded in his *History of The Texas Institute of Letters:*

> In 1952, Dobie won the Collins Award for his *The Mustangs.* Frank wanted to express his thanks in style. Nothing routine, but a real celebration of, as he said in turning to Mr. Collins, "a rich man who knows, unlike most rich men, how to spend his money with benefit to others." Unluckily (or so it seemed at first), Frank was not in possession of some information known to nearly everyone else in the room, namely that Carr P. Collins was a noted tee-totaller and outstanding Baptist layman,

strong supporter of temperance movements, and a large stockholder in a highly successful soft-drink corporation.

"I am going to prove to you, Mr. Collins," said Dobie, "that I too know how to spend my money wisely. Do you know what I'm going to do with this check, Mr. Collins? I'm going to spend half of it laying in a supply of Jack Daniels bourbon, and the other half on Scotch. I have a country place at Cherry Springs. I want you to come to Austin to visit me and we'll drive out to Cherry Springs, build a great wood fire, prop our feet on the mantle and drink toasts to all wise and civilized men, rich or otherwise."

Dobie paused for the pronouncement to be appreciated. He must have sensed an appalled and terrified hush in the audience. All eyes were glued on Mr. Collins. Dobie sensed something that seemed more like anxiety than appreciation. An idea occurred to him.

"I don't know, Mr. Collins, whether you prefer bourbon or Scotch; maybe your choice is rye or brandy. Whatever it is, I'll lay in a supply. By the way, what is your favorite drink, Mr. Collins?"

Mr. Collins rose. The audience sank. Mr. Collins smiled and then burst into a great laugh. He looked at the audience and saw that everybody understood his predicament. He laughed again, then said: "Mr. Dobie, I want to thank you for one of the greatest acceptance speeches I ever heard in my life. But I'm going to let you drink all that whiskey, a thousand dollars' worth of it, by yourself. My favorite drink, Mr. Dobie, is Dr Pepper."[36]

Mabel Major, a professor of English at Texas Christian University in Fort Worth, wrote an article recognizing Baker's accomplishments in the December 28, 1952, edition of the *Dallas Morning News.* The editor of *The Daily Sentinel* in Nacogdoches reprinted the article with a brief introduction:

> As most of our readers know, Nacogdoches is honored to have one of America's most distinguished writers as a citizen. She is Mrs. Thomas E. Baker, 1613 North Street, who writes under the name of Karle Wilson Baker. Mr. Baker, of course, is chairman of the board of the Commercial National Bank and is well-known in Texas banking circles. One of the most interesting reviews the editor has read recently on Baker's accomplishments appeared recently in The Dallas Morning News, being written by Mabel Major of Texas Christian University. The entire article is reprinted herewith in the belief it will be of great interest to Baker's many close admirers in this East Texas area.[37]

Major summarized Baker's career, referring first to her poetry and short stories, then to her essays and novels, but concluded, "Karle Wilson Baker is a versatile writer, who has handled successfully many media, but it is as a lyric poet that she is most distinguished." Major added, "A volume of her collected poems, making available again the out-of-print poems and including recent ones, would be an important literary event for the entire country."[38] She wrote to the editor of Yale University Press in January 1953 and asked that he consider reprinting Baker's collected poems, but he declined.[39] That same year, Baker noted that all of her published books were out of print except *Family Style*.[40] Now, half a century later, Major's wish will be granted when the Center for East Texas Studies at Stephen F. Austin State University reprints selected works of Baker's in a long-awaited collection. As a young woman, Baker had written about herself as a writer: "I can be quite content to be obscure while I am living, but I *must* be recognized after I am dead!"[41]

In May 1953, Baker wrote philosophically in her diary, "I have been concerned with roots and essences; and now, with old age, flowers have come. Flowers, and music, and the mystery and magic of children—of their beauty and inviolable individuality, of their heart-breaking trustfulness."[42] Perhaps she had in mind a tender moment she had shared with her two grandsons, Tom and Jerry (the children of Tom and Jean Baker), the year before:

> Little Duke died during this month. [Little Duke was the family dog.]
>
> Lucy [the maid] went out to call him for his late breakfast (he had lately taken to sleeping until he was called.) He got up, came out of his little house, and started to come to her as she held out her hand.
>
> Then he stopped, lay down, and died.
>
> She came in tears to tell me. "Duke's gone."
>
> I went out, to sit beside him a little, where she had left him, lying on his side, on the grass beside his house.
>
> It was fitting that Lucy should have been with him, I have continued to watch over him, see that he was taken to the doctor when necessary, and so on. But Lucy has given the devoted care, and done what work there was—especially when he needed it after a recent stay in the dog hospital.
>
> John Henry and Lucy buried him in the little "yard" around Strap's house. At the same time he brought up some of the earth from Strap's grave under the pines down the hill where he was buried. He also brought some of the white iris we had planted there and replanted them at the head and foot of both graves.

On the Sunday evening after his death, the boys and I took a little drive before supper. As we were getting out of the car, Tom suddenly said, "Munny, I want to go and tell a prayer to Duke, because I loved him so much. He was such a good little dog, and I want to tell him I'm sorry he had to die."

So he and Jerry went back to the little grave, and I left them to themselves for the while they worked there. Tom made a cardboard headboard, with "Dukey, A Good little Dog" on it. Jerry put at the foot a cardboard cross covered with tinfoil.

Tom is by nature quite reserved, and averse to showing his deeper feelings. But this time he was earnest and unembarrassed, thinking only of what he felt and wanted to express. He is ten now, and Jerry is eight.[43]

Baker continued to receive requests for permission to reprint her poetry. She responded to a petition in 1955 from a publishing house in London, England, asking to print "Let Me Grow Lovely" in an anthology, *The New Silver Lining,* based on a well-known BBC program. She granted permission to use the poem and requested a copy of the anthology when it came out.[44] Also that year, Jesse Andrews of Houston wrote to Baker for advice on program ideas for the Philosophical Society of Texas, which planned to hold its next meeting in Nacogdoches. Baker admitted in her reply that her health was uncertain and that she made few social engagements. She was unsure whether she would be able to attend the meeting, but she was willing to help before the event and behind the scenes. She wrote, "It goes without saying that, as a member of the 1936 group, I am very proud of the Society." She also reflected on what she felt had been the society's best sessions and why they had been successful:

> First, the delightful and enthusiastic ones that gave birth to the rejuvenated Society back in 1936. Then the afternoon program at Liendo Plantation, followed by a dinner in Houston the same evening. Then the wonderful meeting in San Antonio with Maury Maverick. . . . Finally, the resplendent one in the Hall of State, surrounded by priceless historical treasures, with Mr. George Dealey as the leading spirit. What all these had in common was that they were built around something local and tangible that could be interpreted and illuminated.[45]

By these criteria, Nacogdoches was a perfect choice for the site of the next meeting. Baker wrote another letter to Andrews on November 2, 1955, recommending a replacement for herself as a program presenter: "My husband

and I thought it might fill out the afternoon program acceptably to ask Lois Foster Blount to make the short talk on East Texas Lore that you suggested for me. . . . Lois (Mrs. Guy Blount) is a member of the history faculty at the college. Her husband's family includes a signer of the Texas Declaration of Independence, and research in the field has been one of her chief interests for many years. She is a practiced and attractive speaker."[46] Baker and her husband invited a number of family and friends to be their guests at the dinner held at the Fredonia Hotel in Nacogdoches on November 5, 1955: Charlotte, Tom W., Ben T. and their spouses; Baker's niece Floy Lewis; Stephen F. Austin President Boynton and his wife; the "Cheese-eaters"; Victor Fain, the editor of the *Daily Sentinel*, and his wife; Mr. and Mrs. Frank Hathcock, Mr. and Mrs. T. E. Ferguson; and Mr. and Mrs. Blake from Center, Texas.[47]

One year later, tragedy struck the Baker family when on November 8, 1956, Thomas Ellis Baker died. The loss was felt throughout East Texas. He had served as president of Commercial Guaranty Bank since 1929, and under his guidance the bank survived the crash of 1929 and the Depression of the 1930s. His obituary in the *Daily Sentinel* reflected his importance to the East Texas community. In the late twentieth century, J. L. Jackson, the writer of the "SFA Heritage Series" in the Nacogdoches *Daily Sentinel*, paid tribute to Baker: "He helped many men meet their obligations and, in the end, to build great enterprises."[48] On November 11, 1956, Baker expressed her grief through poetry and wrote "All Clear," a poignant poem in memoriam to her husband of forty-nine years. The two had always been supportive of one another: Thomas E. Baker had been Karle Wilson Baker's most ardent champion; she had dedicated her published novels and books of poetry to him.

> So it was as you lay so still and did
> Not speak to me.
> My comings and goings you always
> Knew, as by an inner ear,
> Almost before I started, almost before
> I stirred.
> Tonight you lay in your golden peace and
> The still air said, "All Clear."
>
> If I only opened a shutter, or watered the
> Pot on the sill,
> "Where are you going?" you always asked,
> And did not care what I said,
> Not taking your eyes from your paper,

Or the quiet game in your hand.
Tonight you answered but did not ask,
And the light was about your head.

I came and went through the loving
Door so softly closed behind me,
And the stars were waiting among
The boughs, the kind boughs reaching
Near.
I came and went and you did not
Ask, for the asking years were over
And so it was when you lay so still,
Tonight, my only dear.

In their early years of marriage, the Bakers had studied the stars in the evening sky by telescope from their balcony on Baxter-Duncan Street. They had often walked together among the trees near the home.[49] Now the stars and boughs offered solace to the poet in her bereavement.

Three years later, Baker received a surprise and something of a revelation when in May 1959, Ralph Steen, president of Stephen F. Austin, presented her with a new book by Walter Prescott Webb that mentioned her in the preface. On June 3, in her note of thanks she wrote, "I have admired him [Webb] and his vital and original work. . . . This unexpected book with its treasured and most unexpected inscription has moved me more than I can say."[50] She wrote to Webb on the same day:

> . . . Now I am not only a dictating writer but a "read-to" reader, which has made me very slow about telling you how delightful I found the new book which the Steens have given me. Among other special things, I have always admired your work for a sort of intellectual uprightness; some others have the quality but not the flavor or the force.
>
> But as you have written an honest preface I shall write a shameless personal confession: your kind words about me overwhelmed me. For all these years I had thought that you took small stock in me and my work—the only kind of work I could do. And, as I have said, I liked yours.[51]

Baker's distrust of Webb was justified, and she probably was not swayed from her longtime sense that he had a negative assessment of her. Even at age eighty-one, she still had a clear picture of how some of her contemporaries had viewed her in the past. The celebrated male writers in Texas at the time she had been most productive had been largely indifferent toward women writers in the state. That is not to say that Baker had no male supporters, but they were often men of lesser lights than Walter Prescott Webb or J. Frank Dobie, who had dominated the literary scene. Her early supporters had included George P. Garrison and George L. Crocket, and later W. H. Vann, Hilton Greer, Leonidas Payne, A. J. Armstrong, and John McGinnis. Because of her national recognition, Baker had often been the rare exception as the only female invited to join literary organizations and societies in the state. Her male counterparts found it difficult to overlook the woman who was the foremost poet in Texas and a novelist of national acclaim. But in the face of all of Baker's successes and accomplishments, the question remains: Why has the Texas poet most frequently anthologized in the first part of the twentieth century fallen from memory? And why are her historical novels about Texas practically unknown today? The majority of her works, whether poetry, fiction, or nonfiction are based on Texas and its history. One answer might be that after her death, when Texas literature began to appear more frequently in textbooks and works by Texans gained a larger portion in the marketplace, publishers and scholars who directed the market maintained the tradition of focusing on male writers. The biases that Baker had often defeated in her lifetime may have overtaken her in death. Always self-analytical, Karle Wilson Baker's own words suggest that she was unsure of the place she would hold in literature. On September 8, 1950, when she was seventy-two years old, she wrote about herself as a writer and about being in fashion or not:

> As a writer I have fallen through the crack between two eras. But the man who falls out of time may fall into immortality, and the writer who falls out of time may be a classic, quick with the spark of life that is not the property of any era, but kindles all of them. . . . The more old-fashioned you are, the more likely to live to meet the Old Fashion returning, coming back to do his turn again. He may have a new necktie, but his eyes will be the same.[52]

When Baker died, few other female writers in Texas had amassed the recognition or honors that she had. The acceptance Baker experienced early in her career at the *Yale Review* and Yale University Press established her reputation across the nation, but her great talent ensured her steady climb toward fame. A shy woman from East Texas seized the moment to sing her poetry and pen her prose on a national stage, launching a writing career of nearly five decades. When Baker died on November 9, 1960, the news of her death flashed across the state. Memorials and tributes appeared in many newspapers. In particular, the *Houston Post* and the *Dallas News* printed prominent notices recognizing the distinguished writer from East Texas. The *Nacogdoches Daily Sentinel* paid special tribute to one of its most celebrated citizens, announcing the news of Baker's death on the front page alongside a picture of John F. Kennedy, who the day before had won the office of president of the United States. Underneath the banner headline "Democrats in Sweeping Victory" was a large photograph of Baker with the caption—almost as large as the banner headline—"Mrs. Baker Dies Today." Editor Victor Fain, a former student of Baker, knew that the writer's death was of equal importance to local readers as Kennedy's national victory.[53] The *Sentinel* article informed the public that Baker had died at City Memorial Hospital after a lingering illness that had kept her hospitalized for nearly a year and that funeral services would be conducted the next day at the Christ Episcopal Church with the Reverend John Desel, rector of the church, officiating. Burial was planned at the historic Oak Grove Cemetery in Nacogdoches. The article was lengthy and cited Baker's many publications and accomplishments.[54]

Many of Karle Wilson Baker's poems have inspired others, but the poem most anthologized and most requested for reprint is the lyric set to music in 1953, "Let Me Grow Lovely."[55] Before her death, Baker had become this poem:

Let me grow lovely, growing old—
So many fine things do:
Laces, and ivory, and gold,
And silks need not be new;
And there is healing in old trees,
Old streets a glamour hold:
Why may not I, as well as these,
Grow lovely, growing old?

The Karle Wilson Baker Papers contain example upon example of Baker's contributions to the East Texas community. Her work with young writers and schoolchildren, her speaking engagements at women's clubs throughout the area, and her participation at colleges and universities across the state testify to her tireless dedication to East Texas.[56] The world of Texas writers was particularly hard-hit by her death. The Philosophical Society of Texas included a tribute to Baker in its "Necrology" in the *Proceedings* for 1960. Rebecca W. Smith, Baker's longtime friend and fellow member of the Texas Institute of Letters, wrote the memorial, which began with a brief biographical account of Baker's education and family life and chronicled Baker's published works. She addressed Baker's years as a teacher at Stephen F. Austin State Teachers College, recognized the many organizations Baker had served, and acclaimed the writer's contributions to the East Texas region: "Her abiding interests—in people, in nature, and in the history of the region in which she lived—are recorded for posterity in her work. She was an artist who lived her art, establishing deep roots in East Texas soil and producing rich fruit for the world's spiritual nourishment."[57]

Gustan Davidson, secretary of the Poetry Society of America, wrote to Charlotte Montgomery for data on Baker so that he could notify members of her death in the next *Bulletin.*[58] Faye Carr Adams, secretary of the Poetry Society of Texas, wrote to Charlotte expressing the society's deep feelings of loss over Baker's death; Society President W. E. Bard read "Song of the Forerunners" in her memory at the spring meeting. In 1966, the Poetry Society of Texas dedicated its yearbook to Baker and entered photographs and memorabilia about her in their newly established Poet's Hall of Fame in Belton, Texas. Charlotte sent copies of Baker's three books of verse to the Texas Poets Memorial Collection housed at Mary Hardin Baylor College.[59]

Almost sixty years had passed since that moonlit night at the train station when Karle Wilson Baker felt the illusive mystery of Nacogdoches and a sense of wonder at the majestic old trees as she rode home with her father in the old "depot-hack." Like the trees, she had "pledged hard against the storm to fill her place"; like the birds, she had "soared—wind free."[60] Seven and a half years before her death, on Good Friday, April 3, 1953, Karle Wilson Baker had entered into her diary words that summed up her life and could have been her epitaph:

> I have lived from the centre, from the roots, and I have lived up into the sun and air. If I had been wiser I could have gone farther; but I have come by the right way, and am content.[61]

APPENDIX

THRUSHES

Through Tanglewood the thrushes trip,
As brown as any clod,
But in their spotted throats are hung
The vesper-bells of God.

And I know little secret truths,
And hidden things of good,
Since I have heard the thrushes sing
At dusk, in Tanglewood.

DESIRE OF FAME

See, how I wrestle with the stubborn days,
Morn, noon and eve, and will not let them go
Except they bless me. In the steps of slow
Reticent Time I follow; subtle ways
Of Art and Knowledge spread their baffling maze
Before my feet; but doughty blow on blow
I fight the high, hard battle, and will know
No truce, till on my forehead rest the bays.
Yet, sometimes in the struggle, when the thirst
Of effort tortures, and the thwarted will
Devours the heart, 'tis deeper pain, that this
Is that same soul I used to be, when first,
O early love! thou couldst so surely fill
These dusty wells to brimming, with—a kiss!

AT THE PICTURE-SHOW

She sits with eyes intent upon the screen,
A quiet woman with work-hardened hands.
Beside her squirms an eager, shock-head boy;
Upon her lap a little rumpled girl

With petaled cheek and bright, play-roughened hair;
While, bulwark of the little family group,
Her husband looms, with one unconscious arm
Lying along her chair-back. So they come
Often, and for a few cents, more or less,
Slip through the wicket-gate of wonderment
That bounds the beaten paths of everyday.
The Indians and the horses thrill the boy
With dreams of great adventure; the big man
Likes the great bridges, and the curious lore
Of alien folk in other lands; the child
Laughs at the funny way the people die.
And she?
                    The way the hero's overcoat
Sets to his shoulders; or a lock of hair
Tossed back impatiently; or else a smile,
A visible sigh, an eyebrow lifted, so,—
They touch strange, buried, dispossessed old dreams.
And while her hand plays with the baby's curls
Unthinking, once again she sees the face
That swayed her youth as ocean tides are swayed
Until she broke her heart to save her soul . . .
And fled back to her native town . . . and left
In the grey canyons of the city streets
All the high hopes of youth. . . .
                    She has picked up
Her life since then, and made a goodly thing
Out of the fragments; that is written plain
Upon the simple page for all to see.
I fancy that she hardly thinks of him
Through all her wholesome days; but when, at night
They go a-voyaging across the screen,
And suddenly a street-lamp throws a gleam
On wet pavement . . . a man sits alone
On a park bench . . . or else goes swinging past
With that expression to his overcoat. . . .
She does not pick this player-man, or that,
But all the heroes have some trick of his. . . .

A LITTLE BOY'S BATH

You would have thought he never would come clean,
Yet here he is, shining like a sea-shell.

O Life, thou secret-hearted, ancient mother,
Teach him the hidden paths to thy rock-fountains,
Make them plain to his feet,
And for the insult of thy deep pollutions,
The dust, and sweaty grime, and clinging foulness,
Give him to know thy laughing water-courses,
And the clean brown pools
Among the rocks.

I, his mother, have jealously kept his firm, small body:
Keep thou his soul, O Life!

STILLNESS

As a gull loves the sea-spray,
So I love stillness.
I love to creep
Under a blanket of stillness that muffles even the beat of my heart,
And tuck it in under my chin—or draw it up over my head.
I do not always want the feet of other people
Muddying up the springs of my mind.
Even the feet of the children, as they come whooping and splashing,
Shatter, unknowing, the fragile, bright mirror,
Often,
And send the leaves of my sky-trees flying in every direction,
And drown the strange flowers.
But then—the little feet themselves are so sweet!

BOX-CAR LETTERS

Alone on the hill where the sun goes down
I plunder the earth from my little town;
But the spoils I bring in my fairy sack
Are scattered and spilled on the railroad track. . . .
For there, on the siding, the box-cars doze,

And this is the way their dreaming goes:

"Sault Sainte-Marie and Chicopee,
Miami and San Antonio—"
They call like a lover's song to me,
Call, and I want to go!
Santa Fe, Norfolk and Kalamazoo,
Sacramento, Mobile, Peru—
How, do you think, you could tamely bide
In the one small spot where your heart was tied,
When those haughty drudges came creaking through,
Tearing your anchored heart in two,
Each with a name on its stolid side
Two feet tall and ten feet wide,
That rings like a chime for you?

The wanderer's day will have one good hour,
And every roadside one magic flower;
They wither and droop if you stay too long,
The perfume goes like an ended song.
I would come back to the ways I know
But I would not stay when I want to go!

Wichita, Bangor, and San Jose,
Ypsilanti and Monterey—
They flutter my peace like the tang of spray!
From high dream-pastures homing down
To the fold of my heart in the little town,
I have to wait at the railroad track
On a trundling train with a snorting stack!
The engine's a genie, a grimy scamp
Who turns a philosopher into a tramp.
Denver, Seattle and Calumet,
Natchez, New Haven and Laramie—
Go on with your lumbering lure, and let
A poor philosopher be!

SONG OF THE FORERUNNERS

The men who made Texas
Rode west with dazzled eyes

On the hot trail of the Future,
To take her by surprise:

They were dreamers on horseback,
Dreamers with strong hands,
Trailing the golden Lion
Who couches in far lands:

Old men and young men, little men and tall,
Bad men and good men—but strong men, all.

The women who bore Texas
Could see beyond the sun:
They sat on cabin doorsteps
When the long day was done,

And they crooned to lusty babies,
But their look was far away—
For they gazed straight through the sunset
To the unborn day.

Stern women, laughing women, women stout or small,
Bronzed women, broken women—brave women, all.

The men who made Texas
Laughed at fate and doom—
Dreamers on horseback,
Men who needed room;

And the women in young Texas,
Hanging homespun clothes to dry,
Loved a prairie for a dooryard,
For meeting-house, the sky—

Wide visions and wide spaces, man and land were large of lung:
Texas knew not cheap and easy, slack and small, when she was young!

But the men who made Texas
Left their work half-done—
For nothing stands full-finished
Beneath the spinning sun;

And the women who dreamed Texas
Had much work to do

When they lay down for their last sleep
In a land still new;

And a yet-unbuilded Texas, cloud-paved and glimmering,
Burns yet before the eyes of us, who toil and dream and sing.

TEXAS COWBOY

From garden-bed I tend, it is not far
To those great ranges where he used to ride;
Time's shadowy Door still stands a rift ajar,
And Fancy, glancing backward and aside,

May glimpse him whirling in a storm of dust,
A flashing bronze against a burning sky,
Before a sea of tossing horns up-thrust,
A peril thousand-pronged, to breast or die;

Or lying with locked hands beneath his head,
Watching the stars beside a lonely fire,
About him dim immensity outspread,
Within, dim gulfs of question and desire.
He is a Thought; he is not flesh-and-bone;
He is immortal Youth astride a Dream:
The hungry flame that eats to ash and stone
The gorgeous fruitage of the things that seem;

And I (who sank, with pang and toil enough,
My roots at last down to the nether springs,
Yet, born to coax the shapely from the rough,
Have shunned the red and jagged edge of things),

A woman with a bird, a book, a flower,
Who, sifting life, has kept the quiet part,
Whose days like pearls are sorted, hour by hour—
Why is it that he gallops through my heart?

PRONOUNS

The Lord said,
"Say, 'We'";
But I shook my head,

Hid my hands tight behind my back, and said,
"I."

The Lord said,
"Say, 'We'";
But I looked upon them, grimy and all awry.
Myself in all those twisted shapes? Ah, no!
Distastefully I turned my head away,
Persisting,
"They."

The Lord said,
"Say, 'We'";
And I
At last,
Richer by a hoard
Of years
And tears,
Looked in their eyes and found the heavy word
That bent my neck and bowed my head:
Like a shamed schoolboy then I mumbled low,
"We,
Lord."

NOTES

Abbreviations
CAH-UT: Center for American History, University of Texas–Austin
CBM: Charlotte Baker Montgomery
CBM Collection: Charlotte Baker Montgomery Collection
HRHRC: Harry Ransom Humanities Research Center, University of Texas–Austin
KWB: Karle Wilson Baker
KWB Papers: Karle Wilson Baker Papers
PCBE: Private collection, Baker estate
SLSFASU: Steen Library, Stephen F. Austin State University
SWTSU: South West Texas State University
TEB: Thomas Ellis Baker
TIL: Texas Institute of Letters
TWB: Thomas Wilson Baker

Chapter 1

1. Karle Wilson Baker Papers, box 22/13, Steen Library, Stephen F. Austin State University, Nacogdoches, Texas (hereafter cited as KWB Papers).

2. 2102 Louisiana Street.

3. Karle Wilson Baker, unpublished manuscript, "In Search of Myself" (1922), private collection, Baker estate (hereafter cited as PCBE), folder 19.

4. Ibid.

5. Ibid.

6. Karle Wilson Baker unpublished manuscript, n.d., PCBE, folder 27.

7. Karle Wilson, Ledger Journal, April 22, 1903, PCBE. This diary entry was made when KWB was twenty-five years old. (Baker's family refers to her as "KWB," and she often signed with those initials.)

8. Karle Wilson Baker letter of biographical data to an unidentified student, n.d., KWB Papers, box 44/9. Charlotte Baker Montgomery has shown the author photographs of KWB with her violin. Charlotte has said that her uncle's name was Benjamin Taylor Wilson, but everyone called him "Ben T." Even his tombstone reads Ben T. Wilson. Dr. Ed Gaston commented in an interview that Ben T. Wilson built a tennis court at his home on Mound Street across from Tanglewood, the Bakers' home. Ben and KWB often played tennis together there.

9. PCBE, folder 35.

10. Karle Wilson to Kate Floy Montgomery Wilson, 1898, PCBE. The letters also reflect KWB's general frugality and her consciousness of saving money for her education. The Wilsons were in San Antonio, where W. T.'s brothers lived.

11. Charlotte Baker Montgomery (hereafter cited as CBM), interview with Sarah Jackson, May 23, 1997. CBM does not recall the exact date when her grandfather first

stopped alone in Nacogdoches. According to Ben T. Wilson's daughter, Florence (Toncie), when the Wilsons moved to Nacogdoches, Ben T. helped his father with the new business. For this reason, he was not able to continue his education. She wrote, "Ben Wilson should have been a professor—a scholar—not a business man. He had a lot of intellectual curiosity, and because he had read widely on many subjects, I considered him to be well educated—though he had no degree." Florence Wilson Reavley to the author, September 8, 1997. Judge Thomas M. Reavley, Florence's husband, expressed similar feelings to the author in a letter dated September 11, 1997.

12. Karle Wilson, Ledger Journal, June 26, 1905, PCBE. *Harper's* published the poem in 1903.

13. Karle Wilson, *University of Chicago Weekly,* March 14, 1901, PCBE. The poem appeared after KWB left the university. KWB's poem in the *Weekly* was untitled, but its subject, trees, continued to be a favorite throughout her career as a poet. The poem appears as a single sentence superimposed over of a drawing of barren trees in winter (the illustrator's initials are "E. B."): "A line of gray trees soft as mist, still as phantoms, a background of unbroken white, —the Midway snow covered,—and like a curtain stretched across a window, gathering darkness and falling snow." Her short story published in the same issue, "A Man Without a Purpose," is set at the university, as was the poem. The young woman in the story "has a purpose in life." Most likely the piece is partly autobiographical, which was typical in KWB's early stories.

14. PCBE, folder 14. The letter, written in 1957, identifies the young man as Bertram Griffith Nelson, who became a teacher in the speech department at the University of Chicago. While Karle was teaching in Little Rock, he tried to renew the relationship, but by that time she was no longer interested and never answered his letter.

15. Personal essay, written between 1924–28, KWB Papers, box 44/8.

16. KWB, "In Search of Myself," PCBE.

17. KWB Papers, box 22/13.

18. Ledger Journal, April 4, 1903, PCBE.

19. Ledger Journal, June 3, 1903, PCBE.

20. April 1903, PCBE, folder 5.

21. PCBE, folder 38.

22. Ledger Journal, May 2, 1903, PCBE.

23. Ledger Journal, August 30, 1903, PCBE.

24. Ledger Journal, February 11, 1905, PCBE.

25. Ledger Journal, December 29, 1903, PCBE.

26. Kate Floy Montgomery Wilson journal, April 12, 1904–May 12, 1905, PCBE.

27. CBM unpublished manuscript, "The Magnolia Tree," PCBE.

28. Kate Floy Montgomery Wilson journal, 1908, PCBE.

29. KWB, Diary, Sept. 4, 1905, PCBE. KWB based *The Birds of Tanglewood* (1930) on her birding observations.

30. KWB, Diary, Sept. 6, 1905, PCBE. Ben T. Wilson played a major role in KWB's life. Because of their similar dispositions and interests, she often consulted him. Florence Wilson Reavley wrote about their shared spirit, "My father, Ben T. Wilson, shared with KWB a love of literature and music, of nature, and of philosophy. They enjoyed discussing ideas. Both were kind, sensitive, imaginative, contemplative souls, friendly,

but private people with a delightful low-key sense of humor. Thus, they were much alike in temperament, which made them very close. There was much love and empathy between them." Florence Wilson Reavley to the author, September 8, 1997.

31. Ledger Journal, June 5–July 10, 1906, PCBE.

32. Ibid.

33. Ibid.

34. KWB, unpublished manuscript, "In Search of Myself" (1922), PCBE, folder 19.

35. Manuscript Record Book, PCBE.

36. KWB Papers, box 23/18.

37. *Daily Sentinel*, January 24, 1907.

38. *Daily Sentinel*, KWB letter to the editor, February 18, 1907, KWB Papers. According to CBM, her father was very proud of this letter and made certain that a copy was filed with the KWB Papers. Locally, this letter has become one of the best loved and most repeated of any of KWB's writings.

39. CBM, interview with the author, August 7, 2003. CBM commented that about 1898, her father acted in a local production of *Snow White and Rose Red*. She had a photograph of him in costume to prove it.

40. E. C. Marsh to Karle Wilson, July 17, 1907, KWB Papers, box 23/15.

41. KWB draft letter to E. C. Marsh, July 25, 1907, KWB Papers, box 23/15.

42. KWB Papers, box 23/15.

43. Ibid.

44. CBM, interview with the author, August 7, 2003. Thomas Ellis Baker was not a man to "throw money away," but he spared little expense on the extensive honeymoon trip to New York. CBM has shared with the author photographs of the honeymoon trip showing KWB on the "Sleepy Hollow Bridge" (North Tarrytown, N.Y.) where the headless horseman allegedly rode; KWB at the house across the street from where President Lincoln was shot at Ford's Theatre in Washington, D. C.; and pictures of Mt. Vernon, Virginia, and Niagara Falls.

45. Thomas M. Reavley to the author, September 11, 1997; Edwin Gaston, interview with the author, May 12, 1997.

46. Bryan Holt Davis, interview with the author, July 1, 1999; Mr. Davis put the author in touch with Dorothy Clay Perkins, who confirmed this information.

47. Chronology Folder, PCBE.

48. KWB Papers, box 23/15.

49. G. P. Garrison to KWB, October 22, 1907, KWB Papers, box 23/15.

50. Lt. Augustus W. Magee, a U.S. Army officer who had engaged in dispersing the outlaws in the neutral ground between Louisiana and Texas, conceived the idea of conquering Texas to the Rio Grand and establishing a republican government. Don Bernardo Gutierrez, a Mexican revolutionary, joined him in this enterprise. Samuel Davenport of Nacogdoches joined the expedition and used his wealth to gather provisions and munitions. In August 1812, the little army of filibusters advanced toward Texas under Gutierrez's command. The Spaniards retreated from the Sabine to Nacogdoches. The citizens of Nacogdoches would not join the Spaniards, and when the army advanced to Nacogdoches, the Spaniards fled. Col. Davenport and Capt. James Gaines came up with more recruits and the army swelled to about eight hundred men and set

out along the La Bahia road to San Antonio. April 1, 1813, the city was defeated and a "Declaration of Independence of the State of Texas" was issued, but at this point, the expedition began to fall apart. Magee had died, and Gutierrez cruelly ordered the execution of many prisoners. See G. L. Crocket, *Two Centuries in East Texas* (Austin: Hart Graphics, 1932).

51. "The Story of Texas," unpublished manuscript, PCBE.

52. KWB Papers, box 23/15.

53. E. C. Marsh to KWB, September 21, 1908, KWB Papers, box 23/15.

54. KWB, Autobiographical Writings, PCBE, folder 28.

55. Ibid.

56. KWB, Diary, February 1908, PCBE. Travis Hughes and his wife moved the Baxter-Duncan House to 809 Texas Street in Nacogdoches on July 4, 1988, and restored the home.

57. Ibid. KWB and her husband, Thomas E. Baker (hereafter cited as TEB), used a telescope to stargaze from their balcony on Baxter-Duncan Street.

58. KWB Papers, box 23/15.

59. KWB Papers, box 23/16. KWB used her research from "The Story of Texas" project in some of her historical writings in the 1930s and 1940s.

60. KWB, Diary, 1910, PCBE.

61. KWB, unpublished manuscript, "In Search of Myself" (1922), PCBE, folder 19.

62. Fern Lake Ledger, 1911–25, PCBE.

63. For example, when Karle was young, her mother limited her daughter's reading to thirty minutes a day; KWB entered this fact in her journal, April 22, 1903.

64. Carolyn Sturdevant Miller, interview with the author, January 20, 1997. Miller recalled many enjoyable visits to Fern Lake; Thomas Wilson Baker (hereafter cited as TWB), interview with the author, May 12, 1998. TWB told the author about the rifle. KWB became an animal protectionist in later years.

65. KWB, Fern Lake Ledger, 1911–25, PCBE. TWB said the cook, Lucy Jackson, had a small cabin behind the Bakers' cabin at Fern Lake. TWB, interview with the author, July 8, 1997.

66. TWB, interview with the author, May 12, 1998; Miller, interview with the author, January 20, 1997. TEB's sister, Carrie, was Carrie Baker Sturdevant, Miller's mother.

67. TWB, interview with the author, May 12, 1998. The black man was Henry Mathews.

68. KWB, Ledger Journal, 1913, PCBE.

69. KWB, Diary 1913, PCBE.

70. Manuscript Record Book, 1913, PCBE.

71. *The Craftsman*, February 1915, PCBE, folder 25.

72. CBM, interview with the author, August 7, 2003. CBM said that after school, she and her brother, Tomby, would stop by the Stripling Hazelwood Drugstore (where their father was part owner) for ice cream. She added that she was never allowed to "charge" anything, however.

73. "Camping with the Kiddies: By One Who Has Tried It," unpublished manuscript, PCBE.

74. Ibid.

75. CBM, interview with the author, November 25, 2002.

76. Fern Lake Ledger, 1911–25, PCBE. By 1925, Tomby and Charlotte were enrolled at Stephen F. Austin State Teachers College, and KWB was teaching there. The following year, the three attended the University of California–Berkeley, so there was little time for leisure at Fern Lake.

Chapter 2

1. KWB, Notebook Diary, 1913, PCBE.

2. KWB, Diary 1917, PCBE.

3. KWB draft letter to Walter Pitkin, 1922, PCBE.

4. KWB, Diary 1955, PCBE. The lyric poem, "Thrushes," illustrates KWB's use of imagery and simile in eight concise lines. See appendix for "Thrushes." The thrush was her favorite bird. A good example of her use of the universal in the particular is found in "The Tree," which is quoted later in chapter 2.

5. For Baker's poetry to appear in the same journal with works by Robert Browning was an honor itself. All of Baker's sonnets were publicly well received, but critical recognition came when the literary critic William Stanley Braithwaite published his honor roll of poetry for 1914 in the *Boston Evening Transcript,* choosing "Evening" as one of seven poems on his list. The poem appeared later in *Blue Smoke* and *Dreamers on Horseback.*

6. Edward Reed to KWB, February 25, 1914, KWB Papers, box 1/1.

7. KWB draft letter to E. Reed, about March 1914, KWB Papers, box 1/1. The number of rejection slips for poems found in the KWB Papers, box 31, indicates that she was not always successful, for instance, with the *Atlantic Monthly* and *Century Magazine.*

8. W. L. Cross to KWB, October to November 1915, KWB Papers, box 1/1.

9. All three of the above letters are in the KWB Papers, box 1/1. See Appendix for "Desire of Fame."

10. W. L. Cross to KWB, October 22, 1914, KWB Papers, box 1/1.

11. W. L. Cross to KWB, January 12, 1915, KWB Papers, box 1/1; see appendix for "At the Picture Show."

12. W. L. Cross to KWB, January 27, 1915, KWB Papers, box 1/1.

13. KWB, Diary 1934, PCBE.

14. W. L. Cross to KWB, May 29, 1914, KWB Papers, box 1/1.

15. W. L. Cross to KWB, June 23, 1914, KWB Papers, box 1/1.

16. *Texas Review* (June 15, 1915): 9. KWB Papers, box 54.

17. Baker, an ardent birder and naturalist, often expressed her thoughts through bird imagery in both poetry and prose. In "Poet Songs" the quatrains in parts 1 and 2 express the poet's frustration when writing will not come. In the two beautiful quatrains of part 3, she identifies her verses as mere cast-off thoughts from Heaven. Yet these inspired words from God are her inspiration to write, and they nurture her soul.

18. W. L. Cross to KWB, November 22, 1915, KWB Papers, box 1/1. See appendix for "A Little Boy's Bath." This poem, written for the Bakers' son, Tomby, along with "Apple and Rose," written for Charlotte and Tomby, illustrates KWB's devotion to her children. In November 1930, KWB spoke in Houston at the Central Library in a recital of her works for Book Week. She gave two lectures: an adult evening speech and a children's

hour the next day, where she read "A Little Boy's Bath" and "Apple and Rose." She commented on the poems, "I don't dare read these when the children are around. . . . When they are older I do not think they will mind."

19. KWB, Diary 1915, PCBE.

20. W. L. Cross to KWB, November 22, 1915, KWB Papers, box 1/2. See endnote 18 for comments on "Apple and Rose." When KWB wrote "Stillness," she had in mind the everyday interruptions that continued to concern her. When her children were small, they sometimes interrupted her work, and during those years of demanding family life, she limited herself to writing short pieces, so poetry took precedence over prose. The poet concedes at the end of the poem that even though she is interrupted by her children, the interruptions are sweet. See appendix for "Stillness."

21. CBM, interview with the author, May 23, 1997.

22. TWB, interview with the author, July 8, 1997; also Florence Wilson Reavley letter to the author, September 8, 1997.

23. CBM supplied this information to the Perkins family files. Copies were sent to the author on July 17, 1999, and are still in the author's possession.

24. Florence Wilson Reavley to the author, September 8, 1997. Reavley was living in Bellingham, Washington, at the time of this letter.

25. CBM, interview with the author, August 29, 2002. In 1916, the Old Stone Fort (now on the SFA Campus) was located on the northeast corner of Washington Square. CBM has said that Jenny Harris and KWB became close friends with common interests in nature, especially cocoons and butterflies.

26. CBM, "The Magnolia Tree," PCBE. "Good Company" and "The Tree," discussed later in this chapter, demonstrate KWB's affinity for trees.

27. W. L. Cross to KWB, December 5, 1917, KWB Papers, box 1/2. The theme of finding God through nature occurs throughout KWB's poetry. Even though she saw that she must fight interruptions and "cluttered days" that interfered with her opportunities to write, she knew she had special talents and expressed gratitude to God for this. A musician from Concord, New Hampshire, wrote to KWB in August 1918 asking permission to set this poem to music—which she granted.

28. W. L. Cross to KWB, February 7, 1918, KWB Papers, box 1/3; KWB had sent "William Vaughn Moody" to Harriet Monroe at *Poetry: A Magazine of Verse.*

29. Harriet Monroe, the editor of *Poetry: A Magazine of Verse,* described "Eagle Youth" and "Graves of France" as moving and expertly handled, with a quiet simplicity and sincerity. In 1919, Katherine Lee Bates, author of "America the Beautiful," reviewed a new anthology of war poetry: *A Treasury of War Poetry: British and American Poems of the World War.* She commented in her review, "There is nothing here with the spring and splendor of Karle Wilson Baker's 'Eagle Youth.'" "Leaves" was originally titled "November at Tanglewood." Tanglewood was the name of KWB's home at that time; perhaps she changed the title to make it more general.

30. Wilhelmina Day to KWB, April 22, 1918, KWB Papers, box 1/9.

31. KWB Papers, box 1/9.

32. KWB Papers, box 1/10.

33. CBM, interview with the author, May 23, 1997.

34. Ibid. KWB had been fascinated by train travel since childhood when she visited her maternal grandparents at Linden Grange outside Little Rock, Arkansas.

35. Another poem about trains, "Box-Car Letters," became one of her most popular poems and a favorite of TEB. See appendix for "Box-Car Letters."

36. G. G. Wyant to KWB, August 25, 1919, KWB Papers, box 2/18. In April 1920, KWB signed a contract with Yale University Press to publish *Old Coins*, but she would have to wait three years for publication to become a reality. KWB Papers, box 2/1.

37. G. G. Wyant to KWB, January 27, 1919, KWB Papers, box 1/10.

38. W. S. Lewis to KWB, April 29, 1920, KWB Papers, box 2/1.

39. Katherine Lee Bates to KWB, August 14, 1922, KWB Papers, box 1/11.

40. KWB Papers, box 1/19.

41. Ibid. KWB would refer to this characteristic of her writing as finding the universal within the commonplace. KWB, Diary 1955, PCBE.

42. Rebecca W. Smith to KWB, February 3, 1921, KWB Papers, box 38/21.

43. KWB draft letter to Rebecca Smith, February 1921, KWB Papers, box 38/21. Sara Teasdale wrote to KWB in 1919 that she had liked KWB's work "a long time." KWB Papers, box 40/22.

44. KWB draft letter to G. G. Wyant, December 1919, KWB Papers, box 2/18.

45. KWB Papers, box 40. Dorothy Scarborough was a loyal supporter of KWB's writing throughout the poet's career.

46. KWB draft letter to G. G. Wyant, December 1919, KWB Papers, box 2/18.

47. KWB Papers, box 2/1.

48. KWB draft letter to G. G. Wyant, [March or April 1920], KWB Papers, box 2/1.

49 Ibid. KWB refers to two stories in *The Reindeer's Shoe* (published posthumously in 1988).

50. W. S. Lewis to KWB, April 29, 1920, KWB Papers, box 2/1.

51. KWB draft letter to G. G. Wyant, May 1920, KWB Papers, box 2/1.

52. This information came from interviews with both CBM and TWB, summer 1997.

53. G. G. Wyant to KWB, April 9, 1920, KWB Papers, box 2/1.

54. G. G. Wyant to KWB, April 15, 1920, KWB Papers, box 2/1.

55. KWB Papers, box 2/1.

56. KWB Papers, box 2/4.

57. KWB draft letter to Norman Donaldson, n.d., KWB Papers, box 2/4.

58. W. S. Lewis to KWB, October 26, 1920, KWB Papers, box 2/4.

59. KWB draft letter to W. S. Lewis, c. November 1920, KWB Papers, box 2/4.

60. Ibid.

61. Ibid.

62. Norman Donaldson to KWB, March 13, 1929, KWB Papers, box 2/6.

63. Ibid.

64. Helen McAfee to KWB, November 1920, KWB Papers, box 1/5.

65. KWB draft letter to Helen McAfee, November 1920, KWB Papers, box 1/5.

66. Ibid.

67. Helen McAfee to KWB, November 29, 1920, KWB Papers, box 1/5.

68. W. L. Cross to KWB, September 20, 1921, KWB Papers, box 1/5.

69. KWB, Diary 1922, PCBE. The storm occurred in April 1922.

70. Katherine Lee Bates to KWB, September 27, 1921, KWB Papers, box 2/13.

71. All three letters are in the KWB Papers, box 2/10.

72. Ibid.

73. KWB draft letter to Wilson Follett, March 1922, KWB Papers, box 2/11.

74. "Courage" was one of three short lyrics that KWB grouped under the title "Three Small Poems." When the Texas writer Dorothy Scarborough wrote about the poems, she commented that KWB's thoughts "were crystallized in deft phrases that express her philosophy. No one can read Mrs. Baker's poetry without being impressed by her strong religious feeling, her faith in God, her steady optimism."

75. KWB Papers, box 2/9.

76. According to CBM, "Good Company" was one of KWB's favorite poems. The nourishment she gained from trees and birds was a recurring theme in her poetry. In his *Anthology of the Year 1916,* the famous literary critic and columnist William Stanley Braithwaite selected this poem as one of the thirty best of the year. He also published the poem in the first issue of his new magazine devoted to poetry, *Poetry Review* (1916). Hilton Greer included it in his 1923 anthology of Texas verse, *Voices of the Southwest.*

77. KWB wrote in her diary: "Dead trees have a claim upon my heart somehow. . . . I have so often noticed the color of pine-trunks in the evening light but there is no name for it that I know." Quotation among miscellaneous notes from 1901–1906, PCBE, folder 17.

78. KWB draft letter to Wilson Follett, March 1921, KWB Papers, box 2/19. KWB would wait eleven more months before Yale University Press published "Old Coins."

79. KWB draft letter to Walter Pitkin, August 1, 1921, PCBE. Pitkin must have been a man of great persuasion. In her scrapbook, KWB saved a picture of Pitkin from an advertisement that contained the caption, "Let Walter B. Pitkin show you how some men do TWICE as much in only HALF the time." Another clipping gives a brief biographical sketch of Pitkin and states that he taught journalism at Columbia. Obviously, he was a man of many talents. Undated magazine clippings, in the author's possession. No date or origin available.

80. KWB draft letter to W. Pitkin, October 1921, PCBE.

81. KWB, Diary 1923, PCBE.

82. KWB draft letter to W. Pitkin, October 1921, PCBE.

83. KWB draft letter to W. Pitkin, October 5, 1921, PCBE.

84. W. Pitkin to KWB, October 13, 1921, PCBE. Since she first aspired to be a writer, KWB had kept drafts of letters written to editors and others. These drafts are invaluable in a study of her life, opinions, and writing techniques.

85. KWB draft letter to W. Pitkin, August 1, 1921, PCBE.

86. W. Pitkin to KWB, February 2, 1922, PCBE.

87. W. Pitkin to KWB, February 5, 1922, PCBE.

88. KWB draft letter to W. Pitkin, September 1921, PCBE. The advice to KWB to write "busy, plotty stories" had come from the fiction editor of the *Delineator* in October 1920.

89. W. Pitkin to KWB, October 8, 1921, PCBE.

90. W. Pitkin to KWB, November 16, 1921, PCBE.

91. KWB draft letter to W. Pitkin, January 1922, PCBE.

92. KWB Papers, box 34/1.

93. KWB Papers, box 34/5.

94. KWB draft letter to Wilson Follett, April 4, 1922, KWB Papers, box 2/19.

95. KWB Papers, box 2/19.

96. KWB Papers, box 2/20.

97. KWB Papers, box 2/16.

98. Hilton Greer, review of *Old Coins,* April 29, 1923, newspaper clipping, KWB Papers, box 3/4.

99. KWB Papers, box 3/4.

100. Ibid.

101. Upshur Vincent, "KWB Texas Poet and Essayist," 1923, newspaper clipping, KWB Papers, box 44/10.

102. See appendix for "Song of the Forerunners" in full. With her national reputation firmly established, KWB turned to her adopted state for the subjects of her verse. In her third published volume, *Dreamers on Horseback,* Baker praises the early pioneers of the state in this "Song of the Forerunners." On February 19, 1946, the University of Texas made a special radio broadcast called "The Texas Destiny" celebrating the centennial of Texas statehood. At the conclusion of the program, the narrator referenced Baker's book: "The Texas Destiny. . . . forecast by the 'Dreamers on Horseback' who settled the new state. . . ." This introduction, with appropriate patriotic music, led to a reading of "Song of the Forerunners" by KWB.

103. Harriet Monroe, *Poetry: A Magazine of Verse* (November 1922): 91. KWB Papers, box 55.

104. KWB draft letter to Wilson Follett, April 2, 1923, KWB Papers, box 1/7. The published book, *The Birds of Tanglewood,* was not as expansive as Baker describes here.

105. TWB, interview with the author, May 12, 1998. In her later years, KWB wrote to a friend about her earlier absorption with moths: "At one time my most absorbing pastime was rearing moths and butterflies from the egg." Letter to Robert Avrett, May 26, 1956, KWB Papers, box 32/18.

106. KWB draft letter to W. L. Cross, April 2, 1923, KWB Papers, box 1/5.

107. Helen McAfee, letter to KWB, May 1, 1923, KWB Papers, box 1/5.

108. John Rosser to KWB, August 30, 1923, KWB Papers, box 3/10.

109. KWB draft letter to J. Rosser, August 31, 1923, KWB Papers, box 3/10.

110. John Rosser to KWB, October 1, 1923, KWB Papers, box 3/10.

111. KWB draft letter to J. Rosser, December 5, 1923, KWB Papers, box 3/10. CBM recalls that Floy had lived "several years" with her family when Charlotte was small (about 1913).

112. KWB, speech to The Poetry Society of Texas, KWB Papers, box 25/10.

113. KWB draft letter to W. Pitkin, February 1922, PCBE.

Chapter 3

1. "Rotary Luncheon," *Daily Sentinel,* May 1, 1924, p. 1.

2. Southern Methodist University Catalogue Calendar 1924, Fondren Library, Southern Methodist University; "Degrees Conferred upon S.M.U. Class," *Dallas News,*

June 11, 1924, DeGolyer Library, SMU. The ceremony at SMU took place on Tuesday, June 10, 1924. According to the *Dallas News,* the university presented 128 degrees in addition to the three honorary degrees to Dr. Morgan Callaway of the English Department at the University of Texas, the Rev. J. W. Mills of Beaumont, and KWB. TEB accompanied his wife to Dallas.

3. Mildred Wyatt, "The Pine Tree Hymn," *Daily Sentinel,* October 12, 1948, PCBE.

4. KWB draft letter to Harriet Monroe, March 1924, KWB Papers, box 32/31.

5. Dorothy Scarborough, "Karle Wilson Baker: Poet of Quiet Things," *Dallas News,* March 16, 1924, KWB Papers, box 45/10. Later articles written about KWB refer to the Scarborough tribute. In her diary, KWB had written, "I shall be loved as quiet things are loved." *Poetry: A Magazine of Verse* turned down this poem, "I Shall Be Loved For Quiet Things," but *Harper's Magazine* published it in the September 1920 issue. KWB included the poem in the collected verse of *Burning Bush.*

6. *Bulletin,* Stephen F. Austin State Teachers College, Summer 1924, SFA Archive, Steen Library, SFASU (hereafter cited as SLSFASU).

7. *Pine Log,* May 31, 1924, no. 1.

8. *Bulletin,* Summer 1924, SFA Archive, SLSFASU.

9. KWB Papers, box 10/2.

10. From Della Thompson's "My Speech," February 17, 1938. This text was in a copy of *Family Style* given to the author by Betty Burr of Nacogdoches.

11. Ibid.

12. Oral and written interviews conducted by the author, 1996–98. More than seventy-five former students responded to the survey; most were in their late eighties or early nineties. Hereafter cited as S. Jackson Survey.

13. In August 1998, former students Felix Burrows, Alice Beasley Dullye, and John C. Whitaker provided letters with such examples, S. Jackson Survey.

14. James Langston to the author, August 25, 1997, S. Jackson Survey.

15. Albert Thompson to the author, August 8, 1998, S. Jackson Survey.

16. Inez Washburn Gilmore, interview with the author, January 8, 1996.

17. KWB Papers, box 44/3.

18. Victor Fain to the author, January 20, 1997, S. Jackson Survey.

19. Francis Rudisill, introduction to "Poetry in Our Times," winter term 1929, KWB Papers, box 44/2.

20. KWB Papers, box 44/10.

21. KWB Papers, box 44/5.

22. Bella Wade to the author, July 24, 1998, S. Jackson Survey.

23. Curry Herrington to the author, summer 1997, S. Jackson Survey.

24. KWB draft letter to J. B. Hubbell, July 1924, KWB Papers, box 33/16. In reference to leaving, KWB may have already been thinking about enrolling at the University of California at Berkeley, which she did in 1926.

25. KWB Papers, box 43/11.

26. J. B. Hubbell to KWB, July 15, 1924, KWB Papers, box 33/16. The new title became the *Southwest Review.*

27. KWB draft letter to J. B. Hubbell, July 1924, KWB Papers, box 33/16.

28. KWB to Leonidas Payne Jr., July 20, 1925, Harry Ransom Humanities Research Center, University of Texas, Austin (hereafter cited as HRHRC.)

29. KWB Papers, box 5/19.

30. KWB, Diary 1925, PCBE.

31. Vaida Stewart Montgomery Memorial Collection, DeGolyer Library, SMU. Montgomery had asked W. H. Vann (Baylor-Belton), John C. Beaty (SMU), and Hilton Greer (Poetry Society of Texas) to act as "jurors" to help her select Texas poets worthy of her anthology. All three men strongly recommended KWB.

32. *Pine Log*, October 31, 1926, PCBE.

33. See KWB Papers, box 3/14.

34. CBM, interview with the author, August 7, 2003. The Craig Class was a literary study club. The membership invited KWB to speak many times. CBM identifies two of the members as Mrs. Speer and Lena Rogers. KWB sometimes stayed in their homes when she spoke in Dallas. Rogers was the mother of John William Rogers of the Southwest Press and the *Dallas Times-Herald*. Also see KWB Papers, box 44/10, for mention of other engagements.

35. KWB Papers, box 44/10. Ben T. Wilson had a "listening party" of about twelve guests to hear the program. CBM says that her uncle had one of the first radios in Nacogdoches.

36. Ibid.

37. CBM, interview with the author, May 23, 1997. In an interview on July 8, 1997, TWB told the author that his mother rented a small house in Berkeley where they lived while the three were in college together.

38. Hilda Barfield (among others) to the author, summer 1997, S. Jackson Survey. KWB must have repeated this anecdote from the Berkeley days to her poetry classes; many of the former students surveyed referred to the incident. I first learned about this from Peggy Wright of Nacogdoches.

39. KWB Papers, box 25. Mildred Wyatt, SFA librarian, commented that KWB was very successful teaching athletes: "I heard she could get big old brutes of boys, perfectly unarticulate [*sic*]—she had a way of being able to bring them out. . . . They would get up before the class and not think it was sissy to read some poetry." Mildred Wyatt, interview with Dr. Joy Reeves, sociology department, October 10, 1974, SFA Archive, box 4, tape 1.

40. *Pine Log,* November 13, 1926, PCBE.

41. KWB, telegram to TEB, December 15, 1926, Family Correspondence, PCBE.

42. *Pine Log,* December 10, 1926, PCBE.

43. CBM, interview with the author, August 7, 2003; TWB, interview with the author, May 12, 1998. Tomby and Charlotte had completed their sophomore year at Berkeley. Before KWB returned to Nacogdoches, she arranged for Charlotte to transfer to Mills College (an all-female school) in Oakland, California, because it was small and private. KWB's good friend, Elizabeth Tucker, had attended college at Mills, and CBM thinks that is one reason her mother chose that school for her. Tomby remained another year at the University of California at Berkeley.

44. KWB to Leonidas Payne Jr., February 7, 1928, HRHRC.

45. *Pine Log*, February 25, 1928, PCBE.

46. KWB to Leonidas Payne Jr., February 7, 1928, HRHRC.

47. *Daily Texan*, March 30, 1928, KWB Papers, box 45/10.

48. KWB to Leonidas Payne Jr., February 7, 1928, HRHRC. Several years later, KWB wrote to Payne that TEB had found a copy of the book in their bank vault, and she sent Payne a copy of *Blue Smoke* at that time.

49. KWB to L. Payne, March 8, 1928, HRHRC. Bess and Ben Wilson were moving to Nashville, Tennessee. Ben T. sold the Ford agency and hoped to gain his fortune in the stock market. Unfortunately, things did not turn out that way, and in a few years the Wilsons returned to Nacogdoches. At that time, Ben T. purchased the Chevrolet dealership with financial help from TEB. TWB, interview with the author, May 12, 1998.

Annie L. Perkins Garrison is the wife of George P. Garrison.

50. KWB Papers, box 34/2.

51. The new owner of Tanglewood decided to tear the house down.

52. KWB, Diary 1928, PCBE.

53. Carolyn Sturdevant Miller, interview with the author, January 20, 1997.

54. KWB Papers, box 44/10.

55. KWB Papers, box 38/30. Bates was ill and could not meet KWB's train. The day excursion that included Longfellow's Wayside Inn was the only time KWB was actually with Bates because of her hostess's heart ailment. The visit to the Wayside Inn was of particular interest to KWB. Longfellow's long poem *Evangeline* had been an early favorite of KWB, who purchased a copy in 1892 when the John Adler Company published it. She was only fourteen years old, but the book contains many notations of interest. (This book is in the private collection of Dr. Patricia Russell of Nacogdoches.) KWB wrote that she liked Katherine Lee Bates very much. Bates died six months after KWB's visit.

56. KWB Papers, box 38/30. A copy of the program of the Boston Authors' Club's annual dinner, November 10, 1928, is in KWB's file. Also a copy of the *Bulletin* of the Boston Authors' Club for December 1928 refers to the dinner and "Mrs. Karle Wilson Baker, of Texas, who read several of her lovely poems."

57. KWB Papers, box 44/9.

58. Julia Schmalz, Letter File, PCBE. Many of the letters discuss Schmalz's publication plans.

59. *Pine Log*, February 25, 1928, PCBE.

60. KWB, Diary 1928, PCBE.

61. CBM, interview with the author, August 11, 1998.

62. All letters are in KWB Papers, box 4/20.

63. KWB, Diary 1929, PCBE.

64. KWB, Diary 1929, PCBE. TWB told the author that he left UC Berkeley to enroll at the University of Texas. TWB, interview with the author, May 12, 1998.

65. KWB, Journal 1929, PCBE.

66. KWB Papers, box 44/9.

67. By the following April, KWB realized that the possibilities for publishing the Moody book with Schmalz were completely lost. Anna McCaleb Sheets commented in a letter, "I was sick no less, at the fate of 'the book.'" Anna McCaleb Sheets to KWB, April 7, 1930, PCBE.

68. KWB Papers, box 5/8.

69. KWB draft letter to H. S. Latham, December 10, 1929, KWB Papers, box 5/8.

70. KWB Papers, box 38/28.

71. A. J. Armstrong to KWB, December 15, 1929, KWB Papers, box 38/10.

72. KWB Papers, box 38/28.

73. KWB, Diary September 20, 1930, PCBE. Also see PCBE, folder 7.

74. KWB, "Account of a Visit to Harriet Monroe, Chicago," September 20, 1930, PCBE, folder 7.

75. KWB, "Account of a Visit to Harriet Moody, Wife of William Vaughn Moody," September 13, 1930, PCBE, folder 7.

76. KWB Papers, box 4/20.

77. Largely due to her mother's influence, CBM was an avid birder. She had read KWB's bird essays many times and drew illustrations that complemented the essays. Charlotte was twenty years old when Southwest Press published *The Birds of Tanglewood.* One drawing in the book is a portrait of KWB sitting in a grove of trees with books and field glasses, watching and waiting to write comments on the birds. In 1922, when an ice storm downed many birds in Nacogdoches, Charlotte, only twelve years old, had tried to help her mother save some of them.

78. KWB Papers, box 5/2-7.

79. KWB Papers, box 5/25, box 9.

80. *The Birds of Tanglewood,* (Dallas: Southwest Press, 1930), 1–2.

81. KWB Papers, box 38/28.

82. KWB Papers, box 5/7.

83. KWB Papers, box 36.

84. *Pine Log,* February 25, 1928, PCBE.

85. TWB, interview with the author, July 8, 1997. CBM told the author that KWB could drive a car but preferred to be driven. CBM recalled KWB driving on several occasions to Kilgore to pick her up. CBM, interview with the author, May 12, 1998.

86. TEB, letter to D. Wade, November 2, 1923, KWB Papers, box 36/8, an example of TEB's admiration and pride in KWB's work.

87. Rebecca W. Smith, "Birds of East Texas in Mrs. Baker's New Essays," review of *The Birds of Tanglewood, Texas Outlook,* June 1931, KWB Papers, box 5/7.

88. KWB, *Birds,* 86, 89.

89. KWB Papers, box 45.

90. KWB, Notes 1929, PCBE.

91. Ibid.

92. Ibid.

93. Ibid.

94. Ibid.

95. Ibid.

96. She also expressed this abiding desire in an early poem, "The Tree" (see chapter 2).

97. KWB, *Birds,* 62.

98. KWB Papers, box 37/13.

99. "Texas Poet Tells How She Finds Time to Write and Lead Home Life," *Houston*

Post, November 20, 1930, KWB Papers, box 45/6. In an interview before his death in 2001, TWB said that he could no longer read his mother's verse because it made him too nostalgic. TWB, interview with the author, July 8, 1997.

100. Ibid.

101. *Pine Log,* February 25, 1928, PCBE.

102. KWB Papers, box 41/10. See appendix for "Pronouns."

103. KWB Papers, box 42/21.

104. KWB Papers, box 10/2.

105. Ibid.

106. KWB Papers, box 23/19.

107. KWB Papers, box 45.

108. KWB, Diary, December 1, 1930, PCBE.

109. KWB Papers, box 5/9–10. Evidently P. L. Turner saw potential in *Dreamers* that he had not seen in *White Elephant.*

110. KWB draft letter to Leonidas Payne Jr., KWB Papers, box 38/28.

111. Leonidas Payne Jr. to KWB, January 12, 1931, KWB Papers, box 38/28.

112. KWB to L. Payne, January 15, 1931, HRHRC.

113. KWB Papers, box 44/9. KWB wrote this poem about 1920.

114. Ibid. Each of the six short lyrics in this grouping offers a moral or lesson about how to grow closer to God. KWB's great-niece, Carol Willis, has told the author that this group of poems is her favorite. In March 1933, KWB received a letter from Margaret Hipps at the University of Shanghai, China, asking permission to set "Free" to music.

115. KWB, Diary 1931, PCBE.

116. KWB Papers, box 45.

117. Ibid.

118. "Karle Wilson Baker Lectures on Woman Poet at Texas University," *Pine Log,* February 7, 1931; and J. Frank Dobie to KWB, March 14, 1937, KWB Papers, box 37/6.

119. KWB Papers, box 38/28.

120. Leonidas Payne Jr. to KWB, April 2, 1931, KWB Papers, box 5/19.

121. Dorothy Scarborough to KWB, April 1, 1931, KWB Papers, box 5/19.

122. KWB Papers, box 5/22.

123. Hilton Greer, "Collected Poems of Texas Poet Have Depth and Texture," *Dallas News,* April 12, 1931, review of *Dreamers on Horseback,* KWB Papers, box 5/27.

124. John Rogers to KWB, May 18, 1931, KWB Papers, box 5/10.

125. John Rosser to KWB, June 4, 1931, KWB Papers, box 5/22.

126. See appendix for "Song of the Forerunners."

127. KWB to W. H. Vann, September 16, 1936, South West Texas State University Archive, San Marcos, Texas (now Texas State University).

128. See appendix for "Texas Cowboy" in full.

129. KWB Papers, box 40/5. Elinor Frost was the wife of the American poet Robert Frost. In 1933, Robert Frost spoke in Nacogdoches at KWB's request. KWB and Elinor Frost became friends at that time.

130. KWB Papers, box 10/12.

131. KWB, Daily Diary 1929–1932, PCBE.

132. KWB to L. Payne, October 6, 1931, HRHRC. "The Seeker" had been published in a private printing of only one hundred copies.

133. KWB, Diary 1932, PCBE.

134. KWB Papers, box 25/10.

135. CBM, interview with the author, June 25, 2002.

136. KWB, Diary 1932, PCBE.

137. KWB Papers, box 10/1, box 10/2, and box 25/10. KWB delivered this speech, "Literary Wildcatting: The Background of *Family Style*," on January 17, 1938. She also gave the speech to the Craig Class in Dallas (April 6, 1938), the Beaumont AAUW, and a study club in Henderson, Texas, that spring.

138. KWB, Daily Diary 1929–32, PCBE.

139. CBM, interview with the author, November 2002. Dr. Ed Gaston made the author aware of the criticism that only a man could really write about the oil field in an interview May 7, 1997.

140. KWB Papers, box 10/2.

141. KWB Papers, box 9/15.

142. KWB Papers, box 10/1.

143. KWB Papers, box 10/2.

144. KWB Papers, box 10/1.

145. KWB draft letter to John McGinnis, August 12, 1937, KWB Papers, box 9/5.

146. KWB Papers, box 10/2.

147. Ibid.

148. Ibid.

149. KWB Papers, box 10/1.

150. KWB Papers, box 25/11.

151. KWB Papers, box 10/2.

152. KWB to L. Payne, February 23, 1931, HRHRC.

153. KWB Papers, box 10/2. CBM has identified the family in KWB's speech as the Ginter family.

154. KWB Papers, box 10/1.

155. Ibid.

156. KWB Papers, bundle 3. Baker used newspaper articles to revise and update her manuscript. Some of the exciting headlines from the *Houston Post* included "Wave of Woodbine Wildcatting to Follow Cherokee Strike" (June 5, 1934); "Rusk Woodbine Find Maintains Gusher Flow" (June 6, 1934); and "Major Firm Lays Line to Rusk Gusher" (June 7, 1934). Also see bundle 3 for KWB's hand-drawn maps.

157. KWB, Charts, PCBE.

158. KWB to A. J. Armstrong, May 15, 1932, Armstrong Browning Library, Baylor University, Waco, Texas.

159. KWB to L. Payne, May 1932, HRHRC.

160. KWB Papers, box 44/8.

161. KWB made a sketchy outline of the origins and sources for *Family Style* under the heading, "Gathering the Material and Writing the Book." In the list she included "Charlotte at Kilgore." KWB Papers, box 10/4. April 27, 1937, KWB wrote to Thomas R. Coward at Coward-McCann and asked him to allow Charlotte to send proposed

sketches for the jacket cover of *Family Style.* CBM Collection. Rose Dobbs at Coward-McCann wrote to Charlotte on May 25, 1937, that they were using her illustration for the dust jacket of *Family Style* and that she was enclosing a check for thirty-five dollars. She mentioned that KWB had said that she and Charlotte were working together on a book for children ["The Reindeer's Shoe"], and she would like to see it when it was ready. Dobbs addressed the letter to Charlotte Baker Paine in Chicago. Charlotte and her first husband, Henry Paine, were married for only a short time before they divorced. Later she married Roger Montgomery. KWB Papers, box 38/13. CBM's oil field watercolors and drawings are housed at the Museum of East Texas in Lufkin.

162. KWB Papers, box 38/31. She used Mexico as a resource when she wrote *Star of the Wilderness.*

163. KWB, Notes 1931, PCBE.

164. CBM, interview with the author, May 23, 1997; Bryan Holt Davis, interview with the author, August 7, 1997. Dr. Jere Jackson has told the author that Blount was the first faculty member hired at the new SFASTC.

165. KWB Papers, box 7/8.

166. W. B. Goolsby to KWB, March 23, 1932, KWB Papers, box 42/11; W. B. Goolsby to Cammie Henry, March 24, 1932, Melrose Collection, Cammie G. Henry Research Center, folder 202, Northwestern State University, Natchitoches, La.

167 Cammie G. Henry to KWB, March 28, 1931, KWB Papers, box 41/11.

168. The copy of *The Birds of Tanglewood* sent April 6, 1932, is in the Melrose Collection, Cammie G. Henry Research Center in Natchitoches.

169. TWB suggested the Melrose connection to the author on July 29, 1997. CBM spoke of the Melrose visit in an interview as well. In particular, CBM recalls that she became ill there from the food. CBM, interview with the author, July 1, 1999.

170. All three books are housed in the Melrose Collection, Cammie G. Henry Research Center.

171. KWB Papers, box 42/12–13. In addition to the first visit from November 9–19 in 1932, KWB visited Melrose Plantation in February 1933 and again in June 1933.

172. KWB Papers, box 36/22.

173. KWB Papers, box 36/5, 6, and 10.

174. KWB to A. J. Armstrong, December 6, 1932, Armstrong Browning Library, Baylor University, Waco, Texas.

175. KWB draft letter to Elinor Frost, December 26, 1932, KWB Papers, box 40/5.

176. KWB Papers, box 40/5.

177. KWB, Diary 1933, PCBE.

178. Sarah Jackson, "Frost in Texas," *Robert Frost Review* (Fall 1995): 27–29.

179. Lawrance Thompson, ed., *Selected Letters of Robert Frost* (New York: Henry Holt and Company, 1964), 392.

180. Sarah Jackson, "Karle Wilson Baker Brings Robert Frost to Nacogdoches," *East Texas Historical Journal* (Spring 1996): 71–77.

181. Frost, Elinor. In Thompson, *Selected Letters,* 392.

182. CBM, telephone interview with the author, October 15, 1993.

183. Jackson, *Robert Frost Review* (Fall 1995): 32.

184. "Foremost Poet of America," *Sam Houston State Houstonian,* April 19, 1933.

185. Jackson, *East Texas Historical Journal* (Spring 1996): 71–77. The original postal wrapping for the book, bearing Robert Frost's distinctive signature, is in the Steen Library, SFASU.

186. Information on Saxon is from the dust jacket of *Children of Strangers* (PCBE) and from Mary Linn Wernet, the director of the Cammie G. Henry Research Center at Northwestern State University. Wernet has identified Saxon (1891–1946) as "Mr. New Orleans," a southern gentleman who championed the romance and tradition of old New Orleans in history, biography, and fiction. He was also the director of the Louisiana Federal Writers' Project of the Workers Progress Administration. Wernet identified Rosenbaum as an amateur writer who had an insurance business. E-mail correspondence with the author, July 2003. Saxon wrote from Melrose to KWB thanking her for a copy of *Old Coins,* which she had sent him after their visit together at the plantation. KWB Papers, box 3/2.

187. KWB, Diary 1933, PCBE.

188. KWB Papers, box 2/9.

189. KWB, Loose Leaf Diary 1913, PCBE.

190. CBM, interview with the author, August 24, 1998.

191. See KWB Papers, box 27/4, for article on "Bells." See box 28/16 for article and illustrations on lighthouses. Dr. Archie McDonald has given the author folders containing some of KWB's research from magazines about lighthouses.

192. KWB Papers, box 33/18.

193. KWB Papers, box 36/11. The letter from the Twentieth Century Club in Gilmer came from the author's aunt, Virginia Marshall.

194. KWB Papers, box 36/6.

195. KWB, Diary 1934, PCBE.

196. KWB Papers, box 25/10.

197. KWB Papers, box 38/18. KWB's grandson, Jerry Baker, suggested that the author contact KRLD in Dallas for the 1934 script. Unfortunately, their records do not go back that far.

198. KWB Papers, box 36/11.

199. *Bulletin,* Summer 1932, SFA Archive, SLSFASU.

200. KWB Papers, box 25/10.

201. Ibid.

202. KWB, Diary, July 4, 1934, PCBE.

203. KWB Papers, box 8/6.

204. KWB, Diary, July 1934, PCBE.

205. KWB, Diary 1934, PCBE.

206. KWB Papers, box 25/10.

207. KWB Papers, box 34/7.

208. CBM, interview with the author, fall 1999. Charlotte showed me the Grosz picture.

209. KWB, Diary 1934, PCBE.

210. KWB Papers, box 25/10.

211. Anna McCaleb Sheets to KWB, March 12, 1935, KWB Papers, box 9/9.

212. CBM, interview with the author, fall 1999. Statistics on New London come from

Dr. Bobby Johnson, history department, SFASU, who gave me a copy of *Family Style.* Johnson's family lived in New London at the time of the explosion.

New London was located in the center of the East Texas oil field. Dr. Johnson also maintained that the explosion at the New London School happened because the school heated its buildings using gas from waste–gas lines from nearby oil wells. The school, he said, also did not take proper precautions regarding the regulators on the lines. Since the gas had no odor, the explosion occurred without warning. The state later passed a law to add a scent to gas so that it could be detected in the event of a leak in a faulty line.

213. KWB, Diary July 1934, PCBE.

214. KWB, Journal 1914–20, PCBE, folder 5.

Chapter 4.

1. Henry Smith to KWB, September 25, 1935, KWB Papers, box 33/8. KWB would contribute "Nacogdoches: the French and Spaniards." She was one of two women on Smith's list of eighteen proposed contributors.

2. KWB Papers, box 33/8.

3. H. Smith to KWB, October 25, 1935, KWB Papers, box 33/8.

4. KWB draft letter to H. Smith, October 28, 1935, KWB Papers, box 33/8.

5. H. Smith to KWB, November 22, 1935, KWB Papers, box 33/8. Charlotte's two ink drawings are filed among the PCBE folders. CMB identified these drawings for the author.

6. Because it was belated, the October 1935 issue (printed as vol. 21, no. 1 of the *Review*) has the same volume and number as the January 1936 issue. For various reasons, the *Southwest Review* continued to have late printings. In August 1938, John McGinnis wrote to KWB: "We have resumed publication, bringing out five issues in about the interval usually given to one. We are now current." KWB Papers, box 33/10.

7. H. Smith to KWB, January 27, 1936, KWB Papers, box 33/8.

8. KWB draft letter to H. Smith, February 1936, KWB Papers, box 33/8.

9. *Pine Log,* April 10, 1936, KWB Papers, box 29/5.

10. "Notes on Texas History," KWB Papers, box 48/1. Reverend Crocket was the minister of the Episcopal Church in San Augustine for forty-two years and a part-time pastor in Nacogdoches for twenty-four years. In 1929, Crocket became professor emeritus of history at Stephen F. Austin, where he collected and organized data relating to the history of East Texas.

11. Ibid.

12. KWB Papers, box 47/16.

13. KWB, "Nacogdoches: Indian and Spanish Town," *Southwest Review* 21, no. 1 (October 1935): 11, KWB Papers, box 29/5.

14. KWB Papers, box 48/1.

15. See G. L. Crocket, *Two Centuries in East Texas* (Dallas: Southwest Press, 1932), 149–57.

16. See Eugene Barker, *Life of Stephen F. Austin* (Dallas: Cokesbury Press, 1925).

17. KWB Papers, box 48/2. The papers of Henry Raguet and the papers of Mirabeau B. Lamar are now in the R. B. Blake Collection of the Steen Library at SFASU.

18. KWB Papers, box 29/4.

19. KWB, "Notes on Texas History," KWB Papers, box 48/1.

20. See Marquis James, *The Raven* (Indianapolis: Bobbs-Merrill Company, 1929).

21. KWB Papers, box 49/15. In *The Raven,* Marquis James describes Col. Henry Raguet of Nacogdoches as "a Pennsylvanian of Swiss Descent—merchant, landowner, and substantial citizen—the sort of man Austin would have welcomed to San Felipe. He lived in the best house in town" (199). Raguet's daughter, Anna, was a beauty and was courted by many young men in Nacogdoches, including Sam Houston, who lived there in 1833. Later, when Houston moved away because of the Revolution, Robert Irion, Houston's personal secretary, carried messages to Anna Raguet from Houston. Robert Irion later married Anna Raguet, and they named their first son Sam Houston Irion. See James, *Raven,* 318. The Raguet Papers are housed in the Steen Library at SFASU.

22. In her article, "Nacogdoches: The Gateway of the Pioneers," that appeared in *Southwest Review* 21, no. 1 (January 1936): 150, Karle Wilson Baker states that James Starr and his family chose to settle in Nacogdoches in 1839 because of the "intelligent, cultured, and well established society." He led a group to establish a "college for Eastern Texas" in Nacogdoches. KWB writes: "One issue of *The Texas Republican,* published in Nacogdoches for about two months in 1819, contained an invitation to residents to meet at the house of a Mr. Cargill, for the purpose of selecting trustees for a 'seminary of learning.'. . . In 1845, Dr. Starr and his friends got the charter for their college; by this time it had swelled into 'Nacogdoches University.'"

23. KWB Papers, box 47/1.

24. KWB draft letter to H. Smith, KWB Papers, box 33/8; CBM, interview with the author, June 1998. In addition to the articles for the *Southwest Review,* KWB published a short article the following month, February 1936, "A Great Neighbor," in the *Torchbearer,* which Charlotte illustrated.

25. KWB Papers, box 37/6.

26. KWB to W. H. Vann, April 13, 1936, Texas Institute of Letters Microfilm 1935–36, South West Texas State University Archive, San Marcos, Texas (hereafter cited as SWTSU). Also see KWB Papers, box 34/10 for more about the members of the formation committee.

27. KWB to W. H. Vann, August 1, 1935, Xerox copies from Texas Institute of Letters Microfilm 1935–36, SWTSU.

28. J. Frank Dobie to W. H. Vann, August 1, 1935, TIL Microfilm 1935–36, SWTSU.

29. Walter Prescott Webb to W. H. Vann, July 4, 1936, TIL Microfilm 1935–36, SWTSU.

30. W. H. Vann, *History of the Texas Institute of Letters 1936–1966* (Austin: Encino Press, 1967), 4–7. Also see KWB Papers, box 34/10.

31. KWB had saved articles about Mexico from the *Houston Post* for some time. Typical headlines were: "Mexico City Trip Holds Thrills for Motorist," "Monterrey is Favorite Week End Spot for Houstonians," "Where to Go, How to Go, What to See In Romantic Old Mexico," and "Houston Mexico City Road Will be Ready for Travel in May." These articles, and others dating from 1933–42, were in a folder given to me by Archie McDonald of the East Texas Historical Association. They were clearly marked "KWB–Mexico," and he thought that they may have been in Lois Foster Blount's possession at one time.

In the fall of 1999, CBM provided me an itinerary of the trip: they stayed at the Hotel Regis in Mexico City, then went to the Hotel Monte Carlo, Senora Amor's, Cuernavaca, and Tasco, Borda Ceardeus. On August 11, Thomas E. Baker joined them. They stayed at the Imperial in Mexico City and then traveled to Puebla, Cholula, Tlascala, Ocotlan, Santa Ana, and San Marlin. They left Mexico City and went to Queretaco and traveled by train back to Jacksonville, Texas, arriving on August 24. KWB used information that she learned on this trip in *Star of the Wilderness.*

32. TIL Microfilm 1935–36, SWTSU. See KWB Papers, box 34/11 for Vann's letter to KWB telling her she was selected as one of the ten. See box 34/10 for other fellows from the first list: KWB, Eugene C. Barker, Grace Noll Crowell, J. Frank Dobie, Hilton R. Greer, John A. Lomax, Walter P. Webb, Donald Joseph, and Henry N. Smith.

33. J. Frank Dobie to W. H. Vann, September 14, 1936, TIL Microfilm 1935–36, SWTSU.

34. Dobie to Vann, September 28, 1936, TIL Microfilm 1935–36, SWTSU.

35. TIL Microfilm 1935–36, SWTSU.

36. KWB to W. H. Vann, October 27, 1936, TIL Microfilm 1935–36, SWTSU.

37. KWB Papers, box 45/36.

38. "Regent Head in Acceptance Talk," *Daily Sentinel,* October 16, 1936, PCBE.

39. Vann, *History of TIL,* 8.

40. Dorman H. Winfrey: *A History of the Philosophical Society of Texas 1837–1987* (Austin: The Philosophical Society of Texas, 1987), 77.

41. Dobie to KWB, KWB Papers, box 37/6.

42. Ibid.

43. KWB Papers, box 40/3.

44. KWB Papers, box 38/32–33.

45. KWB Papers, box 33/9.

46. KWB draft letter to H. Smith, July 2, 1937, KWB Papers, box 33/9.

47. KWB Papers, box 30/6.

48. Ibid.

49. KWB, "Extensive Notes on W. F. Gray's Diary," KWB Papers, box 47/16 and box 48/1.

50. In her article for the *Southwest Review,* KWB credited Ehrenberg's diary, *Texas und Seine Revolution,* as the fullest account of the New Orleans Greys. She also says she used an abridged translation of the diary by Charlotte Churchill, published in 1935 and titled *With Milam and Fanin,* along with an introductory article on Ehrenberg by Herbert P. Gambrell that appeared in the July 1935 issue of *Southwest Review.*

51. See KWB Papers, box 48/1 for additional sources. Sources from her notes include John Henry Brown, *History of Texas,* vol. 1 (St. Louis, 1892). (The book included a muster roll of sixty-four men in the Greys representing many states and several foreign countries.) KWB also consulted the muster rolls in the General Land Office. She records from Clarence F. Wharton, *Texas Under Many Flags,* vol. 1 (New York: American Historical Society, 1930) the arrival of the Greys in San Antonio in October 1835, when they joined one hundred men in command there. In her novel *Star of the Wilderness,* she used Wharton's comment that the Greys helped keep the troops from breaking rank and returning to their homes. She took notes from Henderson K. Yoakum's *History of Texas*

(Austin, 1935) about the meeting in New Orleans when Adolphus Sterne offered muskets to the first fifty men to volunteer for the Greys. Box 48/1 contains more examples of her notes from materials that were available at the time.

52. KWB Papers, box 30/7.

53. KWB Papers, box 49/10.

54. KWB, "Trailing the New Orleans Greys," *Southwest Review* (April 1937), KWB Papers, box 30/8.

55. KWB Papers, box 23/8.

56. KWB Papers, box 35/7.

57. Philosophical Society of Texas folder, PCBE. This poem, "Elisabet Ney," appeared in the *Philosophical Society of Texas Proceedings*, 1937.

58.KWB draft letter to H. Smith, July 2, 1937, KWB Papers, box 33/9. When CBM and the author discussed *Star of the Wilderness*, CBM agreed that KWB was "obsessed" with James Grant.

59. KWB draft letter to H. Smith, August 18, 1937, KWB Papers, box 33/9.

60. KWB to Vann, August 31, 1937, TIL Microfilm1935–36, SWTSU.

61. KWB Papers, box 23/23.

62. KWB, *Family Style* (New York: Coward-McCann, 1937), 53–55.

63. Ibid., 105.

64. Ibid., 260.

65. Ibid., 77.

66. Ibid., 36.

67. C. M. Joiner to KWB, September 14, 1937, KWB Papers, box 9/7.

68. KWB draft letter to John McGinnis, August 1937, KWB papers, box 9/5.

69. Ibid.

70. Mrs. E. M. Decker to KWB, May 26, 1938, KWB Papers, box 9/16.

71. KWB draft letter to Mary Ruth Holmes, October 26, 1937, KWB Papers, box 9/16.

72. KWB Papers, box 10/2.

73. The four reviews of *Family Style* used here were gifts to the author from Dr. Edwin Gaston Jr. of Nacogdoches.

74. CBM Collection, PCBE. The CBM Collection refers to papers that are not in the indexed and numbered PCBE folders. Sometimes Charlotte's extra materials, such as those in the CBM Collection, are duplicates of items in the numbered and indexed folders, but often the extra materials are new, such as in this case. CBM has much extra information that the SFASU library chose not to include in the KWB Papers.

75. KWB Papers, box 37/8. KWB was asked to join the association in July 1938.

76. KWB Papers, box 25/10.

77. Ibid.

Chapter 5

1. KWB Papers, box 21/4.

2. KWB Papers, box 23/24.

3. KWB Papers, box 23/5.

4. KWB Papers, box 37/13.

5. Ibid.

6. KWB Papers, box 25/6. The dedication took place on April 21, 1938.

7. KWB, Daily Diary 1938, PCBE.

8. KWB Papers, box 21/4.

9. For letters from colleagues congratulating KWB, see KWB Papers, box 34/13.

10. Vann, *History of TIL,* 10.

11. *Pine Log,* "Heads Writers," October 29, 1938, PCBE.

12. W. H. Vann, Council of TIL minutes, KWB Papers, box 34/14.

13. W. H. Vann to TIL membership, June 3, 1939, KWB Papers, box 34/15.

14. KWB Papers, box 34/16. The speaker selection had been a pain for months. In addition to speakers already mentioned, Stephen Benet had also been asked. Finally J. Frank Dobie consented to speak at the luncheon meeting, and he suggested John Lomax for the evening session.

15. Vann, *History of TIL,* 10–11.

16. KWB Papers, box 21/8. When asked, CBM told the author that KWB hired a Spanish teacher in Mexico, but she did not take formal lessons. CBM, interview with the author, November 20, 1999.

17. KWB to W. H. Vann, November 5, 1939, TIL Microfilm 1935–36, SWTSU.

18. Vann to KWB, November 24, 1939, KWB Papers, box 34/16.

19. KWB Papers, box 21/9.

20. KWB draft letter to S. Sanders, August 1940, KWB Papers, box 21/9.

21. KWB, *Star of the Wilderness* (New York: Coward-McCann, 1942), dust jacket.

22. The *chalan* was a flat boat used to ferry horses, wagons, and people across the Sabine River at Gaines Ferry in *Star of the Wilderness.* The chalan was propelled by two men with long poles, pushing it along the river current; it had no railing or guard of any kind.

23. KWB, *Star,* 84–85.

24. Ibid., 107–108.

25. KWB Papers, box 20/4–5. All entries from the bibliographic list that follows come from box 20/4–5, unless otherwise indicated.

26. KWB Papers, box 21/1.

27. Ibid.

28. KWB Papers, box 49/15.

29. KWB Papers, box 20/3.

30. KWB Papers, box 22/13.

31. CBM, interview with the author, October 1999. KWB was prepared for the trip to Mexico. She had clipped many articles about Mexico from the *Houston Post* prior to the visit. Many of the clippings are reviews of books or reviews of art exhibits relating to Mexico. KWB also subscribed to the magazine *Lands of Romance: Travel Topics of the New World—Mexico, West Indies, Central and South America.* A folder of these items was a gift to the author from Dr. Archie McDonald of the department of history and the East Texas Historical Association at SFASU.

32. KWB Papers, box 21/7. Her original title, "A Letter from Jamie," reflects her focus on Grant.

33. KWB Papers, box 20/4.

34. CBM, Interview with the author, October 1999.

35. KWB Papers, box 22/13.

36. KWB draft letter to G. L. Crocket, September 1, 1933, KWB Papers, box 28/9.

37. KWB Papers, box 28/9.

38. KWB Papers, box 20/6.

39. KWB, Charts, PCBE.

40. KWB, Scrapbook, *Saturday Evening Post,* December 26, 1931, in the author's possession (gift from CBM).

41. KWB Papers, box 10/10.

42. KWB, *Star,* 66.

43. Ibid., 74.

44. KWB Papers, box 10/10.

45. KWB, *Star,* 147.

46. KWB Papers, box 48/1.

47. Ibid.

48. KWB Papers, box 23/8.

49. KWB, interview with John Y'Barbo, May 21, 1939, transcript in the author's possession (gift from Dr. Frances Abernathy of Nacogdoches).

50. KWB Papers, box 30/6.

51. KWB Papers, box 20/3. L. J. Wortham, *History of Texas,* vol.1 (Fort Worth: Wortham-Molyneaux, 1924), 311–12, attributes this information to Guy M. Bryan, and KWB quotes from Wortham. A cousin of Stephen F. Austin, Mary Austin Holley, makes an identical statement about the balls in her history, *Texas* (Baltimore, 1836). On page 145, Holley writes: "All visiting is done on horseback, and they will go fifty miles to a ball with their silk dresses, made perhaps in Philadelphia or New Orleans, in their saddle-bags." (Holley does not add the part about "Sundays.") Wortham did not mention Holley's work, and KWB must not have known it in regard to this quotation. After her death, the family of Lois Foster Blount gave Wortham's five-volume work to the SFA library. KWB had probably borrowed Mrs. Blount's history for her research.

52. KWB, *Star,* 138.

53. KWB, Journal 1920, PCBE.

54. Ibid. William Vaughn Moody became another "channel" for communication into the spirit world. KWB based her ability to recognize Moody's handwriting in automatic writing experiments on examples from notes he had written on her themes at the University of Chicago. When her work on Moody's biography showed little progress, she sought help by going to him in the spirit world.

55. Ibid. Besides TEB, Ben T. Wilson was probably the strongest influence on KWB. She often sought his advice.

56. TWB, interview with the author, July 8, 1997.

57. KWB, Journal March 1941, PCBE.

58. KWB, Psychic Notes March 1941, PCBE.

59. Ibid.

60. Ibid.

61. Ibid.

62. KWB, Psychic Notes April 1941, PCBE.

63. KWB, Psychic Notes March 1941, PCBE.

64. Ibid.

65. Ibid.

66. KWB, *Star,* 93.

67. KWB, Psychic Notes March 1941, PCBE.

68. KWB, Psychic Notes May 1941, PCBE.

69. Ibid.

70. Sugene Spears to KWB, May 1, 1940, KWB Papers, box 21/6.

71. KWB Papers, box 23/13.

72. Charlotte Baker Montgomery to the author, November 20, 1999.

73. KWB Papers, box 21/2.

74. Ibid.

75. KWB Papers, box 21/13.

76. KWB Papers, box 21/14.

77. KWB Papers, box 22/12.

78. KWB draft letter to George B. Dealey, April 13, 1942, KWB Papers, box 23/6. KWB's letter reflects her typical modesty, but she was a recognized historian and a member of the Texas Historical Association. In December the year before, Arthur Vanderbilt had invited her to become one of two hundred founding members of the Phi Beta Kappa association in New York.

79. KWB, Journal 1954, PCBE.

80. KWB, Philosophical Society of Texas folder, PCBE.

81. KWB Papers, box 22/13. KWB refers to the J. R. Montgomery/Paul McAlpine similarities in "In Search of Myself," PCBE. KWB's copies of legal documents between Sam Houston and James Starr and Sam Houston and John Durst reflect her detailed interest in Houston. These also helped her understand Starr and Durst. In the author's possession (gift of Dr. Archie McDonald).

82. KWB Papers, box 21/4.

83. KWB Papers, box 22/13.

84. KWB Papers, box 21/4.

85. KWB Papers, box 22/13.

86. KWB draft letter to Mrs. M. Burke, February 28, 1943, KWB Papers, box 23/1. The booklet KWB refers to is *Historic Nacogdoches Texas* prepared by R. B. Blake and Rev. George Crocket in 1936 as part of the local celebration of the Texas centennial. The booklet has been printed three times since then. In the author's possession.

87. KWB draft letter to CBM, c. April 1942, KWB Papers, box 23/4.

88. George B. Dealey to KWB, April 14, 1942, KWB Papers, box 23/6.

89. Floy Lewis to KWB, July 12, 1942, KWB Papers, box 23/13.

90. Laura Krey to KWB, September 11, 1945, KWB Papers, box 23/2.

91. Eugene C. Barker to KWB, May 21, 1942, KWB Papers, box 23/3.

92. Herbert P. Gambrell to KWB, April 25, 1942, KWB Papers, box 23/3.

93. CBM to KWB, April 15, 1942, KWB Papers, box 51/20. CBM had sent some jacket drawings to Coward-McCann for the novel, but the publisher did not select them.

94. Copies of the full text of the Barker, Acheson, Vann, and Field reviews were gifts to the author by Dr. Edwin Gaston Jr.

95. KWB Papers, box 23/14.

96. KWB, Diary 1913, PCBE.

Chapter 6

1. KWB Papers, box 21/4.

2. KWB Papers, box 23/8.

3. KWB Papers, box 23/27.

4. KWB Papers, box 39/17.

5. KWB draft letter to Sister Agatha, July 16, 1942, KWB Papers, box 39/17.

6. KWB draft letter to Sister Agatha, July 28, 1942, KWB Papers, box 39/17.

7. Sister Agatha to KWB, August 17, 1942, KWB Papers, box 39/17.

8. KWB draft letter to Sister Agatha, August 1942, KWB Papers, box 39/17. Later, KWB returned Sister Agatha's favors by reading the nun's manuscript of a juvenile book and making helpful suggestions. KWB Papers, box 39/19.

9. KWB Papers, box 39/19, box 48/7, and box 48/8. Don Manuel de Salcedo was governor of the Texas Territory in 1812 (Yoakum). After Don Bernardo Gutierrez murdered prisoners at San Antonio during the Magee-Gutierrez Expedition, he was replaced by Gen. Don Jose Alvarez Toledo as chief of command. Under Toledo, the disastrous battle of Medina was fought, in which American soldiers were almost annihilated, and the whole Magee-Gutierrez Expedition of 1812–1813 was overwhelmingly defeated. See G. L. Crocket, *Two Centuries in East Texas* (Austin: Hart Graphics, 1932).

10. KWB Papers, box 48/7. The manuscript for "It Blows from the Spanish Country" is in the PCBE.

11. Thomas Coward to KWB, September 15, 1947, KWB Papers, box 23/27.

12. John Farrar to CBM, September 17, 1948, PCBE. Roger Montgomery was practicing law in Portland; Charlotte was curator at the art museum.

13. Ned Bradford to CBM, June 9, 1949, PCBE.

14. Allen Maxwell to CBM, February 22, 1949, KWB Papers, box 23/17.

15. "It Blows from the Spanish Country," CBM Collection, PCBE.

16. Jacques Chambrun to KWB, September 25, 1952, PCBE.

17. KWB Papers, box 34/3–4 and box 34/25. As late as 1958, when she was eighty years old, KWB was still judging poetry contests for the Poetry Society. That year, the society bestowed the title of honorary vice president on KWB. When the Poetry Society of Texas met the following June in Dallas, KWB's health did not allow her to attend the meeting, but she was a presence there nevertheless. One of her short lyrics adorned the program: "The Stars are so far apart / My steps so small; / I must haste who would / Set foot in all."

18. Winifred Kittredge to KWB, December 1942, KWB Papers, box 37/7.

19. KWB, "If You Want to Write," unpublished manuscript, PCBE.

20. Ibid.

21. Ibid.

22. KWB, Manuscript Record Book, PCBE.

23. Ibid.

24. KWB, "If You Want to Write," PCBE.

25. KWB Papers, box 34.

26. KWB, "Full Circle," February 1944, PCBE, folder 33.

27. John William Rogers, "A Round-up of the Most Interesting Texas Books of All Time," *Dallas Times Herald,* October 7, 1945, PCBE, folder 38.

28. Ibid.

29. KWB Papers, box 25/5. The broadcast took place on February 19, 1946.

30. Herbert Gambrell to KWB, November 19, 1951, KWB Papers, box 35/11.

31. KWB draft letter to H. Gambrell, November 22, 1951, KWB Papers, box 35/11.

32. In his *History of TIL,* Vann explains the term *fellow.* At the TIL organizational meeting in 1936, the idea was put forward to name the most worthy of the institute as "fellows," but the proposal did not pass. Members revived the idea in 1948. Vann wrote, "The provisions were that there should not be more than 5 living Fellows at any one time, that not more than 3 be named the first year, and that no one should be chosen who did not receive the votes of two-thirds of the active members." In 1949, members voted to give the council of the organization the authority to name the recipients. Council members named J. Frank Dobie the first fellow in 1949, Walter Prescott Webb in 1951, and KWB in 1952. Vann, *History of TIL,* 59–60.)

33. W. H. Vann to KWB, October 4, 1952, KWB Papers, box 34/22.

34. KWB Papers, box 34/23.

35. Ibid.

36. Vann, *History of TIL,* viii. Vann also records in his book that CBM became the first second-generation member of the TIL in 1953. She won the institute's award for best juvenile book that year for *Magic for Mary M.*

37. KWB Papers, box 45/5.

38. Ibid.

39. KWB Papers, box 38/21.

40. KWB, Diary May 1953, PCBE.

41. KWB, Ledger Journal 1903–5, PCBE. Dr. Jere L. Jackson, director of CETS, has undertaken the project to reprint selected poetry and prose. The author will provide essays to accompany the reprinted works.

42. KWB, Diary May 1953, PCBE.

43. KWB, Diary May 1952, a typescript, PCBE, folder 7. In an interview with the author on July 8, 1997, TWB told the author that he and Jean Blount married in 1940. The Blounts lived just up North Street from the Bakers. She was the "girl next door"—a very creative, vibrant person. Her father was Sen. Eugene A. Blount.

44. KWB Papers, box 5/26.

45. KWB, Philosophical Society of Texas folder, PCBE.

46. KWB Papers, box 35/14. Andrews had already printed the program and did not ask Lois Blount to take part.

47. Ibid. TWB remarked in an interview with the author on July 8, 1997, that he remembered the event clearly and that the speaker that evening was the president of Rice University. He said it was one of the most inspiring and well-informed speeches he had ever heard.

48. Jere L. Jackson, SFA Heritage Series, *Nacogdoches Daily Sentinel,* August 9, 1998, sec. E.

49. KWB, Diary 1908, PCBE. Many diary entries refer to the Bakers' interest in the stars. The early poem "Altair" came about as a result of stargazing. So many of KWB's poems are about trees that CBM has remarked that she associates trees with her mother's poetry even more than she does birds. KWB had these words inscribed on TEB's tombstone: "And he shall be like a tree planted by the rivers of water," and planted a magnolia tree at the grave site. It is now a very large tree and shades both their graves.

50. KWB to Ralph Steen, June 3, 1959, KWB Papers, box 38/19.

51. KWB to Walter Prescott Webb, June 3, 1959, KWB Papers, box 38/19.

52. PCBE, folder 8.

53. The *Daily Sentinel* was an afternoon paper at that time, so the news of KWB's death that very day received coverage along with the election results from the day before, Tuesday, November 8.

54. "Mrs. Baker Dies Today," *Daily Sentinel,* November 9, 1960, KWB Papers, box 45/8. Articles in the *Houston Post* and *Dallas News* appeared on November 10, 1960; newspaper clippings in PCBE.

55. Many of KWB's poems were set to music; see KWB Papers, box 26/9–18.

56. KWB Papers, boxes 38 and 39; KWB Papers, box 36; KWB Papers, box 37.

57. KWB Papers, box 45/8.

58. Gustan Davidson Letter to CBM, June 27, 1961, PCBE, folder 23.

59. PCBE, folder 22.

60. See "The Tree" from *Blue Smoke* in chapter 2.

61. KWB, Diary, PCBE, folder 7.

WRITINGS OF KARLE WILSON BAKER

SELECTED UNPUBLISHED MANUSCRIPTS

"AE: Practical Mystic," n.d.
"The Anarchist and the Puritan," [1905]
"The Barnhoff Account," n.d.
"Bella against the Elements," n.d.
"Breaking into Society—of the Birds," n.d.
"Camping with the Kiddies, by One Who Has Tried It," 1916
"The Car Door Slams," n.d.
"Carl Sandburg: Brother of Stars and Cinders," n.d.
"The City of Magnificent Distances," 1935
"Crepe Myrtles," n.d.
"The Crop," [c. 1923]
"A Day on the Campus," n.d.
"Differing in Glory," 1921
"The Dissolution of Miss Bee," n.d.
"The First Thousand," [1930s]
"Full Circle," 1944
"Galveston," n.d.
"Gone to Texas," n.d.
"Grandma's Marigolds," n.d.
"Great Things with Small," n.d.
"His One Hunting Story," 1914
"Homes of the Presidents," 1936
"Honey from the Thorn," June 27, 1936
"Horns of Elfland," [c. 1921]
"A Hundred Miles of Memories," 1934
"I Face the New Year," [c. 1916]
"In Search of Myself," 1922
"It Blows from the Spanish Country," 1943–44
"The Life of David Crockett," n.d.
"Lighting the Sea," 1935.
"The Little Carpet-Bagger," 1906
"Milking the Cow," n.d.
"The Moon-Month," [1921]
"The Mother Prays after a Hard Day," n.d.
"Must One of them Dominate?" 1937
"The Name Was Wainwright," [c. 1945]
"The New Religion and Women's Problem," 1913

"Number Five," n.d.
"Of Leisure," n.d.
"Of Stitches," n.d.
"On Accosting Strangers," n.d.
"On Being a Stream of Consciousness," n.d.
"On Communing with Boulders," n.d.
"On the Trail of a Dream," [c. 1935]
"The Pan-Handle," n.d.
"The Paradoxical Profession," n.d.
"The Pneumatic Dollar," 1930
"The Reconstruction of Rebby," n.d.
"Robert Frost, Neighbor," [1930s]
"Rooms, Houses, Walls, and Taverns," n.d.
"Sam Houston Steals the Show," [1930s]
"See What I've Found!" n.d.
"So It Was When My Life Began," n.d.
"Still Sits the Schoolhouse by the Road," n.d.
"The Story of the Roosevelt House," 1935–37.
"The Story of Texas," 1907
"A Sturdy Oak," n.d.
"Sweet Are the Uses of Prosperity," n.d.
"The Talisman," n.d.
"A Taste of Gregariousness," n.d.
"Through the Back Gate," n.d.
"Twenty Miles of Elm Trees," n.d.
"A Villager Goes to Town," n.d.
"White Elephant," [1920s]
"William Vaughn Moody: An Informal Study,"1921–22
"William Vaughn Moody: The Firebringer to the Classroom," [c. 1931]
"Woman and Song," n.d.

PUBLISHED WORKS

Books

Baker, Karle Wilson. *Blue Smoke.* New Haven: Yale University Press, 1919.
———. *The Garden of the Plynck.* New Haven: Yale University Press, 1920.
———. *Burning Bush.* New Haven: Yale University Press, 1922.
———. *Old Coins.* New Haven: Yale University Press, 1923.
———. *Texas Flag Primer.* New York: The World Book Company, 1926.
———. *The Birds of Tanglewood.* Dallas: Southwest Press, 1930.
———. *Dreamers on Horseback.* Dallas: Southwest Press, 1931.
———. *Two Little Texans.* New York: The World Book Company, 1932.
———. *Family Style.* New York: Coward-McCann, 1937.
———. *Star of the Wilderness.* New York: Coward-McCann, 1942.
———. *The Reindeer's Shoe and Other Stories.* Austin: E. C. Temple, 1988.

Short Prose

"An Accidental Saint," *Collier's*, December 21, 1907, 14–16.

"An Artistic Temperament," *Broadway*, 1908.

"An Averted Catastrophe," *Smart Set*, 1907, 25–81.

"Being True to the Ghosts," *Nacogdoches Daily Sentinel*, January 24, 1907.

"Bells," *Torchbearer* 15, no. 15 (April 12, 1936).

"The Birds of Tanglewood," *Yale Review* 11 (October 1921):118–29.

"Bread and Hyacinths," *Woman's World*, December 1916, 9–12.

"The Bully," *This Week*, April 18, 1937.

"Busman's Workday," *Yale Review* 26, (Spring 1937).

"The Busy Flower-Lover," *Holland's Magazine*, October 1913, 47–48.

"Charmed Days," *Texas Review* 7, no. 1 (October 1921): 70–74.

"The Choicest Book in the World," *Portal* 97, no. 18 (May 1937): 4.

"Colors," *Texas Review* 5, no. 3 (April 1920): 249.

"The Commonest Fault in a Guest," *McCall's*, 1915, 104–105.

"The Corduroy Man," *Smart Set*, 1907.

"Creation and June," *Home Magazine*, 1907.

"To Cure the Poverty-stricken Consciousness," *Nautilus*, 1923.

"Diversities of Gifts," *The Red Book*, 1907, 345–57.

"The End of a Philosophy," *Putnam's*, 1909.

"A Good Shot," *Everybody's*, August 1907, 274–78.

"Gran'ma's," *Everybody's*, 1907, 132–36.

"A Great Neighbor," *Torchbearer* 15, no. 7 (February 16, 1936): 4.

"Helpful Facts in Building a Summer Camp: By a Woman Camper Who Knows," *Craftsman*, 1915.

"Her Husband's People," *Success*, 1909.

"How Padre Antonio Buried the Bells," *Sunset*, December 1909, 564–72.

"How We Prepare for Christmas," *Holland's Magazine*, December 1912.

"Howdy Stranger," *Globe* 1, no. 2 (May 1937): 17–19.

"In Texas," *Motor Print*, September 1914, 11–12.

"The Island of the Saints," *Classmate* 43, no. 9 (February 29, 1936): 5–6.

"The Kite Flies High," *Target* 96, no. 10 (1936): 5.

"Listening," *Nautilus*, 1937.

"A Man without a Purpose," *University of Chicago Weekly*, March 14,1901.

"A Modern Incompatibility," *Home Magazine*, October 1907.

"Nacogdoches: The Gateway of the Pioneers," *Southwest Review* 21, no. 2 (January 1936): 137–54.

"Nacogdoches: The Indian and Spanish Town," *Southwest Review* 21, no. 1 (October 1935).

"On a Certain Condescension of Natives," *Scribner's*, October 1920, 503–504.

"On Writing for the Best Magazines," *Atlantic* 97 (April 1906): 571–72.

"The One City," *Scribner's*, February 1920, 247–49.

"The Oracle's Window-Seat," *Housekeeper*, April 1910.

"Padre Antonio," *Sunset*, 1910.

"Playing Geography," *Home Progress*, 1914.

"A Poet of the Lean Years," *Forum* 68, 1922.
"A Point of Honor," *Century Magazine,* 1908, 261–66.
"The Prose and Poetry of Karle Wilson Baker." P*amphlet,* c.1931.
"The Porch Swing," *Century Magazine,* 1920.
"Red Roads," *Southern Review* 1, no. 1 (January 1920): 33–34.
"The Rubber-Tired Boy," *Century Magazine,* 1906.
"Sand-Ugh," *Motor Print,* 1915, 9.
"The Small Town Audience," *Movie Pictorial,* June 20, 1914.
"A Toast for June," *People's Home Journal,* 1913.
"Trailing the New Orleans Grays," *Southwest Review* 22, no. 3 (Spring 1937).
"Washington: An Arkansas Town with a Texas Shrine," *Dallas News,* December 29, 1935.
"Washington's Home Town, "*Lutheran Young Folks* 33, no. 11 (February 15, 1936): 81–82.
"William Alexander Percy's Notable Poetry," *Dallas News,* November 14, 1943.
"William Vaughn Moody: A Recollection," *Boston Monitor,* December 1922.
"Window Lore," *Yale Review* 12 (April 1923).
"A Writer's Camera," *Photo Era,* July 1915, 17–19.
"Your First Camping Tour," *Holland's Magazine,* June 1914, 51–53.

SELECTED SPEECHES BY KARLE WILSON BAKER

"If You Want to Write"
"Literary Wildcatting"
"On the Poetry of Emily Dickinson"
"On the Poetry of William Vaughn Moody"
"Poetry and People"
"Poetry and the Modern Spirit"
"When a Poet Turns Novelist"

SELECTED ANTHOLOGIES THAT INCLUDE WORKS BY KARLE WILSON BAKER

American Poetry Since 1900. Edited by Louis Untermeyer. New York: Henry Holt, 1924.
American Speech. Edited by Wilhemina Hedde and William Brigance. New York: J. B. Lippincott, 1942.
Anthology of Magazine Verse for 1918. Edited by William S. Braithwaite. Boston: Small, Maynard, 1918.
Anthology of Magazine Verse for 1921. Edited by William S. Braithwaite. Boston: Small, Maynard, 1921.
A Book of Yale Review Verse. Edited by W. L. Cross. New Haven: Yale University Press, 1917.
A Canticle of the Year: A Birthday Book for Girls. Edited by Elvira J. Slack. New York: The Womans Press, 1920.
A Century With Texas Poets and Poetry. Edited by Vaida S. Montgomery. Dallas: Kaleidograph Press, 1934.
Children's Bookshelf. Edited by R. B. Buckingham. Boston: Ginn and Company, 1936.

Children's Hour. Volume 5, Edited by Marjorie Barrows. Chicago: The Spencer Press, 1947.

Enjoying Literature. Voices of America Series. Edited by Leonidas W. Payne, Mark A. Neville, and Natalie E. Chapman. New York: Rand McNally, 1940.

The Golden Year: The Poetry Society of America Anthology (1910-1960). Edited by Melville Cane, John Farrar, and Louise Nicholl. New York: Fine Editions Press, 1960.

Literature We Like. Edited by Winifred H. Nash and Russell Blankenship. New York: Charles Scribner's Sons, 1939.

The Lyric South. Edited by Addison Hibbard. New York: The Macmillan Company, 1928.

Modern Verse, British and American. Volume 1. Edited by Anita Forbes. Revised edition. New York: Henry Holt and Company, 1938.

My Mother's Bible: A Scrapbook Treasury of Verse and Wisdom. Edited by D. E. Lurton. New York: Wilfred Funk, Inc., 1941.

New American Speech. Edited by Wilhemina Hedde and William Brigance. New York: J. B. Lippincott, 1957.

The New Silver Lining: A Second Anthology of Readings, Poems and Prayers. Edited by Richard Tatlock. London: Bodley Head, 1955.

New Trails and Wide Horizons: Our Reading Heritage Anthology Series, Book 7. Edited by Eleanor McGehan. New York: Holt, 1957.

Prose and Poetry of America (Southwestern Edition). Edited by H. W. McGraw. 1934. Reprint, Syracuse, N.Y.: L. W. Singer Company, 1940.

Principal Poets of the World: The Biography, Detailed Bibliography and a Representative Poem of Leading Poets of the English-Speaking Countries. London: The Mitre Press, 1937.

Roycroft Birthday Book. Edited by Elbert Hubbard. East Aurora, N.Y.: The Roycrofters Publishing Company, 1924.

Southern Poetry. Edited by B. D. Taylor. Livingston, Texas: Enterprise Printing, 1922.

Southern Treasury of Life and literature. Edited by Stark Young. New York: Charles Scribner's Sons, 1937.

Strength for Service to God and Country: Daily Devotional Messages for Men in the Services. Edited by Chaplain Norman Nygaard. Nashville: Abingdon-Cokesbury Press, 1942.

Texas in Poetry: A 150-Year Anthology. Edited by Billy Bob Hill. Denton, Texas: Center for Texas Studies, University of North Texas, 1994.

Texas Poets: An Anthology of Verse of 83 Contemporary Poets. Edited by Henry Harrison. New York: Henry Harrison, 1936.

Texas Sampler. Edited by Eula Phares Mohle. New York: Oxford Book Company, 1955.

Types of Literature. Edited by E. A. Cross. New York: Macmillan, 1944.

Victory! Celebrated By Thirty-eight American Poets. Edited by William Stanley Braithwaite. Boston: Small, Maynard, 1919.

Voices of the Southwest: A Book of Texan Verse. Edited by Hilton Greer. New York: Macmillan, 1923.

Writers and Writings of Texas. Edited by Davis Foute Eagleton. New York: Broadway Publishing Company, 1913.

BIBLIOGRAPHY

ARCHIVES

Armstrong, A. J. Archive. Armstrong-Browning Library, Baylor University, Waco, Texas.

Baker, Karle Wilson. Papers. Steen Library, Stephen F. Austin State University, Nacogdoches, Texas.

Baker, Karle Wilson. Private Collection. Baker Estate. In possession of Charlotte Baker Montgomery.

Baker, Karle Wilson. Vertical File. Center for American History, University of Texas, Austin, Texas.

Doe/Moffitt Libraries, University of California, Berkeley.

Fondren Library, Southern Methodist University, Dallas, Texas.

Mary Couts Burnett Special Collections Library, Texas Christian University, Fort Worth, Texas.

Melrose Collection. Watson Memorial Library, Cammie Henry Research Center, Northwestern State University, Natchitoches, Louisiana.

Montgomery Memorial Collection. DeGolyer Library, Southern Methodist University, Dallas, Texas.

Payne, Leonidas W. Papers. Harry Ransom Humanities Research Center, University of Texas, Austin, Texas.

Selecman Papers. Bridwell Library, Southern Methodist University, Dallas, Texas.

Southwestern Writers Collection. Albert B. Alkek Library. Center for the Study of the Southwest, Southwest Texas State University, San Marcos, Texas.

Texas State Archive. Extension Loan Library, University of Texas, Austin, Texas.

PERSONAL COMMUNICATIONS BY AUTHOR

Baker, Edward (Jerry), grandson of Karle Wilson Baker. Interview by author, May 12, 1998; July 10, 1998. Letter to author, May 12, 1998.

Baker, Thomas Ellis II, grandson of Karle Wilson Baker. Interview by author, May 12, 1998

Baker, Thomas Wilson. Interviews by author, July 8 and 29, 1997; September 15, 1997; May 12, 1998.

Davis, Bryan Holt. Interviews by author, August 11, 1997; July 2, 1999.

Fain, Victor. Interview by author, January 20, 1997.

Gaston, Edwin W. Jr. Letter to author, April 27, 1997. Interview by author May 12, 1997.

Gilmore, Inez Washburn. Interviews by author, December 8 and 11, 1996; January 8 and 9, 1997.

Miller, Carolyn Sturdevant. Interviews by author, January 9 and 20, 1997.

Montgomery, Charlotte Baker, daughter of Karle Wilson Baker. Multiple interviews by author, 1996, 1997, 1998, 1999, 2000, 2001, 2002, 2003, 2004.

Perkins, Dorothy. Letter to author, July 3, 1999. E-mails to author, July 17, 19, and 23, 1999; August 22, 1999.

Reavley, Florence Wilson (Toncie), niece to Karle Wilson Baker. Letters to author, August 26, 1997; September 8 and 15, 1997; July 20 and 24, 1999.

Reavley, Judge Thomas M., Toncie's husband. Letter to author, September 11, 1997; November 20, 2003; December 16, 2003.

Wells, Gordon. Interview by author, August 20, 1997.

Winfrey, Dorman H. Letter to author, June 6, 1997.

BOOKS, ARTICLES, AND PAPERS

Barns, Florence E., ed. *Texas Writers Today.* Dallas: Tardy, 1935.

Beaird, Miriam G., ed. *Leading Women of America.* Thompkins: New York, 1938.

Cross, Wilbur. "Ten Years of The Yale Review." *Yale Review* 11 (October 1921): xxix–xxxii.

Gaston, Edwin W., Jr. *The Early Novel of the Southwest.* Albuquerque: University of New Mexico Press, 1961.

———. "Karle Wilson Baker." In *New Handbook of Texas,* edited by Ron Tyler, 349. Austin: Texas State Historical Association, 1996.

———. "Karle Wilson Baker: First Woman of Texas Letters." Paper presented at annual meeting of the East Texas Historical Association, Nacogdoches, September 18, 1976. Also printed in *East Texas Historical Journal* 15, no. 2 (1977): 45–51.

———. "Karle Wilson Baker: The Other Southwestern Woman." Paper presented at annual meeting of the Southwestern American Literature Association, February 1, 1978.

Grider, S. A., and L. H. Rodenberger, eds. *Texas Women Writers.* College Station: Texas A&M Press, 1997: 87–91.

Hibbard, Addison. *The Lyric South: An Anthology of Recent Poetry from the South.* New York: Macmillan, 1928.

Howes Durward, ed. *American Women.* Los Angeles: Richard Blank, 1935.

Jackson, Sarah. "*Family Style* and the East Texas Oil Field." Paper, annual meeting of the East Texas Historical Association, Nacogdoches, September 2000.

———. "Frost in Texas: Lecture 1933." *Robert Frost Review* (1995): 26–35.

———. "Image and Text: Collaborative Works by Karle Wilson Baker and Charlotte Baker Montgomery." Paper presented at Image and Text II Symposium, Stephen F. Austin State University, Nacogdoches, November 6, 1998.

———. "Karle Wilson Baker and Charlotte Baker Montgomery." Paper, C. B. Montgomery Art Exhibition, Steen Library, Stephen F. Austin State University, February 25, 1997.

———. "Karle Wilson Baker Brings Robert Frost to Nacogdoches." *East Texas Historical Journal* 34, no. 1 (Spring 1996): 71–76.

———. "Karle Wilson Baker: First Lady of Texas Letters." Center for East Texas Studies, Stephen F. Austin State University. http://www.cets.sfasu.edu. June 1998.

———. "Karle Wilson Baker: Nacogdoches Laureate." Paper presented at annual meeting of the East Texas Historical Association, Nacogdoches, September 21, 1996.
———. "Karle Wilson Baker: Texas Laureate." Paper, annual convention of Texas Council of Teachers of English, San Antonio, February 5–7, 1998.
———. "Karle Wilson Baker: Texas Teacher and Writer." *English in Texas* 28, no. 3 (Summer 1998): 12–19.
———. "Karle Wilson Baker: The Making of a Texas Poet." *WILLA Journal of the National Council of Teachers of English* 7 (Fall 1998): 23–30.
———. "Laureate of Texas: The Poetry of Karle Wilson Baker." *East Texas Historical Journal* 36, no. 2 (Fall 1999): 68–75.
———. "Reading the Land: Karle Wilson Baker's Poetry of Place." Paper presented at Image and Text II Symposium, Stephen F. Austin State University, Nacogdoches, November 6, 1998.
———. "Remembering Karle Wilson Baker: Texas Poet." Paper presented at annual convention of Council of College Teachers of English and College English Association, San Antonio, April 2–4, 1998.
———. Review of *Texas Women Writers*, eds. Grider and Rodenberger. *East Texas Historical Journal* 32, no. 1 (Spring 1999): 79–80.
———. "S. F. A.'s First Star: Karle Wilson Baker." SFA Heritage Series, *Nacogdoches Daily Sentinel*, September 6, 1998, sec. E.
Larkin, Thomas III, ed. *Who's Who in Texas.* Boston: Larkin, 1941.
Luker, Winnie Davis. "Karle Wilson Baker, Local Colorist of Texas." Master's thesis, Stephen F. Austin State University, Nacogdoches, Texas, 1943.
Majors, Mabel, ed. *Southwest Heritage: A Literary History with Bibliography.* Albuquerque: University of New Mexico Press, 1938.
McLennan, Mary. "A Short Biography of Karle Wilson Baker." Illustrated student paper, Stephen F. Austin State Teachers College, Nacogdoches, Texas, 1937.
Palmer, Pamela Lynn. "Dorothy Scarborough and Karle Wilson Baker: A Literary Friendship." *Southwest Historical Quarterly* 91 (July 1987–88): 19–32.
———. "Karle Wilson Baker and the East Texas Experience." *East Texas Historical Journal* 24, no. 2 (1986): 46–58.
———. "Subjective Regionalism to Cosmopolitanism: A Study of Three Texas Poets." Master's thesis, Stephen F. Austin State University, Nacogdoches, Texas, 1973.
Pearce, T. M., and A. P. Thomason, eds. *Southwesterners Write.* Albuquerque: University of New Mexico Press, 1953.
Perring, R. W., ed. *Contemporary Personalities.* London: Merville Press, 1930.
Queen, Mary Jane. "Karle Wilson Baker: the Muse of 'West Window.'" *Junior Historian,* Nacogdoches High School (November 1954): 11–12.
Smith, Goldie C. *Creative Arts in Texas: A Handbook of Biography.* Dallas: Cokesbury Press, 1926, 13–14.
Thompkins, Virginia L., ed. *Leading Women of America.* New York: Author's International, 1938.
Thompson, Lawrance, ed. *Selected Letters of Robert Frost.* New York: Holt, 1964.
Turner, Martha Ann. *Old Nacogdoches in the Jazz Age.* Austin: Madonna Press, 1976, 42–58.

Vann, W. H. *The History of the Texas Institute of Letters 1936–1966.* Austin: Encino Press, 1967.

Winfrey, Dorman H. *A History of the Philosophical Society of Texas 1837–1987.* Austin: The Philosophical Society of Texas, 1987.

Wynn, Thomas, ed. *Southern Literature.* New York: Prentice-Hall, 1932.

SELECTED REVIEWS OF KARLE WILSON BAKER'S WORK AND NOTICES OF PUBLIC SPEECHES

Acheson, Sam. Review of *Star of the Wilderness. Saturday Review of Literature,* May 16, 1942, 33.

Austin Daily Texan. "Baker Reads Moody Poetry Friday at 8," March 28, 1928.

———. "Poetry of Moody Subject of Baker Lecture Tonight," March 30, 1928.

———. "Moody's Poetry Analyzed by Baker in Talk," March 31, 1928.

———. "Poet Interprets Dickinson's Life," February 28, 1931.

———. "Mrs. Baker Reads Original Poetry," March 1, 1931.

———. "Karle Wilson Baker to Speak at Texas University March 30," March 29, 1932.

Barker, Eugene C. Review of *Star of the Wilderness. Southwestern Historical Quarterly* (July 1942): 88.

Barnes, Florence Elberta. *Texas Writers of Today.* Dallas: Tardy Publishing Company, 1935, 57–58.

Book Review Digest. Review of *Star of the Wilderness,* June 1942, 36.

Bowyer, John W. "Tragic Era of Texas Told by Poet Karle Wilson Baker." *Dallas News,* April 26, 1942.

Campbell, Killis. "A Collected Edition of Mrs. Karle Wilson Baker's Poems." Review of *Dreamers on Horseback.* Books and Branding Irons. *Texas Outlook,* June 1931.

Collins, Mrs. C. F. Review of *Dreamers on Horseback. Texas Federation News,* August 1931.

Dallas News. "English Anthology will contain Works of Nacogdoches Poetess," December 16, 1923.

———. "Indigenous Texas Material is Used in School Primer," May 9, 1926.

———. "East Texas Oil Field is Setting for Fine Novel: Karle Wilson Baker Knows her People," September 19, 1937.

———. "Mrs. Thomas E. Baker, 82 Etex Author and Poet, Dies," November 10, 1960.

Dobie, Bertha. "Texas Poet Gives Some Sidelights on Birds at Home." *Dallas News,* December 21, 1930.

Fain, Lucille. "News Praises Mrs. Baker's Recent Historical Novel." *Redland Herald,* April 30, 1942, 3.

Field, Louise M. "*Star of the Wilderness.*" Review. *New York Times Book Review,* April 26, 1942, 22.

Frye, Mattie Lou. "Karle Wilson Baker." *Texas Weekly,* April 4, 1931, 8–9.

Greer, Hilton R. "Collected Poems of Texas Poet Have Depth and Texture." *Dallas News,* April 12, 1931.

———. "Prose Writers of Texas." *Dallas Journal,* November 20, 1935.

Houston Post. "Texas Poet to Appear Here," November 8, 1930.
———. "Dinner for Texas Poet," November 16, 1930.
———. "Through the Porthole," November 16, 1930.
———. "Texas Poet Tells How She finds Time to Write and Lead Home Life," November 20, 1930.
———. "Texas Woman Poet is Heard," November 21, 1930.
———. "Texas Woman's First Novel Gripping Drama of Texas Oil fields." Review of *Family Style,* December 5, 1937.
Houston Washington Square News. "Mrs. Baker, Texas Poet, at Public Library." November 14, 1930.
Kansas City Star. "Collected Verse of a Poet of the Southwest," 1931.
Lufkin Daily News. "Famous Poetess Honored at SFA College," July 3, 1960.
McGinnis, John. "Forthcoming Novel Depicts Oil Boom." Review of *Family Style. Dallas News,* September 5, 1937.
———. Review of *Family Style. Dallas News,* 19 September 1937.
Major, Mabel. "Karle Wilson Baker's Lyrical Gift is Assessed." *Dallas News,* December 21, 1952; reprinted in *Nacogdoches Daily Sentinel,* January 6, 1953.
Nacogdoches Daily Sentinel. "In Honor of Mrs. Baker," January 16, 1922.
———. "Karle Wilson Baker's Novel of East Texas," September 20, 1937.
———. "Local Author Honored," November 19, 1952.
———. "Famous Poetess at SFA College," July 2, 1960.
———. "Works of Karle Wilson Baker on Display at SFA Library," July 2, 1960, 6.
———. "Mrs. Baker Dies Today Rites Thursday," November 9, 1960, 1.
———. "1966 Book of the Year Dedicated to Karle Wilson Baker," March 9, 1966.
———. "Nacogdoches Street Named for Karle Wilson Baker," September 7, 1966.
New Republic. Review of *Burning Bush,* October 25, 1922.
New York Herald Tribune Books. "Turns with a Bookworm," April 26, 1931, sec. 9.
New York Times. Review of *Old Coins,* March 18, 1923.
New York Times Book Review, "Queries and Answers," March 24, 1935.
Philosophical Society of Texas. "Necrology: Karle Wilson Baker." *Proceedings,* 1960.
Pine Log. "Will Teach in Summer School," May 31, 1924.
———. "Karle Wilson Baker Speaks to Poetry Society," February 20, 1926.
———. "Karle Wilson Baker Speaks to Craig Class," December 10, 1926.
———. "SFA Poet-Teacher Finds Chosen Field in Instruction of Youth," February 25, 1928.
———. "Karle Wilson Baker Lectures on Woman Poet at Texas University," February 7, 1931.
———. "Karle Wilson Baker at UT," February 28, 1931.
———. "Mrs. Karle Wilson Baker Fulfills an Ambition to Write Fiction," September 20, 1937.
———. "Heads Writers," October 29, 1938.
———. "Mrs. Baker is Honored," February 21, 1958.
———. "Mrs. Baker Succumbs Rites Held Thursday," November 11, 1960.
Redland Herald. "Mrs. Baker's Poem 'The Tree,' is Used by English Author in Preface of Best-Seller," July 11, 1940.

Rugel, Clara H. "Karle Wilson Baker: An Authentic Poet of the Southwest." *Texas Monthly,* November 1929, 524–37.

Scarborough, Dorothy. "Karle Wilson Baker: The Poet of Quiet Things," *Dallas News,* March 16, 1924, sec. 3.

Smith, Rebecca W. "Birds of East Texas in Mrs. Baker's New Essays." Review of *The Birds of Tanglewood.* Books and Branding Irons. *Texas Outlook,* June 1931.

———. "Pre-San Jacinto Novel Depicts Values of Past." Review of *Star of the Wilderness.* Books and Branding Irons. *Texas Outlook,* July 1942.

———. "What Would You Do If You Struck Oil Tomorrow?" Review of *Family Style.* Books and Branding Irons. *Texas Outlook,* November 1937.

Southern World. "Old Coins Garnered by Karle Wilson Baker," Review of *Old Coins,* July 27, 1923.

Tinkle, Lon. "Time to Reconsider Our Regionalism." *Dallas Morning News,* August 22, 1948, sec. 6.

Trombly, Albert E. "Americanism and Blue Smoke." *Texas Review* (January 1920): 155–162.

Vann, W. H. "Texas in Revolt: *Star of the Wilderness.*" Review. *Houston Post,* May 10, 1942, sec. B.

Vincent, Upshur. "Karle Wilson Baker Texas Poet and Essayist." Fort Worth *Star-Telegram,* 1923.

Weems, John E. "Texas Institute of Letters: Looking After Texas Letters." *Dallas Morning News,* April 5, 1981.

Winchell, Walter. "On Broadway." *New York Times,* May 17, 1942.

Wyatt, Mildred. "The Pine Tree Hymn." *Nacogdoches Daily Sentinel,* October 12, 1948.

INDEX